The House of Abraham Phillips

On December 6th 1875, defective ventilation led to an explosion in the Lan pit, Gwaelod y Garth. Sixteen men and boys were killed, many more injured. It was described as the most serious explosion of the year. The Overman, Abraham Phillips, was found guilty of negligence.

The House of Abraham Phillips is a fictitious interpretation of the effect the Lan disaster had on one family's history. It is told through the mouth of Phillip Phillips, Abraham Phillips' second son. Haunted by his father's action, steeped in memories and the words of the Old Testament, Phillip Phillips muses his history to seek resolution.

All of the characters in this story lived. The main incidents are part of recorded history. While the facts around the disaster are taken from contemporary reports in the press and records in professional journals, the interaction within the family is pure fiction. This story is a memorial to those who lost their lives in the winning of coal.

First published November 2012

second edition 2014

©Norma Procter

ISBN 978-1-291-24482-3

THE HOUSE OF ABRAHAM PHILLIPS

Norma Procter

This story is dedicated to the Phillips family.

It is a Memorial to the men and boys who lost their lives or were injured in the Lan Explosion, Gwaelod y Garth, 1875.

Abraham Phillips, 53; Thomas Llewellyn Senior, 45; Thomas Llewellyn Junior 16; William Llewellyn 29; Henry Sant, 51; William Peters 33; Robert Taylor, 21; Moses Llewellyn, 12; Daniel Evans, 28; John Thomas, 18; John Pritchard, 16; Shadrach Davies; John Flyn; Evan Howell; William Harding; Charles Mills; David Rees.

Morgan Morgan; Evan Davies; Abraham Williams; William Morgan 18 and his father, Morgan Morgan 48, Evan Howell and William Harding died within a week of the explosion.

Old Testament Quotations in italics

are taken from

The King James Bible

The House of Abraham Phillips

1880

There is a ghost reflected in the darkening window frame of *Ty'n y Coed*, a reflection, clouded over by Taff Gorge. I see the face of Phillip Phillips and know it is my own. With my finger, I trace the features mirrored there - they are not the strong and Celtic image of my father, Abraham Phillips, but the finer lines, the frailty of my mother Elizabeth's face. Breath after breath, my history speaks through the misting glass. *For now we see through a glass, darkly; but then face to face: now I know in part; but then shall I know even as also I am known.* Am I known? Does this place remember me? I am now twenty seven - much the age of my parents when first they came to *Ty'n y Coed*. Turning, leaning against the glass, looking over the valley floor, down to the snaking Taff, over the landscape that shaped my history - I see only ghosts of men, those silhouetted trails of gaunt faces who scurried through my childhood, people who strode or dawdled, bent, to work. These are the origins of my memory. Tired, emaciated humanity, etched in the labyrinths of my despair. No-one hurries to the Lesser Garth today, no children dragging children dressed in rags. I listen. Business is bad, the iron works near closed. As poverty blows with the westering wind, as the window reflects my face, I use this mirror of the valley, this captured microcosm, to revive my dead. The window sash has settled to an angle, but the wood is sound. I have brought myself back home to where I drown in memories. The house stands still as time stands still. Eyes to the glass, I peer into the empty room. As I wipe the breath of condensation from the glass, my image dies and I am conscious of my every loss. I have sustained grief and the death of kinsman. I have seen in this tiny pane every ill that has befallen man. I have opened wide the door to *Ty'n y Coed*, my childhood home, and all the sorrows of my world return.

I am condemned to pitiless investigation. *Woe is me! for I am undone; because I am a man of unclean lips, and I dwell in the midst of a people of unclean lips.* Nothing has replaced my troubled soul. *One of the seraphims flew unto me, having a live coal in his hand, which he had taken with the tongs from off the altar: And he laid it upon my mouth, and said, Lo, this hath touched thy lips; and thine iniquity is taken away, and thy sin purged.* But I cannot put down Isaiah's burning coal or return to summers on the mountain - those happier times, when I could fly with the warm breeze, flowers opening, grass waving, sing in time with the sun rising and setting and the high and resonant echoes of the blackbird and the thrush. Those days are long since passed, frail memories that now that die, insensible.

As I stand here, outside *Ty'n y Coed,* the polluted Taff throws off its skull of industry and glows in morning sun. I am haunted by the ghostly spectres that walk the damp tracks of its trail, know I will feel their presence as gaunt shadows flit across the sun. My mood is sombre. I have stepped backwards to my childhood home. I look down to the Square row, to New Level, and to Orles Cottages. Built for the furnace workers, they will now be sold. Their meagre walls reflect my different faces, mark my childhood, mark the face of my destruction. Even the Forgie Line that transports castings is silent now. I turn towards the Garth and feel spontaneous joy, but know black crows still hover over dead lambs and hungry flies hum into the hot air.

I will lift my eyes up to the hills from whence cometh my help. Pulling myself from my despair, I head for Coed Rhiw Ceiliog. There, on the edge of the coal seam, Maesarail still stands, reflecting sun much as it did when as a boy I would run, run, run through the trees up to the hill. I do not run now. I walk. I listen. No sad reflections now for my soul is alive remembering those endless days before I learned to think. Happy I was, a child there on the mountain near the Colliers' Arms. My memory is replete with colliers raising glasses, raising voices, drinking outside in the new-born sun, their rich Welsh voices singing out to my young mother as we passed. I do not hear them now, but can easily recall how my mother would shake her head, making her long hair dance with all the sultry defiance of a mountain breeze. Fair the summer, the men chorused together, Fair as heaven, and laughing together as they joined in harmony, Fairer yet the face of Elin.

Mor hardd yw natur Mehifin
On harddach fyth wyneb Elin

'Elin?' my mother would giggle back. 'Not me, lads. You sing to the wrong girl! Don't let my Abraham hear you, anyway.' She would call out to them as she swept past, tossing her head in obvious pleasure at their song. Laughing she was, always laughing, beautiful, always admired, but she had eyes only for my father. I wish I had her temperament. Now, I seldom smile.

No longer able to resolve anxiety, I, Phillip Phillips, subsume my grief in memory. As I walk the hill, as I hear the skylark overhead, my mood lightens. As I walk alone, as I have always walked alone, I see my father hold my mother's hand while I run free. I smile, recall how he was ever kissing her, ever teasing as they laughed together. In those days, those far-off and halcyon days, I was always happy. I see still my father, his big eyes shine white through his coal-grimed face, his thick black Celtic hair hanging heavy across his eyes. Those were the good times up there by the Colliers' on the hill, house full of callers, heart full of laughter and of song. There was no anxiety then. Those were the times before I held the seraph's burning coal.

As the shadows move with the sun across the hill, I walk the mountain road down to our gate. As I pass the disused Cribbwr level, as I pass the silent Lan, I hear the plaintiff cries of history's distress.

I belong nowhere, this place no longer home. I hide my office hands, feel only shame I left the valley. I cannot take reality and sink again to memory, my safe retreat. As I walk in air, the sky my ceiling, I recall the long shifts underground my father had. As he stooped to tunnelled passage ways, as I walk under the clouds, I wondered how he made the time for me, how he found the patience to take me on his knee and sing. There were days when he would swing me by the hands, up to the sky. I remember from early, a child in arms, the group of us going to the *pigyn* - the very peak of the Garth - and sitting there, my father leaning back, my mother's head on his shoulder, smiling to the sun. I remember, too, rolling alone down the hillside, the world dizzying round me, round to isolation. Alone, always alone. I watch in my mind's eye my older brother, Evan, running fast with John, all legs my brothers then, my father a giant in those distant days.

I am always restless now. I remember my mother, would never stay long at the top. 'Busy I am,' she would say when Dada was reluctant to go down. 'Can't we stay here in the air, Elizabeth,' he'd beg, but it would be back down the steep path to home, no arguing.

Clouds scud across the horizon, sun catching them quickly as the storm clouds loom. As I head back to *Ty'n y Coed*, I recall how small our cottage on the Garth with its smell of roses round the door and midges skating the water butts. Scrubbed clean the step and windows glistening, my mother in her apron, always washing, always cooking. Often-times, my sister Susannah watched over me. She would hold my hand in her tight fingers till her fist was white and my hand sweating, while Evan and John ran reckless, unobserved, disturbing pigs and chickens as they dashed among the cottages. Our little community of cottages clung tenaciously to the hillside by the Colliers' Arms, much as I cling to my memories now. Their rough thatch and sun-caught windows glisten like paradise in my mind, against the bleak, grey squares of houses in the valley.

I realise now how lucky we were. While we walked the Garth, children from the Levels walked the pits or climbed the steep ascent towards the iron mine - colliers, horse drivers, air boys, carters and skip hauliers - children of John's and Evan's age, up at five and working twelve hour shifts regardless of the Ten Hour Rule. Law never holds the Masters in its thrall, never can bring sense to bear on poverty.

Strange how tall the colliers seemed in those far-off days of childhood ignorance. I see them now diminished, ravaged men and brave, wending their tired way to savage industry. In those days on the mountain, though, how big they were, how high the latches on the cottage door - and me, a boy on giant's shoulders as my father held me, towering, head up in the clouds. I looked down on everyone as we ambled over hills, calling our *shw mae's* and the names of fellow workmates as we passed.

I am diminished now. My cottage keeps its secrets, but I remember looking from our window to the sea. Fair was the sight and magical, another world that sometimes sank beneath the Cardiff mist. I craved to travel there, was told the city was too big, too busy and too distant from our hill for more than dreams. Sometimes, when I woke and it lay hidden in swirling cloud or morning mist, I thought it gone and grieved, but then the sun broke clear and I could see for miles. Magic, my life was then -*y ddraig goch* - the red dragon, flying my dreaming skies by night with the singing from the Colliers' as its guide.

No magic now. I am the friend of grim reality. I know that people struggled in my valley to bring out the coal. I watched them dragging up the hill after their shifts, bewildered that at closing these same men came ambling from the Colliers', post-drunken wranglers then. From my window, I watched as colliers who shovelled coal by day danced, jubilant by night. I have listened while the eerie owls called to their mates and heard loud voices when the moon was in the sky.

I have seen girls out walking, arms entwined with men, seen miners use their fists as they engaged in Colliers' law to settle scores. This is my memory of childhood on the hill.

But I have lived with guilt. While I sat at my books, I saw the iron workers, children and fathers struggling to their work through night and day, their grey pain-ridden faces, the weary human machine of industry, dragging their emaciated bodies from the tunnel head to the back of furnaces, where little tip-girls cleared the cinders. While I went to school, I saw young women breaking limestone flux, its small pieces to be mixed with coal my father's men had hewn. Hard and fatiguing labour, seven days a week in twelve hour shifts for little more than a shilling a day. While I ran the hills and pastures of the Garth, children watched iron ore run to the bottom of its furnaces into moulds. While I ate well and fed our family pig, pig iron fed the puddling furnaces and a boy of just my age, the under-puddler, opened and shut the treacherous furnace door with his lever and chain. While I learned to read, the pullers-up, seven year old boys and girls, lost their dreams to monotonous work, high temperatures and toxic fumes. While I looked from my window, complaining of the noise, shinglers with heavy hammers prepared the ore for rolling mills, catchers put it to the rollers for six year olds to pile, while seven year old straighteners and roughers with their unwieldy tongs, used all their meagre strength to barrow it away. Quiet, the iron works now, dire poverty replaces its hard labour. Men who were gaunt from work grow thin in hunger. Children who had no time to play sit idle, empty outside cottage doors.

Honour thy father and thy mother: that thy days may be long upon the land which the LORD thy God giveth thee As I go through the doors of *Ty'n y Coed*, as I look again at its old stone, I shout aloud to empty rooms, 'God, did you intend men to live the way we live in the land you gave to us?' And I curse aloud the iron masters, the coal masters, curse the natural wealth of Wales. With every step I take in *Ty'n y Coed*, I see my father, hear his old *helo* as he calls out his tales of work with all the *hywl* of any reverend *Capel* man. As I look out the back, the old tin bath hangs on the wall. I hear the clatter that brought it in. I see the steam of kettles and the scrubbing by the fire. And when I pause my steps, when all the echoes cease, I hear them tired but laughing, and I understand. But honour my father? I find acceptance hard.

Honour thy father? I honoured him in those distant days when talk of food and street, when gossip of community filled the lamp-lit night. I honoured him while he spoke of wages dropped, of the falling price of coal. I honoured him, as yawning, he put me into the bed with John. But I question honour now.

Honour thy father that thy days may be long? While I dreamed of *Mabinogion*, of dragons, I woke daily to the pressing horrors of cholera in Merthyr, pit accidents and death, poverty and distress. Will honouring my father make my days be long? I cannot pray. I cannot honour him. I have come back to his house and now I wait. I wait for resolution in this empty room. And I carry in my hands the seraphim's burning coal.

1857

I remember it was the end of June when Deborah came. Four summers had passed up by the Colliers', roses were arching in the garden and the sun streaming in to light the best front room. Four, I was, but I remember so well the sun that day - strange how when nothing persists, some images are fixed as pictures in the mind. I see it still, me sitting in the window, dreaming, with flies crawling on the window panes. I hear myself through time, struggling to sing the Ponty weaver's song that everyone was singing. I heard it nightly from the Colliers', heard it as the men went home. '*Mae hen wlad fy nhadau,*' I started, my voice thin and hesitant. I was no singer then or now. As I searched my mind frantically for the next line, I remember that the sun streamed past the flies, their buzzing giving me confidence to sing. '*Gwlad beirdd a chantorion,*' came Evan's voice from the garden, '*enwogion o fri.*' I climbed on the window ledge to open the sash to him. He looked up at me, danced a little jig for my amusement. We both wanted to be free.

If I could believe I would grow old and lose all my anxieties, I would not delve so deeply in the past. I lean back against a beech tree that was just a sapling when first I came here. My heart is empty for all but resolution. I cannot pray for solace to my mother's God. I do not read the Book she taught me daily at her knee. I know well its song, its words, which echo mindless in my heart, but it is a cruel god I see.

Hot it was the day that Deborah came. Welsh summer at its best. Sun spotted the edge of tree leaves, the trunk dark against the light of sky. I remember how still it was, how calm. I did not hear the hammers of the work places on the valley floor, did not notice how the smoke from furnaces obliterated light. Instead, sun painted the garden and a buzzard overhead was calling to its mate. I watched it soar into the blue, fly over the Gorge and pass from sight. And I wanted to be a bird, wanted to see the world beyond Taff Gorge.

As I watched, as I listened to the buzzard's high pitched call, I started. No buzzard then. The sound was frightening. Better to be outside like Evan, I thought, got up to leave my bedroom but was trapped. The still cottage was wracked with endless sounds of pain that lasted for eternity. As my father paced the floor, as the kettles boiled, as *Mamgu* Deborah shut tight doors, I sat imprisoned by my dread. The birth of a child should be a joyous thing. At Deborah's birth I only felt great fear. *In sorrow thou shalt bring forth children* it is written in the Book. I heard that sorrow when our Deborah came.

When my father came to take me to the bed where my mother was almost sleeping, pale and small, I remember that her eyes would not go wide and sparkle as they did. 'Why is your hair wet, Mam,' I asked her with the innocence of a child, 'too long it is to have it wet in bed.' She did not have the energy to smile; her arms were limp, not there to draw me in.

'Look who has come to us,' my father said. 'Her name is Deborah.' Holding her gently, he pulled back her swaddling, so we all could see. 'How beautiful she is, this tiny one,' he breathed. John stood behind me, proud that he was five and me, ashamed of only being four, on tiptoes beside Evan, almost ten. Susannah was eight then, and mothering before her time. She was shushing them because they spoke too loud. The wooden cot that my father made was by my mother's bed, scrubbed clean and painted for this child. Dada leaned over and put the new-born Deborah on the bed. I remember how small she was, just like Susannah's doll. And she was pale, transparent, like petals on the rose outside the door - and still she was, as if she were not born.

'Deborah in the book of Judges is a prophetess,' Evan declared, always pedantic, his head full of books. I heard that up at *Penuel*, he added proudly. 'She is too small to be called prophetess.' Susannah pushed him aside. 'Oh, Evan,' she said with great superiority, 'Always you are bookish. She is so beautiful. Can I hold her now, Dada?' The tiny child, bound tight, was placed into Susannah's arms. I recall how comfortable my sister looked, maternal, satisfied. I stood there, arms ready, bewildered, apprehensive, waiting for my turn, not quite sure where this child had come from, not quite sure what I should do. When no one offered her to me, my arms fell slowly to my sides. It was my first taste of rejection and I found it bitter. Looking towards my mother, I saw her eyes were closed. 'What does it mean, Da,' I recall asking in a whisper. 'In the Book - what does it mean that *in sorrow thou shalt bring forth children*? Is my Mam in sorrow still? Are you?'

I remember my father's face as he told me the Book also says *fill the earth and subdue it*. 'This country is full of men who are breaking their backs to feed their children,' he said. 'We can fill the earth, Phillip, but how, oh, how, can we subdue it!' I remember how puzzled I was by his words, how sad I was that my mother was in sorrow. 'The best man, Phillip,' my father laughed, 'is he who can rear the best child and the best woman is she who can bear the pain of birth. It is hard for women,' he said, looking with love at my exhausted mother on the bed. 'We should sing praises to the women who bring into the world a little boy or girl. Tired your mother is now. Asleep. It is time to go.'

Time passes slowly when you are four. I know I felt lost and jealous of the little one. My days were life-times spent alone, my mother always busy with this child. I remember Deborah took so long to feed that she was ever at my mother's breast. I felt angry that my mother's arms were always full.

As I stand here now, my back against the tree I hear baby Deborah's whimpering, remember how she always cried when my father went to her. Life was different after she came, our house more hostile, more quarrelsome, more silent as we ate. What am I that I carry still this grief? As my mind turns, the words of the Book fall around me, stones in the mountain spring. *I will greatly multiply thy sorrow and thy conception* I breathe thinking of this bitter world where women produce children who, like the cursed snakes, crawl to the headings in the coal face, breathing dust. *On thy belly shalt thou go,* said the Lord, *and dust shalt thou eat all the days of thy life.*

Early that year, the summer sun bleached grass to autumn colours, and with the drought, as leaves fell, the garden grew more wild. My father went as usual to his shifts, but no one seemed to laugh or smile. 'Our Deborah does not thrive,' I heard my father say repeatedly. 'She is so pale, Elizabeth, she does not grow.' 'Hist, man. You are jealous,' my mother would reply. 'Lovely is the child. Look at her skin, her golden hair. Curly it grows.' I can still see my mother's lips pursed in defiance as he shook her head and turning her face from my father, down to baby Deborah, she would sing, '*Calon lân yn llawn daioni* - a pure heart is full of goodness -*Tecach yw na'r lili dlos* - more lovely than the pretty lily.' Evening after evening moved to darkness, my mother nursing, fondling, Deborah's fine hair round her fingers, as her arms gently enfolded the child.

'A full hour you have fed her now,' my father would complain. 'Should she not sleep?' I listened, watching, as I always do. 'Abraham, away with you,' my mother would reply. 'Tired I am from feeding her at night. Long she takes, I know.' 'The Book you keep beside your bed,' my father once said bitterly, 'that Book of yours says *and thy desire shall be to thy husband.*' I remember his sadness as he looked at her there in the nursing chair, rocking, rocking back and forth, the old wooden rockers knocking the flag stones as she moved. Standing then, I heard my father say beneath his breath and with unusual sarcasm, '*And he shall rule over thee?* Not much chance of that in this house, eh,' as rubbing his chin ruefully, he walked outside.

Slowly the months passed. Fading was the garden now. Roses overblown and scattered by the winds. But green was the hill behind us, green and welcoming. Through bracken and through saplings, there I ran alone, set free from my anxiety, free from the hostile atmosphere within my home. I was brown from the sun and lusty as the crows as I ran free. July came, August. Still our mother was preoccupied with Deborah. While I wandered unrestrained and wild as a gypsy, dust gathered on the mantelpiece, flowers grew and fell. I remember how fine I thought our garden then. So overgrown. A place for shanties, a place for me to hide.

As I stand here now, as I look down towards the Lan, I think how seldom as a boy I looked over to the pit. As the summer sun faded the ironworks, the furnaces, into another world, I looked up higher to the hill. In those far distant days, I learned how to escape my grief. Birds sang just for me, falcons flew ahead, but always the buzzard was my soul. I floated with it high, absorbed its cry. And lost I was for time.

'Deborah does not grow.' My father's insistent voice comes back to me, spun fragile like the whispering wind down summer chimneys. I hear him daily now, in the gardens where the leaves began to fall, from the landing where the stairs turn, from where the little window looks straight to the Garth. I hear him when the moon shines in the night, hear his plaintive voice saying, 'Elizabeth, the child is sick. She does not thrive.'

'She sleeps, man. Are you jealous still of time?'

'Transparent is her skin,' Eliza. 'Can you not see? Her eyes are never clear. The focus is awry.'

'Tired she is, Abraham. She knows me well, follows my fingers, and can smile.'

'Her legs, Elizabeth, they are not strong. She does not try to sit.' While they argued together, I looked up at the hill, red then in bracken and late sun. Now, a man, my eyes turn always to the valley, to its grim landscape of devastation. I see it as it is, stripped bald, black in the shadow of the hill, reflecting its dull message to the distant skies. Today, children play in murky holding pools where other care-worn working children struggled as I grew.

September came and with it, our apple tree was full. Evan and John picked apples from the tree while I made baskets full of fallen fruit. Susannah held the house against the rattle of drams crossing from the clay pit down below. My father washed alone as best he could at the end of every shift, while mother still held Deborah, pale, whimpering and fraught.

While we children learned to stand alone, I heard always my mother's constant voice drift from room to room as she sang for Deborah, '*Ar lan y môr mae rhosys cochion* ... red roses growing - *Ar lan y môr mae lilis gwynion* - is your face like the lilies, my darling? Your Dada says you are pale. *Ar lan y môr mae 'nghariad inne* - my true love is going to sleep. As she murmured caressing the child, cajoling her to sleep, I shrugged my shoulders and ran towards the hill. *Yn cysgu'r nos a chodi'r bore*. It haunts me still. I cannot hear that song without seeing Deborah limp there in my mother's arms.

October and the days were cold. No leaves now on the trees and the wind whistled to the hearth. Evan made the fires while Susannah cooked. My father went each day to work, but tired he looked, concerned. Too fast I grew to independence, my mother distracted, pale, no time to speak. Always in her arms, the baby Deborah. Always the chorus that she *does not thrive*. I learned those words, heard them so often they were etched on my young brain.

November and the wind was fierce. I woke to Mama's screams and ran into her room. Dada was there, awake and shouting strong, taking the baby away from Mam.

'She is dead, Elizabeth. Deborah is dead.'

'No, Abraham, No. She sleeps.'

Dada took baby Deborah from our Mam and wrapped her tight in cloth. 'She is dead, Elizabeth,' he said. 'Please do not scream.'

I crept into the corner terrified. A dreadful tug of war there was. Mam pulled the baby back from Da, who took her back again. Exhausted at last, Mam fell unto her bed. Dada sat beside her as he spoke.

'Elizabeth, be brave. Deborah is gone. Cold is the child. And you hysterical. You must be calm.' Turning, he saw me crouching there. 'Out, Phillip. Now. It is no place for you. I tell you. Out.' Taking the bundle that was Deborah, he left.

The present makes the past look ominous. So does the Book. *And I will kill her children with death*, the book of Revelations cries out to me, *and all the churches shall know that I am he which searcheth the reins and hearts: and I will give unto every one of you according to your works.*

As my mind goes back to that day, I know that I was young and had not then faced death. I crawled in bed with my mother but she did not look at me. Instead, she made a howl that turned into a scream. Long was that scream. Long as she had breath. Exhausted then, she slept. Quiet I crawled out from that room and went back to my window and the moon.

Silent was our house when my mother stopped screaming. Cold was the bed I crept back in. I remember that even John, John who was not weak like me, covered his ears, pushed close to Evan, still asleep. Frightened I was. I recognised then the chill of insecurity. How could our little prophetess create such fear?

Changed was our life from then. My mother cut a little twist of hair, a curl from baby Deborah's head. Quiet she was, my father, too. No singing now, no laughter. *'The Lord gave, and the Lord hath taken away,'* whispered my mother as they put the baby in her coffin. Small the box they put our Deborah in. Small the tiny child who lay inside, unnatural white the lace they wrapped her in.

I know now that we all come with a date to die but I was afraid that night. The moon hung large behind the black of the beech. No prophetess, I thought. More like Death's Angel. Grief was everywhere in our small house, filling the air with suffocating gloom. Her baby dead, my mother still sang lullabies. '*Yn cysgu'r nos a chodi'r bore,*' she sang over and over. 'My true love sleeps within her dwelling,' her voice weak, piercing the silent, stagnant air.

1857-8

We took no flowers to the grave where Deborah lay, but scattered the ground with rosemary leaves instead. 'Rosemary for remembrance,' my father said, as he spread the spiked and perfumed herb. What better way to cover the fresh earth. '*Nos da,* Deborah,' he whispered as he threw in a handful of the new turned soil, '*nos da,* little one, goodnight.' Then, holding my mother close, he ushered us through the graveyard of St Catwg's, through the funeral arch and down the steep hill home. The sound of Deborah's death knell stills rings across the years into my head.

November blew chill and drear. Damp air hung round us like the mist rising from *Afanc*'s lake, fixed in my mind from our mythology. Cold winds blew the few remaining leaves to air, shrivelled and spent, the trees naked. A sad lot we were, huddled together against the loss of Deborah, my mother white, shrivelled, transparent like a purse of honesty. Her face worn and marked by tears, I watched as she held Deborah's curl that lay hidden in the box beside her bed. It was a sad November in our house. My mother moved like a ghost, my father serious. I sat beside Susannah, who knitted quietly, while Evan read. John paced the floor complaining and the wind howled.

My mother did not speak much those days after Deborah. She stayed in mourning long. But memories, thank God, retract and hide themselves. Gradually, her cheeks were pink again, more gradually, she smiled.

The year after, young Booker's father died of apoplexy. 'Old Booker-Blakemore's gone,' my father called as he came in. 'He was a fine old chap,' he added as Evan helped him bring in the old tin bath, 'by all accounts, he was benevolent.' As my father took off his pit-grimed shirt, as the water bubbled on the fire, I watched useless as Susannah and my father tipped the cauldron to the bath. As steam hung in the kitchen like a mountain mist, as the chatter of their voices filled the air, I gloried that our house had come alive. 'Old Mr Booker got his cottagers growing vegetables and flowers,' my father said as he stripped off. 'Had a flower show for his men in Whitchurch every year.' Kneeling on the floor then, my mother scrubbing his back, my father slobbering his face clean, head down, he went on, 'Booker-Blakemore's eldest, his boy, Richard, is no good, so I've heard tell.' Head back then, wet hair spraying, he muttered, 'so young Thomas William Booker will be in charge from now. Just twenty eight he is,' he gasped between the ohs and ahs of back scrubbing.

'That's younger than you are, Da,' said Evan scornfully, 'and he will be in charge?'

'Not the skilled work below, Evan,' my father replied. 'That is on my shoulders still. He's a toff, son. He doesn't get this black.' Grinning now, cleaner, he laughed, explaining that Thomas William Booker's job would be investment, and that rumour had it, he was keen. Turning to my mother then, he sang out, *'Dwi'n dygaru di* - I love you -' as she handed him clean clothes.

When she had done the chores each winter night, my mother would go into the front room to play the harp. *Ar lan y môr* would merge with *Cariad y Bardd* or sometimes, *Ar hyd y nos*. I liked that best and oftentimes still sing its melody in my head. It brings back to me evenings, sitting together round the fire, after my father's shift, coal in the scuttle, wood I gathered from the mountain paths, cheese toasting in the embers of the fire. Deborah's death still haunted me, but when I look back to childhood on the Garth it is not her graveyard I recall.

'*Cariwch, 'medd Dafydd, 'fy nhelyn i mi.* Bring me my harp,' my father would tease oftentimes, as my mother's gentle playing filled the house, 'then we can play together.' He would laugh then, ribald, for he could not play a note. I remember how he was amused by his own joke, as music drifted through the air of cooking, floated to where the washing dried.

> *Nid wy'n gofyn bywyd moethus,*
> *Aur y byd na'i berlau mân:*
> *Gofyn wyf am galon hapus,*
> *Calon onest, calon lân*

My mother's voice, singing quietly, plaintively would fill the house. 'She wants only a pure heart, not gold or pearls,' my father would laugh. 'Just as well on a collier's wage with prices rising and wages falling and all of you to feed and clothe!' Sometimes he would muse seriously that the iron works was failing and Lan in problems too, but at that time, mostly it was happy in our home. Going to the door of the front room, he would chorus to my mother,

> '*Calon lân yn llawn daioni,*
> *Tecach yw na'r lili dlos:*
> *Dim ond calon lân all ganu-*
> *Canu'r dydd a chanu'r nos*

a pure heart is full of goodness, more lovely than a pretty lily. Only a pure heart can sing like you, *Cariad annwyl.*' His deep baritone would sing out, his voice resonant, arms open wide, 'Sing day and night, my darling,' he would laugh, 'Sing day and night.'

Happy I was then. The lights twinkled each night from the Colliers' Arms, stars fit to challenge the sky. Many a night I stared at them devoid of sleep. We boys slept at the front of the cottage with my father, my mother sharing with Susannah at the back. My mother had the big bed that my father made when first they wed. We have it upstairs still. Susannah slept on a small bed, low to the floor. Quilts there were on both these beds, quilts stitched by my mother, goodness knows from what or when.

'Have you seen the full moon shine through the naked branches of a tree?' I asked Evan as he slept. 'Magic it is for me,' I whispered as I fell asleep. Frost shone on the floor in winter, painted its delicate ferns on the inside of the window panes. While we huddled together for warmth in the big bed, while I dreamed of dragons, shivered in the cold, sleepy chickens perched and foxes howled on the Garth. Clear moonlight lit the corners of our cottage home. On nights awake, alone, after the Colliers' lights were dimmed, I would watch intently for that giant bird, for the *Adar Llwch Gwin,* to fly. Night was the time it listened to our speech, knew all we said. It brought enticing fear. Grandfather Shôn o'r Lan regularly transported me to this mythology. Such things he told me as I sat, wide eyed, upon his knee. I loved his stories, loved his rolling words, the Welsh that poured so fluid from his tongue. My mother would turn her wheel and tut. 'You'll have him scared with your old myths,' she would say. 'Don't listen to his old magic stuff. You Phillip, you Evan, you must learn from books, not this old man!'

'Oh, Mam! Phillip's still little, he is but five,' scorned John, 'leave him with Grandpa's stories. He doesn't need to learn. I'll keep you. I am going underground.' My mother shook her head. 'Phillip will follow Evan, John. I want them both in school. You, too, lad, in spite of what you plan.' I remember through the years my brother John's perpetual grief. Nothing gets learned in school, he would mutter, quoting his friend John Griffiths who never was a day in school and he was working just a year ahead of him. 'I'll go Sunday School if you like,' he would plead, 'except they would not have me because I do not know the ten Commandments yet.' As my mother shook her head, he would persist. 'They teach you in good Welsh and not in English like in school,' he said. 'I will not go to Booker's school.'

'Enough, John,' Mama would call to him, 'for you will go.'

'I speak good Welsh. Why isn't that enough? I do not want English or to read. They only teach in English,' he spat, 'and I won't understand.' Then, staring directly at our mother, rebellious, he would protest 'You have to learn arithmetic and to read and write - and old Madge hits you if you don't learn fast because he won't get paid.'

'Hush John, Dada will be in. Why don't you meet him down there in the lane?'

'I like Grandpa's stories, Mam,' I cut in. 'He doesn't frighten me with just mythology. He talks about our country. Tells me about the language and the men at work and how they need good friends. And about the Masters of the coal and iron. They are rich, Mam, but I want to be a scholar just like Grandpa Shôn.'

'So I will earn your fee,' shouted John. 'Someone has to pay for school and Dada can't find everything.' John moved towards the door. Opening it wide, he slammed it hard behind him.

'A scholar is worth ten labourers,' I shouted after him.

I remember that my mother shook her head. Drawing me to her, she said quietly, 'Do not heed John. It is not want of means that keeps boys from the school in Dada's house. Keep us all, you will, Phillip, with your good head. You are clever like your granddad Shôn. You have got an independent mind like him. You watch and listen, so you learn. Evan is clever, too, but you can think. No underground for you, my littlest lad.'

'I worry when my Da is underground,' I said to her. 'I don't want John there too. It's a place where *Coblynau* pace, waiting to catch a collier or a miner in his thrall. Appeased, satisfied they have to be, for when angered, they can make rock fall.' I remember looking into my mother's eyes and saying seriously, 'and when rock falls, the airways block and colliers die. Grandfather Shôn told me that, too.'

My mother threw her head back, laughing, the loose strands of her golden hair translucent in the sunlight. 'Appeased Phillip? Where do you learn such words? You are old before your time. Now come to me.' As I stood there she looked directly to my eyes 'No more worrying when Dada is underground, for he is careful. And no more listening to Grandpa Shôn's old magic, do you hear? We want no *Coblynau* here.'

Looking back, I remember that moment with such clarity. I can see the room, still smell the lavender. That moment contained the present in the past. I knew then such things could happen and it bothered me.

1859

The day we came down the mountain from the Colliers to have a look at *Ty'n y Coed*, another door of my life was opening. I think of it now as I sit here at my order books. I did not want to leave the hill and came reluctantly. 'There are trees on the bottom,' my mother said as she dragged me along, 'and wild flowers - look at the meadow sweet and those white daisies.' I agreed that the birds sang but it was against the cacophony of the valley floor. I knew I had no choice and at that moment, I remember, the sun broke through the clouds encouraging me to run into a riot of rose bay willow herb, which danced in the brambles. While bugs swarmed round thistles and copper butterflies dived into tufted vetch, I left the others and ran in alone. Light alters so much. I remember that my spirit rose as I pushed through the yellow pea that scrambled over the unruly bushes.

    The building stood alone, dejected, not yet done. Its shallow slated roof showed naked timbers. Moss streaked the piles of waiting stone. Walls black with damp, the daub grown soft, barely held up the outhouses. I stood there facing the valley, swallowing hard. I felt isolated, drawn alone against the valley floor. To settle my anxious mind, I counted the twelve small panes of the four windows to the Garth. Walking round, I shuddered at the four that looked out to the valley floor. Two worlds in one. Behind me the glorious hill, before, a place where smoke hung low and the sounds of hammers rang against the racket of engines. A place where the brick-works, forge, the holding ponds, the furnace of the iron works, stood like dominant giants in cruel contrast to the light breeze that moved the grasses on the hill. I could see short creatures there bent, with long shadows, making their way from work, knew they were men and children, and I felt afraid.

Landscape does not create our history. We do that quite alone. The mountain shone silver in the late sunlight as we stood in front of *Ty'n y Coed*. Silver, as the wind moved the grasses, silver as the light skittered on the wet slates. But I could not look beyond the devastation of the flood plain, only could think of the gorse, that yellow place, my hill, that we would leave. I loved it on the mountain. Down at *Ty'n y Coed*, looking up at the Garth, I felt a strange longing for its height, the morning mist that hid the distant views of Cardiff leaving only sky. I watched my mother and father standing in that riot of brambles around the moss-stained stone, but could hear only the throbbing heart beat of hammers from the flood-plane, could only feel great sadness in the air.

The truth is, that day we all went see to *Ty'n y Coed* together, my father was especially happy. Booker had made him Overman at the Lan. 'Common Collier no more,' he had joked as he ambled round the land of the cottage. 'Overman!' he chortled as he rolled the word on his tongue, laughing at its sound on his resonant voice. 'You'll all have to watch it now that I'm in charge!' he laughed aloud. 'Overman at the Lan.' He put his arm around my mother, who pushed him away. 'The coal seams are thicker at these lower levels,' he said ignoring her rebuff. 'Booker will be overjoyed to have the good coal we will win.'

'Keep the Lan safe,' was all my mother said, staring directly at him.

'I hear young Thomas William is intent on progress', my father intervened. 'Goodness only knows what investment he has planned.'

My mother threw back her hair. 'He's a young man like you, Abraham,' she said. 'Adventurous. He is known for wanting innovation but they say he has no real experience. Don't let him be a fire-brand intent on getting out more coal at any cost - be safe my only love.' My mother held out her hand to me and it was warm and lovely, but by now I wanted to run ahead with Evan. Six I was then, with John coming seven. Evan was eleven years old. Almost a man. I thought him huge and ancient. Old enough to go to the pit with my father soon. I wondered if he would have cut down trousers like the boys from the Level Houses, wondered how anyone could stand being deprived of light and air. I never wanted to go with my father to his work, yet I knew there were air-boys of my age, sitting all day aside the air-doors, cramped, cold and wet, half fed, with just a solitary candle for a light. I shuddered as I thought of them, beneath me now, opening and shutting the air doors so the haulier with his horse and dram could pass.

Oblivious of us children, my father tried to spin my mother in the grass but she protested. I heard her say, 'Oh, Abraham, no. This place is too big. And what a tumbledown pit it is! Not finished yet and muddle everywhere. Better we are to stay on the mountain.'

I watched my father catch his breath, his spirits daunted by her clear disdain. 'A pit, is it, Elizabeth,' he said. 'Then you know nothing about a pit. Let me tell you there will be no muddle under me, above ground or beneath. Men will know they work for me. I will be fair and organised. I know their lives and want it better for them. Same here in the house. Tumbledown indeed! It may not be finished but there is no terrace of houses here. It stands alone. I want it better for you all.' I watched as my father stood upright then, his face set, serious. 'We will come to live here, Elizabeth,' he said firmly. 'And you will like it well.'

'A stickler for order, are you, Abraham?' my mother said sulkily. 'You let the children get away with anything!' Then, seeing Dada's face fall, she pulled him close to her and whispered, 'I know you well, Abraham Phillips. Work it is, work that will come before making this place habitable.'

'I have been reading Samuel Smiles' Self Help,' Da laughed, undaunted. 'How to work hard, live frugally and then rise in the world.' He laughed again, stopped speaking for a moment, then, holding my mother to him he whispered to her ear, 'I believe in his aristocracy of labour, Elizabeth. Strived, I have, to learn my craft. There are many skilled men in our country - these workers are the aristocrats, not the Dynevor's of our land, not the Butes of Aberdare.' He moved from my mother then, his voice louder. 'We have craftsmen, experts in iron - and look at the furnace arch.' I followed his finger to the valley where the furnace stood. 'It was our craftsmen who set that curve, Elizabeth. The entrance to the Lan, the arcs even to the rat holes - they are all made by our skilled men ....'

'Just skilled men, Abraham? And what of the women? Who cooks you your black beef, I would ask,' put in my mother. 'And who does the washing, scrubs the steps and keeps the children fed on halfpennies ....'

My father laughed, his mellow, resonant Welsh voice ringing around the stones of the half finished house. 'I can keep the pit safe and make this place glorious - and you can keep house diligently for me. I recognise your worth, *cariad*.' My mother beamed at him, satisfied. 'I want this place. I can make it good,' my father said intently, 'make you a cottage you will love. Believe me,' he insisted as my mother's mouth tightened in disbelief. In full voice now, my father went on, 'Dynevor land it is, land leased out to young Booker. If he agrees, I will build more, repair well and make you a palace down here in the woods.'

'Even if it is on the rim of his clay pit,' my mother said bitterly.

'There is garden enough for vegetables,' my father cried out, taking her hand in his. 'Your wash line can be there - and the pump is ours alone. No waiting in a queue. And look, so close to the New Drift. Later I can leave in the morning, earlier I can be home at night.' He took my mother's arm and twirled her round. With the hill rising behind him and the devastation of the valley floor hidden by his dreams, the world was his. He was determined. 'We need more space, Elizabeth,' he said, 'and Booker has given us the chance of this. Booker is interested in me. Friendly. It's a responsible job, Elizabeth. It's more than it used to be in your grandfather's day. A sly grin crossed my father's face as he recognised the need to wheedle my mother. 'I know,' he said, 'let us call this place *Ty'n y Coed* after that colliery your grandfather has between Creigiau and Pentyrch. Down at the Lan, I will have charge of the entire workings just as he did there. I will have to get the pit working every morning. It will be me that attends to all the details of arranging the work and getting out the coal. The ventilation, too. That will be my responsibility. And, yes, it will be me that keeps the daily account of the work wrought. I will have to sort out the dues to every man - write it all out - expenses, wages - give the colliery an account every fortnight of what each man has earned.'

As I think back to that day now, I realise that my mother was happy. 'Well, Abraham, you have come up through the ranks,' she said, 'you were a mere trapper when I first knew you. If Thomas William Booker sees you as an experienced man, he has good sense.' My mother linked her arm in his and smiled.

'The weight of the works will be on my shoulders,' my father grinned proudly. 'Valued within the Booker Empire! I have to do the hiring and firing, too,' he added 'that I will not like. But I can organise the shot firing - and I'm sure I can sustain the output from the Lan.'

'Make the contract with Booker as soon as the papers are drawn up,' my mother urged. 'Evan is eleven now - it's books for him. He will have some quiet here. Susannah - well, she will be ten. She needs more space. All the children in one room is not good. And we have this little one to think of too.' I remember that she patted her stomach. Strange how little we knew of birth those days.

'There are four good rooms upstairs,' my father said. 'Susannah can have a room all to herself. Evan, John and Phillip can still share. And we can at last sleep alone together in that big oak bed I made. We have managed where we are but I want to make it better for us all. Look at John, now. He already wants to be a collier. A man in his head already. And young Phillip maybe just six, but he is seriousness itself. He'll follow Evan. You watch my word. He has my father's ways.' Then, head in the air, my father declared, 'Anyway, Eliza Phillips, the Overman cannot live up there among the colliers that he leads. And Booker wants me here, close-by.'

'Dada, Dada, look at me,' I remember shouting, interrupting him, head over heels.

He laughed and waved to me. 'You want to come here to live, don't you, Phillip,' I heard him say. I could not answer, but just watched him while he ruffled-up my hair. I took my mother's hand and heard my father jest that we would be living close to Ffynnon Taff when we moved here. 'It's the smallest spa in the world!' he teased. 'Cure all your aches and pains they say!' As I looked across to the blackness of the valley, to its soot and grime, its blood red sky, my father, Abraham Phillips, threw back his head to laugh.

'I love living on the mountain... ,' Elizabeth protested, quietly. 'All we are closer to here is smoke and noise.'

'A fine view of the Garth we have from here,' my father said. 'So *lift up your eyes unto the hills,* but live down here.' My father laughed loudly and taking my mother again into his arms, he put his lips to her hair and said seriously, 'Remember you have a position to fill now, Elizabeth - wife of William Thomas Booker's Overman!'

'Dada,' John interrupted, tugging at his sleeve, 'can I come to work with you when I am eleven? A collier I want to be, like you. Maybe I'll be an overman, too, one day. I'll work at it, I will'.

'Not what you think, really, John boy.' My father was suddenly stern. 'Underground is dangerous. You study, man. Follow Evan.'

'But a collier I want to be, Dada.'

'You study first, son. Then we'll see. That way your wages will be higher if you do come down. An extra 3d a week if you can read.'

'I want to leave out the school bit and come down underground with you like the Old Level boys.'

'John. John. Son. Let us settle for you waiting at the end of the lane for me as my Shift ends. You can help me carry my bags. Let's settle for that, eh?'

'But Dada,' John protested, 'I've been doing that since I was five. I want to be underground with you. Other children work. Anyway, one boy told me his mother said you learn less in school than out of it. Said his brother had been there for three years and learned nothing ....'

My father had stopped listening. Instead, he was in deep and intense conversation with my mother. I heard Booker said, Booker will allow, Booker respects this family. A young boy still for all his intent to work, John saw me run off through the long grass with Susannah, Evan in hot pursuit. He forgot his questions to father, questions which hung unnoticed now in the warm air. Screaming with laughter, we all romped around the Dynevor-Booker land while Mam and Dada continued to argue quietly together. Eventually, they called us to them. Arm around my mother, my father asked, 'And what do you think of the house of Abraham Phillips, then?' Not one of us knew what to say, but we all joined in as Dada roared with happiness.

As we trudged back up the hill towards the Colliers', I wouldn't have known that my mother was large with a new baby. It is true I noticed that her black mourning dress had been discarded and folded in the bedroom chest. I knew, though, that she still wore a diamond of black velvet on her sleeve in memory of Deborah and had less time for me. Looking back from manhood to that time, I can see now that she was not well. She did not want her food, spent time in bed. Thin was her face although her belly grew. Evan was in school. John and I battled as usual while Susannah fetched the water, cleared the food, looked after my mother while my father was at work.

Oftentimes, my mother in her bed, I ran alone and paddled in the mountain's springs, watched crystal clear water as it skimmed across the rocks and down behind the Colliers' Arms. I remember sitting there one day, the evening falling fast, and me, as usual, alone. I suppose my father had come looking for me. The sun was sinking behind the *pigyn* and clouds hung over the valley floor. I saw his shadow reach me as he, too, looked over to the scene of industry. I remember that I told him then I did not want to move down to the valley - remember, too, that he looked sad.

I asked my father then why Deborah had to die.

'Some would say that the Lord wanted her, Phillip,' he replied, 'as he squatted beside me, 'that she was too good for this place.'

'How could she be too good, Dada,' I asked incredulously.

My father laughed quietly, his breath rising into the mountain air. *'There is no peace, saith the Lord, unto the wicked.'* I looked up at him, bewildered. 'No peace, Da,' I remember saying. 'It is very peaceful here.' He mused a moment. 'Ask your Mam about God in Heaven, boy. She knows the Book.'

'God in Heaven?' I echoed. 'Has he taken her? Has he got our Deborah?'

'The Lord giveth,' Da said as if he were in *Capel*, *'and the Lord taketh away.'*

'The Lord God, Da?' I asked looking into his eyes.

'That's him,' my father replied.

'You mean the God in our prayers, Dada? You know, the night time prayer for children *Mamgu* teaches us to say at bedtime - *And if I die before I wake,'* I chanted to him, *'I pray to God my soul to take* - Is that who took her?'

'Phillip, you ask too many questions,' my father said. 'I find no answers in the Book, but there is not much space for the irreligious here. We're a lost element in our history, boy. It's all temperance and revival now.' He looked serious then. 'Deborah was very ill,' he murmured softy. Then, gently, taking me on his knee, he repeated,

'She died, that's all. No one took her.' Shaking his head a little, he put me back down on the ground.

I sensed my father then was near to tears. 'Too big you are to sit upon my lap,' he said quickly. 'School for you soon, young man.'

From then on, those prayer lines became less abstract for me. The words took on a ghastly life of their own, started to haunt me till I could not sleep. Often times my mother took me into her bed. My feet came just to her knees as we lay there together. She was sad for the baby, she whispered to me in the dark of the bedroom. Said I would have to fill the space. I never knew what she meant, but it really bothered me. I suppose everything bothered me. It still does. But then, a child, I would sit in the grass wondering how I could fill Deborah's place for my mother. It frightened me. The little wooden coffin they put the baby in floated into my dreams too often - that and the crying of my mother and my father's walking up and down.

Grandpa Shôn always said that I thought too much, that thinking in the abstract weakens you. As I sit here now at the window of *Ty'n y Coed*, a lifetime behind me, I realise how much I loved his world of *Mabinogi*, a world full of omens and enchantment, of good hope. It was easier for me to understand than the world around me where God fights the Devil and takes souls away.

Our second Deborah came in the early morning. We were all asleep. Before long, my mother was busy as ever, making the bread, scrubbing floors and my father's back as day after day he came in black from the drift. When he was scrubbed, he would lean over, take baby Deborah in his arms. Nuzzling into her curls, he would smother her with kisses, leaving me to grieve. If I did not understand her birth, I soon learned to come to terms with death. It was ever on my parent's tongues. 'Accident today at Bryn Coch down in Neath,' I heard my father say. 'There are twenty six men dead. David Morris one of them - and they couldn't even find Tom Reynolds. My age they were. Do you remember Tom Reynolds, Elizabeth,' he said.

My mother shook her head. 'It was only three years ago at Lewis Merthyr in Pontypridd,' she tutted.

'That was nine dead. Accident at Cwmavon last year, too,' Da added.

My mother did not look up at him, her hands busy cutting bread, sawing at top speed, with great meaning. I realised now that she lived with the fear of my father's death. 'There were twelve dead there, as well, Abraham,' she said looking up and wiping her brow. 'I wish you men didn't go underground. Better the days when we were farmers.' She didn't seem to have time to be missing the dead baby. The new Deborah must have filled the gap.

'Not many getting a living from agriculture these days,' my father replied. 'Nearly all in the coal industry now.' My mother worked harder than ever at cutting the bread, piling it up before her on the wooden table. There was a cloud on her face even though these days, she was singing again as she scrubbed, the black diamond for the first Deborah gone from her sleeve.

All this was a long time ago. Life has been cruel to my family. We are asleep to reality. Asleep, in those days, too, to the railways that were being built. Strange how we knew so little of our world. As lines of steel extended to the Rhondda, as the murky Taff linked it to Cardiff dock, as orders came for Welsh coal from Argentina, India, the Far East, I ran the limits of the Garth. While the village developed a stone's throw from the mountain, Dada worked his shifts. While English landowners took the minerals they felt they owned, landowners who could not speak our tongue, we were oblivious to progress and to nature. Babies arrived we knew not how, men died to go to heaven or to hell. We kept the language safe, doffed hats to our betters, worked while other people, *gwerin*, prayed.

We live in superstitious times, and I have returned to the house of my childhood to seek sustenance, to seek the answer to my troubled soul. *The fathers have eaten sour grapes, and the children's teeth are set on edge.* The words of Job fall from the Book, providing me no comfort - *He shall return no more to his house, neither shall his place know him any more.* The truth is there. The village shuns me for my father's name. I am not wanted here. I am estranged.

1859

Today, I travelled but took no orders - thus, I have no books to fill. Think of me as I walk, sleepless, along the twilight passage of my father's house. There are images fixed in my mind, images thrown through the aperture of memory into the labyrinths of my distress. I did not know my father. I see colliers coming from Cwm Llwydrew, men and boys from the brick works, the furnaces, the coal. All grey. Grey against the grey. I do not know these men. I do not give them lives or characters, but see only the black of their boots against the yellow mud. Likewise, I did not see my father. I sleep fitfully and wake to the moon shining through my room. Its silver and chalk mix and darken as it exposes to light, or my eyes make a wet plate of the day we left the mountain, me in tears. I seek to know my mother. Fixed in my mind, daguerreotype, is the way she looked, her face red from the lifting to the cart, her voice huffing and blowing across tight lips. 'There's a cart, Abraham!' she still cries in my memory. 'You really call that a cart fit for our removing? Never big enough,' she declared, as we all crowded round to look. The old dresser had to come, and the beds - the big oak one my father made and the one *Mamgu* had given - Susannah's trundle. too. 'I will not leave my furniture behind,' my mother cried. 'Already, I have to leave my memories.'

'Too many memories lurk like threads of rot in those old stones,' my father said. 'The cottage on the bottom is finished now. We make our home there from today.'

God said, Let there be light: and there was light - but in this village there is none. Even the sky is dull above the valley. I see the chimneys, the forge, the colliery buildings grey with haze, grey with the smoke that hangs trapped in the Gorge, trapped like the workers in this desolate valley, and I realise I never saw my father with objective eyes, know only how he looked.

I remember the day we came down from the mountain like sheep. I sat watching from the branches of the apple tree. No place for me there with the packing and the sadness as everyone rushed around and argued. I remember reddening when John saw me, shouted out for all to hear that I was watching like an owl perched in the tree. *I have been a stranger in a strange land.* I knew that day that I was different to my brothers. I saw John's strong body, lifting and carrying, saw him easy with himself, while Evan happily listed and collated all we had. Loneliness was to be my life-time's destiny, that I would always watch alone. *He that observeth the wind shall not sow; and he that regardeth the clouds shall not reap* is written in the Book. An observer only, I am, thus condemned.

'Every family has someone who just watches,' I heard my father say to John. He must have noticed my isolation, for he came to me. My father was a talker, one for history. Leaning against the tree, he did not ask my feelings but told me how Richard Blakemore got the Pentrych forge, how he opened collieries and built the line that linked the Melingriffith to Pentrych. He told me that Richard Blakemore was the man who had adopted Booker's father, his nephew, a boy of just my age, telling me that one day the boy inherited the whole company which he passed on to his son. 'And that is the Booker,' said my father, 'who owns the Lan and the land we live on. It's all inheritance,' he said to me.

'And what do I inherit, Da,' I asked.

'What about the hill, Phillip. Will that do?' My father outstretched his arms. 'You are a Freeman,' he said to me. 'You inherit this. And a love for Wales.'

'I expect the hill belongs to Booker or Dynevor, too,' I said doggedly. 'They dig everywhere for iron or coal. And the people who live here just help them do it and no one cares for them. Why don't they all say together that they will not wreck the land?'

My father smiled. 'Have you heard of *Shoni ysgubor fawr,*' he asked as he lifted me down the tree. 'He was a Merthyr hero,' he said, hand on my shoulder, 'the first fighting Champion for Wales.' Bumping me to my feet from the branches, my father went on to tell me that when he first came to live in the village with Grandpa Shôn, he didn't want to leave Lan farm. Piling another heap of kitchen pans on the cart, heading back into the cottage to get more, my father called to me, 'Come on, Phillip. We have to help the women pack'. As I walked by his side, he chattered on. '*Shoni ysgubor fawr* didn't like authority,' he said to me. 'Hated the English, especially.' Then, dragging me towards the removal cart, pulling me from my isolation to join in, he said, 'there's a story about his wife - she was alone with an English man in her own house - a Manager at the local iron works, and *Shoni* threatened to kill him. He was heard shouting that no more English men would be Managers in Wales. John Jones his name was, son.' I could never assess what was real and what was *Mabinogion*. My father's stories or those of Grandpa Shôn.

'Are all the English Managers bad then, Da?' I asked, trotting alongside him.

'I'll answer that when Seymour, the new one at the Lan, settles in,' my father grinned. 'You need to speak to Grandpa Shôn,' he added. 'You've got the makings of a true Welsh Ivorite. They say in this village that your Grandpa is Father of the Ivorites, my boy.' My father laughed. 'You would think it enough for him to have fathered me!'

I laughed with him. 'What do the Ivorites do,' I asked.

'It is a Friendly Society to keep the poor from the clutches of the workhouse and the Poor Law,' my father said. 'Grandpa Shôn cares about the rights of working men.'

'And you, Da, what do you believe?' I asked him then.

'A radical non-conformist, me,' he laughed, slapping the donkey who stood there patiently.

Useless at packing, pushed from left to right, it was not long before I again I stood under the branches of our apple tree. While my mother and Susannah fussed and hurried, packed and loaded, folded and wrapped all of our belongings to the cart, I smelled the air of the mountain and did not want the valley floor. It was a sad sight to see the house loaded into one small pile. As my mother or Susannah appeared in the open door, arms full to bursting with pots and pans, blankets and sheets, vases and under-bed china, my father strolled down to the village to get Uncle Hugh from Grandpa's house.

Truly, I was isolated then. I stood useless watching as all the bits and pieces of our life piled-up before me. I watched, empty, as my father and Uncle Hugh, helped by men from the next cottage, lugged the wooden beds down the narrow stairs. I listened, anxious, speechless, glued rigid to the spot. But my mood changed when all was packed. When the frenzy ceased, when the loaded cart trundled its bumpy way past the Colliers', down Mountain Road, with all the family following, I confess to an excitement. Mother held Deborah in her arms, Susannah by her side. Evan walked beside me, and while John helped our father do what could be done to control the pig, I felt proud.

Not far to *Ty'n y Coed* as the black crow flies, all down-hill, but the journey long. The five of us and our parents had said goodbyes to neighbours on the hill, but we were stopped to talk to many another villager. Down the mountain road and along the village to where the Lan shift was coming out. It was *helo*'s then to colliers, to hauliers, and many handshakes as we passed. Then, up the lane to our new place and the chaos of unpacking and scrubbing started all again. I remember that by now my mother was exhausted, sighing but still busy, my father walking round, inspecting, making plans, saying he was hungry and could eat the pig. Evan settled into helping Susannah unpack while baby Deborah slept right through.

Into the long grass I crept, not wanting to be seen, until tired of hiding, I went round to the front and looked out over the desolation of the valley floor. I saw men against the sky like leafless sticks, filing down from the quarry, white faced against work-darkened clothes. Little gaggles of colliers smoked together, while others walked the homeward trek alone. That day, from the vantage point of the new garden, I watched as ragged children filed towards the Level houses after work, too tired to play. Suddenly I had seen the dumb and starving image of my beautiful country. I looked at their tired faces and heard the voice of Isaiah cry *Grind the faces of the poor.* I felt a foreboding then I could not understand. I feel it still and take comfort only that *our time is a very shadow that passeth away.*

1859

My mother taught me much about the Book, but I could not understand her God. The buzzard was a deity to me, the falcon too - but that year we came to live in *Ty'n y Coed*, my mother's God was everywhere. People were fervent. A great Revival was spreading fast through the valleys of my country, rushing like a tide that picks up pebbles and dashes them against the rocks, screaming out 'sinners' with the vengeful wind of clerics. Non-Conformists all, used to their treatment by the established church, people sang out loud paeans and made supplication to an uncompromising God. *We are all infected and impure with sin,* Isaiah's words called out to us. *When we display our righteous deeds, they are nothing but filthy rags. Like autumn leaves, we wither and fall, and our sins sweep us away like the wind.*

I live in superstitious times where ancient Bible words are shouted out to frighten. *Thou shalt not* rules for we are sinners all, grown men and children, too. Though ministers had long decried years of non-attendance at the chapel, while people had blamed poor sermons or the hardness of the times, the spirit of Revival was now filling pews to overflowing. *Capel* was not for me - the Nant my walking space, while other's prayed. When my mother, Susannah and Evan joined those crowded, hard as dolomite, pews, I ambled past the sluices and the clay capped dams which stored the water close to me. While others were praying, and doing all they could to revive the word of God, while thousands of people up and down the country were converted, while my mother waited humbly to be blessed, I walked up to *Ty Newydd* unrepentant for my envy of Astley Thomson, banker and Director of Melingriffith, who lived there. I worshipped God in the snaking waters of Nant Cwm Llwydrew. I did not understand strong, abstract deities, but recognised the power of the holding ponds to drive the water wheel and power furnace blasts.

When I came in from my solitary walk, the house was quiet, my mother and my siblings still at prayer. My father sat pensive at the kitchen window, staring out at clouds that scudded the golden sides of the Garth. A few sheep were there, white against the undergrowth, standing stupidly, and staring back. 'They are as stunned by this bloody Revival as your Mam,' my father said. 'Everyone is on their knees praying - even my colliers and hauliers.'

As he spoke, the door opened and there stood my mother, glowing from her walk down from the chapel - or her prayers 'I heard you, Abraham,' she said. 'Don't you understand? Before the Lord does great work, he first sets his people praying.' My mother walked in, pulling off gloves that only came out for *Capel*. 'That came from the pulpit, Abraham,' she declared. 'The Minister said that last Sunday. The children have gone to Sunday school,' she added, 'The room is really full these days.'

'Mothers send their offspring for redemption while they wear out their knees scrubbing coal-filthy slabs at home,' my father replied bitterly.

'In this village, voices are ringing out, not just in *Capel*, not just in Bethlehem, not just from *Penuel -*' my mother protested.

'And from the hillside, on the banks of the bloody river, anywhere a crowd can gather,' my father cut in. 'They are sheep, Elizabeth, dozy staring sheep like those stragglers out there down from the mountain.'

'Revival is filling us all with hope,' my mother said. 'Times are so hard now that only God can intervene.'

My father tutted. 'Well, you won't see me weeping for my sins, woman. *Speak to the earth, and it shall teach thee,*' he flashed back at her, 'See, my Elizabeth,' he said, 'I can quote the Book as well as anyone!' He shut his eyes as if to sleep.

My mother would have none of it. '*God is our refuge and strength, a very present help in trouble,*' she quoted.

'You take all this stuff into your head as *an ox goeth to the slaughter,*' my father laughed. Mam gave him a disgusted look from where she prepared vegetables at the bosh. 'I saw that, Elizabeth Phillips,' he grinned. 'Just you turn your mind to Lot's wife. Remember? She *looked back from behind him, and she became a pillar of salt.*' Standing then, my father went to the sink and put his arms around my mother, kissing the back of her neck. 'I am tired, woman,' he said, kissing her again. '*Here the wicked cease from troubling, and here the weary be at rest,*' he murmured. He took my mother in his arms, putting his head down on her breast.

Mam was not to be seduced or silenced. 'Have you not heard of Humphrey Jones in Cardiganshire, Abraham?' she asked. 'He came back from America having experienced God first hand - and David Morgan awoke one day while he was actually talking to God,' she declared. 'He is convinced the reign of Christ is here. He said that the holy spirit would descend in July - '

'Woman, have sense. It didn't happen, did it?' my father said. 'Since then, we have had autumn, Christmas and winter. He's a broken man.'

'But Morgan's preaching that the Lord will give us good things is filling the *Capels* with God's presence,' my mother continued. 'The news has spread through all the churches - Non Conformist, Methodist and the Congregational Church, Wesleyans, Baptists - all their pews are full.'

'Elizabeth, everyone is called on to repent?' My father was serious now. 'Repent what? That they work all day for food while the

Masters prosper? That young collier, Evan Roberts, has the Valleys on their knees in prayer - and little good it does them. They come home grimed and tired. Human beings struggle, *Cariad*. That's the deal they have with God.'

'You can *heap coals of fire upon his head, and the LORD shall reward thee,* Abraham,' my mother said shaking her finger. *'The Lord will always be there for you no matter what you say - as long as you repent.'*

'You swallow the rhetoric that flows from these stale Ministers, eh?' my father laughed at her.

'Proverbs, Abraham. It is from the Book - it is not rhetoric.'

'So, no one yawns or sleeps through sermons now?' My father's voice was less gentle. 'That can't be bad. And yes, Elizabeth, wife of mine, sinners we all are, drunkards, gamblers tossing coins outside the Colliers' - but I will not be renounced with *hwyl* from wood-clad pulpits, Eliza.'

'Your father and mother will receive their Baptism by immersion today, Abraham Phillips, and you speak like this. You will come with us to witness their repentance when we go today.'

'I know I am a sinner for I have barely stepped in Chapel since my baptism and I will not come to see my father so abased. Baptism in the Taff at his age......'

'Come, Abraham,' my mother said, moving to him, cajoling, stroking his mass of hair. 'Please come - you father will be wanting it.'

'I cannot have a part in this hysteria, Elizabeth.' I remember thinking how fine my father looked when he was roused to protest. His face fixed, his posture set towards my mother, he said in no uncertain terms, 'This Revival has no place here in this valley where men work to die.' Morose was my father then, serious, dark of face. He sat again at the open window and the song of nesting birds was loud against his silence.

'You must come, Abraham, Shôn will expect you there. Your mother, too. Will you not come down to the gathering just for them?' Both hands on my father's shoulder now, she placed a kiss into his mass of tousled hair.

'Elizabeth, woman. Do you not hear,' said my father, angry, pulling away. 'I will not come. I cannot be part of this Revival.' He stood abruptly, still not facing her. 'I cannot talk to you about religions,' he said. 'All of them underwrite the causes of the Masters. Revolution the men want here, not a Revival.'

'Abraham Phillips. Do you call for revolution? It's black beef I want on the table, not Scotch cattle on the Garth.' Hands on hips then, my mother stared at him in desperation. 'Can you not see? Men need the Lord to fill their lives with meaning. Think of the Newport riots way back. Deaths, too many deaths. We don't want Chartists here. Better the men put their hope in the Lord. The Book means much to them.'

'Superstition, woman. We do not know how to fill the gap, so we use the name of God. Because it is written in the Book, can we stop thinking? Plates are empty here in this village. Working men cannot feed families. No water into wine as in your Book.' Turning to her, my father chanted quietly, do you remember Aberaman 1855, Brynddu, Christmas 1853, 1876, or Cymmer in the Rhondda just two years ago - 114 dead. Remember young Daniel Lewis? He caught it with a ten year old boy alongside him. Dead. So where is this God they praise? He is precisely pouring hot coals on their heads.'

My mother gasped. 'Oh, Abraham. There's wicked you are. God saved many of the men, helped them to heal. He did not make the explosions that brought the coal down onto their heads. He guards us all. It says so in the Book. *Are not five sparrows sold for two pennies?* it says, *yet not one of them is forgotten by God.* I learned that in Sunday School and have not forgotten it. Matthew it is.'

'So,' my Dada sighed, 'you still believe he sees the little sparrow fall, do you, Elizabeth? I wish I could have your faith when I look at those children from the Level Houses, doing shifts that are inhumanely long, without food often. And why do they work? Because husbands and fathers have been splashed at the iron works, injured in the mine - or their mothers are on the straw with yet another child they cannot feed.'

'Your father is already unhappy that we do not send Phillip to Sunday School. A rift it will cause if you do not go to this Baptism. It means so much to them.' As I watched, as I listened, I could see my mother quieter, a peacemaker now, but my Da would have no part of it.

'My father will have to understand I cannot share his faith,' my Da said firmly. 'His commitment to the working man, yes, I follow that. His passion for the language. Yes, I follow that, but Baptism in the Taff? No. I cannot show my face there in a crowd of people lost in the vain hope of their deliverance.' My father paused, took stock and then, walking towards my mother, he took her in his arms and rubbed his nose to hers. 'We cannot quarrel over this, Elizabeth,' he said gently. He looked round the kitchen to where I sat watching. Susannah had brought Deborah in, was holding her on her knee 'Come on you young progenitors of the future,' my father called. 'Go with your mother to see Grandpa Shôn and *Mamgu* Deborah dunked in the Taff in the name of their God.' Laughing, he started to quote one of his favourite passages from the Book. Before he started, my lips were already forming the words from the Book of Romans, chapter eight, verse 35. '*What will separate us from the love of Christ?*' my father chanted, imitating the reverend Thomas, '*Will anguish, or distress, or persecution, or famine, or nakedness, or peril, or the sword?*' Jumping on the kitchen table, he declared, '*As it is written: For your sake we are being slain all the day; we are looked upon as sheep to be slaughtered.* Do Hear that, Phillip? I can see your big eyes watching. Do you hear me, Evan?' he shouted to my brother who had just come in with John. 'All those men who die below are sheep to be slaughtered. Some truth in that, young John. The Masters lead us like sheep to work for a pittance.'

I remember how my mother ignored him, that she busied herself with Deborah who was being clad in her best bonnet, sleepily resisting the ribbons tied beneath her dimpled chin. 'Tut, Abraham,' she declared under her breath, 'What an exhibition you make before the children.'

'But it is the Revival, Elizabeth. I, too, am swept away with it! Anyway, the Book says, *in all these things we conquer overwhelmingly through him who loved us. For I am convinced that neither death, nor life, nor angels, nor principalities, nor present things, nor future things, nor powers, nor height, nor depth, nor any other creature will be able to separate us from the love of God in Christ Jesus our Lord.* The book of Romans, Eliza. I know your Book. That is what takes us underground, woman, that is what gives us subservience to Booker and his like. Believe or not, we cannot escape it. Human beings struggle,' he repeated. 'Masters, too. I recognise humanity has different needs. But I will not go down to the river and testify to sins I cannot own.' My father came alive for me that day. His angry words engraved themselves within my questioning heart.

My father did not repent, would not come down with us to his father's Baptism in the murky waters of the Taff - that same filthy, snaking water that blessed the coal and dolomite. Where of an evening, fish leaped the foaming water of the Weir, the Reverend Thomas would be down from Penuel, in full voice, his body flapping black in passion to urge his people to accept Christ. Loud amens, thanks to the Lord and wonderful - *Diolch iddo* and *Bendigedig* - would be called out from everywhere -

So we left my father in the kitchen and set-off without him. My mother, arrogant, tossed her head towards him in defiance, as she picked-up Deborah and stepped out through the door, calling Evan to follow her. Head in the clouds as usual, the Book under his arm, Evan wandered out after my mother, while Susannah called to me.

As we made our way down the track towards the river, I was thinking only about what my father had said up on the table, trying to understand about Baptism and God. I recall I complained bitterly that John always was allowed to stay with Da. 'Coal in his blood, that one,' my mother had said. 'Better to leave him be.' Then poking my brother Evan, mother complained that he was not saying much. 'Always deep in thought, you,' she said to him. 'None of this rebellion in you, I hope.' She did not question me as together, she and Susannah, their heads together, herded us down the lane.

At the river a crowd was gathering. Hymns rose and fell with the spring breeze. Joyous they all were, ecstatic. First the singing and the loud declamation of Reverend Thomas that God would soon come down. Women were flapping fans, men jumping up to declare that they had found their way - all of them aflame with gospel-glory. I stood at the back of the crowd, listening.

'If we are living in the light,' shouted the Reverend, 'as God is in the light, then we have fellowship with each other, and the blood of Jesus, his Son, cleanses us from all sin.' A pause for the words to sink in, breaths held in the crowd assembled there. 'If we claim we have no sin,' the Reverend's voice rang clear, 'we are only fooling ourselves and not living in the truth. But if we confess our sins to him, if we are faithful, He will forgive us our sins and cleanse us from all wickedness.' I was on tiptoes then. Evan made his way to the front where Grandpa Shôn and *Mamgu*-Deborah stood in line, waiting for their Baptism. Strange how loud it all was. 'You must be humbled before God because of your sins,' the Reverend shouted. 'You must all make an effort. Pray in the streets, in the pits, pray publically,' he commanded. 'We must all encourage sinners to turn to the Lord.' I looked up at my mother worried about our responsibilities to my Da.

Every word the Reverend Thomas spoke echoed clearly over us. Strange. I remember thinking that it was a mystery where the Reverend had found this powerful voice, because in *Capel* it was not so clear and many of the older ones nodded to sleep. The singing down by the Taff was so loud that day it must have been heard in Portobello. I have never heard its like. Everyone was excited, singing with such vigour that sweat ran down their eager faces. A lasting impression it made on me. I have to admit that it was exciting. I remember wishing that my father were there to take me on his shoulders so that I could better see.

A collier from the Coed y Beddw pit that I often saw as he walked up from the village, spoke out as loud as the Reverend, waving his arms, a big black carrion, shouting about repentance and that he wouldn't go drinking to the Colliers' anymore and what a sin it was to drink.

'What do you think of all this?' my mother asked a woman standing in the crowd. 'My Abraham says we have all gone mad with this religion.' The woman shrugged her shoulders. I heard my mother tell her in a whisper, 'He wouldn't come - embarrassing, what with his parents here for Baptism. God doesn't get a fair deal in our house,' she added quietly.

'There are meetings like this everywhere these days,' the woman said. 'Doesn't put bread on the table, that's for sure. It's for the young.'

'Aye. But hard men are taken with it as well.' I remember that my mother looked confused.

I listened to the conversation bubbling around me. Watched bewildered as Grandpa Shôn received his Blessing. He was standing there, wet shirt sticking to him, head put underwater, there in the cold and dirty Taff. I was disorientated by this open show, this excitement amongst the grown-ups of my world, this explosion of religion, this public confession of sin. God and Christ seemed to be everywhere within this teeming crowd. I counted women that I knew, saw colliers that worked down the Lan with my father, saw friends of our Susannah, and the Reverend Thomas sweating cobs. Why did everyone suddenly want deliverance? It was all sin, all God. There was no mention of the pits or Masters.

'God bless you, child,' came the voice of David Llewellyn from *Maes Gwyn*, breaking my reverie, his sweaty hand clasping mine. 'Have you come to the Lord?'

Blankly I stared at him until my mother bustled me away. 'There's late it is, Susannah,' she declared as she made her greeting to Mr Llewellyn. 'Can't stop, David,' she said hurriedly, 'Time we were home now. Abraham will want his food before the shift.'

I recall now the relief, the gratitude I felt to be saved from this encounter. Without a word, it was up the slope to home. Deborah wanted to walk some steps. She took my hand and it was slow then and into the woods before the upward track to home. My mother and Susannah talked nonstop about the Revival and Grandpa Shôn's baptism, while Evan stalked before us, almost man.

Deborah was tired by now and in Susannah's arms. Seeing my brother ahead of us, I called out to him. 'Evan,' I shouted, 'wait for me,' but my voice was dissipated by the breeze. Alone as ever, my step in line with my mother, I fell behind as usual. Sun danced on my mother's hair, the breeze making it fly upwards, hairy fine, free in spite of pins.

The sun had shone throughout that day. Even the Taff had sparkled. April was moving into May with the wild garlic, erect and strong, perfuming the air as we trudged up the lane. A few celandines still bloomed and early buttercups shone through briars, some dancing free on banks where grass still grew in spite of splattered mud. As we tumbled up the steps to home, I remember that our garden was golden in the sunlight, neat with rows of flowers. The windows of the cottage glinted where the sun shone back at us its glory. Worship of a Sun God I could comprehend.

Two decades on, I stand here in the kitchen of *Ty'n y Coed*, the low sun skirting its light to the flagstones on the floor. Am I glad to be back home? The burning coal of my quest is heavy. I think back to that day of the Revival and see only the image of young Deborah, a grown woman now, her eyes shut, long lashes on her soft, warm cheeks, asleep, curled on the chair, magnificent. Glad I was to be back home that day, glad to fall back into normality, my mother laying into the vegetables for my father's dinner, cutting him doorsteps for his snap. Through the open window, I can still hear John asking Dada questions. Always about coal. No interest in the wider world. 'There are lots of old workings on the Garth,' I heard my father say. 'But I don't like those Rat Holes. Lucky I am to be down the Lan. Got more time to answer your questions, now,' he had chuckled, looking over to the window where my mother smiled, complicit as she worked.

'Dada,' John asked, intent on information, 'is it true that the Coed y Bedw Colliery over there is two hundred years old and that it links up with Lan drift?' His finger pointed South, and I remember seeing how big his hands were, strong, not white and small like mine.

'Two hundred years old, John, boy? I don't really know,' my father answered 'All I can tell you is that it belonged to Morgan Thomas and he sold it on to Booker.'

'Is Booker Master of the Lan,' John asked.

'Aye,' said my father, 'And Master collector of our rent, as well.' I remember that he grinned.

'But Dada, Grandfather Shôn said it was two hundred years ago. Booker is now,' John insisted.

'Umm,' mused my father, 'I don't really know its history. Thomas Vaughan worked some place around here a hundred years ago. But Booker is bound to crop up somewhere. Old Booker must have bought it at some time.'

Standing suddenly, pointing out over the little Garth, my father moved his hand across the vista. 'Look at that, son,' he said. 'What Master could hope for more: here in our valley they get all the materials they need in this one place. They do not see it beautiful. They see the trees for the timber or charcoal, iron ore, limestone and coal - and even water power.' He laughed, indicating Pond Mawr. 'There is as much stone as they want for building - and right at the bottom of our garden, clay for their bricks.' Drawing John to him, he added, 'and on top of that he has silly buggers like you and me ready to crawl underground to bring out the coal, while others rush off to mine his iron, man his furnaces or dig out his clay pit. Made they are, the Masters, because the likes of you and me help them make it, help them buy their mansions.'

I remember hearing my father laugh, seeing him stretch and rub his back, sore from working underground. His face was fine, but even as a child I could see coal in the scar marks on his neck. 'Son,' he counselled John, 'it's hard working underground. It's sweat and blood. Everything gets handled many times before you see it up here. Colliers and hauliers, shovels, buckets, wheel barrows to take it to the drams - it all gets hauled by men. And youngsters like you start with the heavy toil. Go to school, John. Make your life elsewhere. One man in our family underground is more than enough for your Mam - even if this praying and Revival does bring some God to help us all.'

'But I want to be a collier, Dada.' John had insisted. I can see now his eager face looking up at my father in great admiration. 'I like it all, Da,' he said. 'I like the outside entrance, the horse stables, the workshops. Some days when I walk out alone, I have looked in the explosive stores and the sorting bays.'

'God, man,' my father cut in, 'don't let your Mam know that! She'll never let you out alone. She'll have your guts for garters, just you see.' My father joked with him, slapping his back just like a boyo. 'It can be bloody hot or cold and draughty down there,' he said, 'and noisy, too. All you will hear is the hammer and clink, the coal falling - and you will get sore arms heaving picks and shovels, sledge hammers - and you have to pay for your own candles, too. It's not exactly heaven, boy.'

'I'd rather work in the coal mine than an iron pit,' John declared.

'Son, you do not have to work in either. School for you along with Evan - and Phillip when his time comes.' My father yawned, moving towards the kitchen. As I listened to John and Dada talk, as I trailed in behind them, I heard John say, 'I'll bring home enough for Phillip's school fee - and I'll get the free coal.' Everything in my life has conspired to make me feel inadequate. I could see the bond between my father and my brother, one I did not have. Looking back, I see my mother intervene and wonder if she understood my isolation. Busy with the peas that Evan had shelled, impatiently waiting still for mine, she moved over to me, taking the basin and doing the peas herself.

'Free coal, indeed,' she jibed at John, 'and then you'll have to shovel it in when they have tipped it in the road.'

'I won't mind that Mam,' John insisted.

'There's strange,' my mother retorted. 'Never seen you rushing out to fill the bucket when I need it. Now to the table you, and no more talk of coal - and mind you get out to the rain butt to wash those hands of yours first.'

Shrugging, John moved to the outside door. Not one to lose an argument, he said, 'If I go underground, I'll still be working when my Da is old. You'll need help then.'

'That boy is all confidence and cheek,' my mother sighed as she watched him at the tub. 'A man he'll be in no time and more worry for us all if he is underground - and as for you, Abraham Phillips, aren't you the least bit interested in hearing about your father's Baptism?' My mother was always admirable when roused.

'I have nothing but embarrassment that my father has been Baptised so publically,' my father declared. And don't worry about John, woman,' he taunted. 'Remember the sparrows, Elizabeth.' He put his arms around my mother's waist, declaring, 'The Lord won't let him fall.' As my mother opened her mouth to protest, my father whispered in her ear, 'You know already that I am a dreadful sinner!' He smiled wickedly. 'But those sparrows, girl? Remember? *Not one of them is forgotten by God*'. Turning to her, he kissed my mother's startled face in front of us.

As I stand here now, a grown man, I dwell on the words of my father to my brother, John. And the words of the testimony of Genesis comes like a song from the depths of my childhood: *And the Lord God said thou art cursed above all cattle, and above every beast of the field, upon thy belly thou shalt go, and dust shalt thou eat all the days of thy life.*

Cursed we were. Forgotten by God.

1860

Exposed to the prevailing Westerlies is Pen y Garn, but our cottage in the Gwaelod is sheltered, unfrozen while the higher ground is solid. There, on the flanks of the Taff Valley, my father had made the moss-ridden stones grow into home. We were rarely cut-off by the ice that froze the lower ground of Nant Cymllewydrew - the frosty bottom of the hill. Sometimes, as the westering sun lit the grass around the cottage, gilding the trees, it seemed a very heaven to be living here. My mother had tended flowers, put in vegetables, their order comforting - and inside, the continuous smell of her cooking - of *cawl* or *bara* pudding - mingled with the homely warmth of burning coal. My mother's life was busy, so oftentimes, when school was finished or it was full summer and the break from lessons, I was left to wander where I would. Then, up then past *Maesaraul* I would go, saying *shw mae* to Mary Morgan, who stood out the back with Mrs George, another to Mr Thomas, digging his vegetables. Then, with Thomas Lewis watching, half running backwards in politeness as I passed, I would take a deep breath and race to reach the Garth. Once there, shouting out loudly, flying with raptors overhead, I was master of the air, alone. While poorer children of my age scrapped coke, I ran under the buzzard's call, saw the swifts swooping, heard the skylarks sing, their song never ending as I galloped through. Or I would sit alone with gold winged dragonflies, take sustenance from the spring water bubbling out for me, or walk the zigzagged paths that crossed the mountain side, running through the bracken, kicking ant hills as I ran. Ignorant, I was, unacquainted then with real distress. I did not fully understand the stark difference between the wages of the boy or man who could read and those that laboured. I knew but did not dream the harsh life of the working child, had seen them entering expenses at the shop, had seen them smoking, heard them swearing like a working man. Perhaps I was afraid - but while Susannah assisted our mother in the house, nursing, cleaning, fetching water, I roamed the craggy path that led to the Lan farm, where Grandpa Shôn had brought my father as a child. I knew the craggy pennant of its rocky face, the rough terrain of badgers, of sheep, grazing their days away. I had not been taken early to my father's Drift or to the iron mines to learn the calcinator's sulphurous vapour. Instead, I lived with knowledge but in ignorance. Instead, I breathed in fine bluebell woods, gathering flowers for my mother, carpets of violets beneath my feet, with blackbirds rummaging spent autumn leaves. This was the careless pattern of my childhood summer.

These two worlds I lived in never merged as one. For some reason, I seldom spoke with children who were working, never took one as a friend. I lived on the Garth, wild, apart. I belonged to the hill, the walk back home slow, reluctant. The valley floor was alien. Tired and slipping on the mountain's downward paths, backed by the setting sun, I would face with disgust the microcosm of its industry, its furnaces, its brickworks, stagnant pools. I measured my progress home by sinking spirits and the ever rising chimneys and the noise.

Autumn passed, with leaves filling the garden of *Ty'n y Coed*. Winter followed quickly that year, my father busy making good the house, my mother was always occupied with the little ones. As the evenings settled down to early darkness, as the weather precluded my visits to the Garth, that old feeling of isolation haunted my days. Evan was deep in books, John had no time for me. I watched while seasons changed. I listened as my father listed jobs he had done to repair the house. Six then, I copied Evan, turning pages but could not yet read.

Christmas approached and snow fell. As I walked in exhilarated from putting footsteps in the virgin snow, my mother said 'Your future is secure, young man.' Her voice was high with excitement. 'Dada has signed the Deeds for *Ty'n y Coed*,' she said. 'Booker has signed an agreement giving our family rights here for nigh on a hundred years,' she purred. 'We have no rent to pay. The cottage comes with your Da's new place,' she laughed. 'Christmas will be good this year.'

I must have looked bewildered, for she said, 'Come, Phillip. Are you not glad? Why look so serious. You can rightly smile.' Pulling me towards her, she went on, 'Dada says Mr Booker was in such a benevolent mood. He has wed this year - linked himself to Caroline Emily Slon from one of the County Families.' I recollect how she stressed the individual names as she spun me round. 'They will live at Velindre,' she said. 'What a house, Phillip! Happy Thomas William Booker must be. That will be why he has been so generous to us.' It was deep winter now and Christmas Eve. Snow had fallen since morning. Everywhere was white and beautiful, but this was the day my dreams turned into nightmare. What is my prospect, then, I thought. I could only assume that Booker's coal fields called me and I would have to work. I knew that coal was bread and butter in my world, that it was everything - it was the friends we had, our conversation, our community. Young though I was, for me, it spelled out tragedy. I recall my father came in then, laden with holly for the house.

'I do not want to work with coal,' I burst out to him.

'Coal is everywhere these days,' he laughed, dropping the armful of holly to the floor.

'But you told John one man underground in this family was enough,' I protested. 'I don't want to go underground even if he does.'

'Not that there is much else of worth round here,' my father said, leaning to warm his hands before the fire. 'Coal is the future, son - especially for boys who can read and do arithmetic. You will settle to it, Phillip. I know you do not want to work underground now, I know that I have advised against it, but the Bute Merthyr field is seething with new people and wanting more - in the Rhondda Fach, they are now mining Ferndale coal. A secure future you would have in coal.'

Silent I was, old for my years, my mother said. I estimate that my father was thirty eight when I was six, but he was very old already in my eyes. 'I want to travel, Da,' I said. 'I like to live in air not underground tunnelling like a mole.' Standing by the fire beside my father, the spitting heat from snow-wet coal steaming to the air, I asked, 'Did you not want to travel, Da? I do.'

My father laughed again, his laughter ringing through the cottage. 'Travel, son? I have travelled if you count coming down from Ystrad Dyfodwg to Pentyrch. I call it travel and I call it progress - the opening of the Taff Vale Railway brought me here. It'll be right up to Treherbert by 1865. Is that far enough for you to travel, boy?' I stood there horrified and cold.

'I want to travel further, Dada,' I said, seriously. 'Not just to Treherbert. I have seen right across the water from the Garth.'

'Mining villages are cropping up all along the valley floors,' my father mused, ignoring my intent. 'You can go further from this village if you want to get away from your Mam and me! Coal mining is vital to progress,' he declared. 'It's the place to work these days. It can lead to other industry, too -.' Then, drawing me close to him, he said intently, 'Everything is associated with it, boy.'

As I stood there quiet, pale faced and miserable, my father said, 'Look across at the brickworks, at the iron works - and there are deeper pits now to find the better coal. It's that stuff of higher quality they need. You aim at that, son, and your life is made. With your good brain, you will earn extra every week. Phillip, cheer-up. It is Christmas Eve - help me put this holly around for your Mam.'

Mindlessly, I bent to sort the holly, but I thought of coal. It was all dirty, low quality stuff or good, it was all coal and it was mined by men down the rat holes that peppered my walks. 'I do not want to follow you underground, Dada,' I said again as I put the smaller pieces of holly to one side. 'I want to go to school and then I want to travel.'

My father was silent. He pushed me gently from his side. 'History has been unkind, eh, Phillip? You hear about the accidents and worry.' He smiled then. 'We'll leave it all to John, shall we? It's a colliers' life for him. He's only eight - and can't wait to follow me into the mine. I want you all in school, first, anyway - you and John, and our Susannah, too.'

'And then underground, Da?' I asked him apprehensively.

'It hasn't done me any harm, boy,' he said, his pile of holly on the floor. Look at this place we have from coal. We'll make it fine with these berries for Christmas Day.' I could tell that my father was proud of our cottage, proud of his position underground. For him at this moment there was nothing else. Standing up, he grinned at me. 'Work calls,' he said. 'I have to work this shift but tomorrow is Christmas and I will be free to talk all day. Listen. That's old Nelson, the steam engine, turning the blades of the Guibal fan, calling me to pick up my step.'

Christmas? Up to my bedroom then and to the window. Breathing hard, I looked out through my mist of breath to the black horror of the place spread out across the valley floor. The snow around it made it look more ominous, more black. Reluctant tears pricked my eyes as I thought of working underground. I knew then I was different. I was not hard and strong like Da and John. The realisation of my weakness shamed me. Down to the coal shed then, fast down the stairs and out. I shut the door. Its black on top of blackness gave me space to think of the air-boys and their solitary, dark days. I wondered how any parent could so sacrifice their child. I felt sick, ashamed of my distress, mortified that I dreaded work with coal so much. I thought of the carters underground, dragging the drams along the narrow passage ways on hands and knees. I thought of the children down with them. There, amidst the coal, I felt true isolation. Opening the door to the frosty cold yard, I crept over to the window and could hear the family in the cottage, knew that Grandpa Shôn and *Mamgu* had arrived. I could hear them singing out *Nadolig Llawen* to Susannah and the girls, could hear *Mamgu* in conversation with John and Evan, could hear Grandpa Shôn congratulating Da on finishing *Ty'n y Coed*, congratulating him on signing Booker's Deeds.

'He's retaining mineral rights,' my father said, 'So there will be no holes dug under kitchen tables in this house.' I heard my father laugh. 'I signed it with a X,' he said, crockery ringing as plates and cups passed round. 'All written in English it was - no attempt to give it to me in Welsh!'

I heard Grandpa Shôn's voice explode, shouting out *'Duw Mawr* - Great God' - over and over again. 'And in our own country too,' I heard him growl. *'Di-Gymraeg* Masters think they own this land and they cannot even use the language!'

While my siblings ate and adults chattered in excluding, fast accelerating crescendos, I watched through the lamp-lit windows as drinks were poured to celebrate. I could see that everyone was excited by Christmas and the signing of the Deeds, angry at the lack of Welsh. I watched. I listened. Then, quietly I slipped from the window back into yard. I leaned against the door of the old coalhouse, thought of the shiny lumps of coal hewn from the earth - thought of miners as beetles, with their black and lustrous backs. Then I remembered the uncovered grave of baby Deborah, felt my loneliness, my solitude would never end. Tears fell from my eyes, rolled down my dust-dirtied face into the wedges of my mouth, dropped like molten insects in the snow. I stared ahead at them knowing that Dada would say: Welsh men don't cry.

A slight chirruping caught my attention, jolted my despair. I watched a thin, bedraggled robin, frantically flying from stone to shed, from window to floor, in search of solace or of food. Its frailty in the shadow of the coal shed startled me. The need for tears had vanished, my loneliness dissolved. I was no longer alone in the backyard. I felt clean. Peaceful. Sure that I would travel from this place. And more than ever sure I would not work in coal.

1861 - 63

I learned that every man has his own ambition and I settled gradually to mine. Life in our house was happy amidst the rabbit warren of old workings and new mines. My father did not mention going underground again and my mother had her way about school. Evan, John and I were bundled off to Booker's Bethlehem, which opened weekdays, resounding to the cries of fortunate children. Some, like my brother, John, came reluctantly, but I set off daily, my head high. The tuppence a week paid, I buttoned the round collar to the white shirt that I had after Evan, tucked into trousers never made for me and set out joyously. Grandpa Shôn had forgotten his rift with my father. In the evenings, after school or at weekends, they would sit in the kitchen talking. This was my education, my insight into adult thought. I would shrink to nothing in the corner, listening, while Susannah minded Deborah, John walked and Evan read.

Time had passed since my father had extolled the virtues of a life in coal. As I delve into my mind to find him now, I hear him banging on the table as he did when he was moved. I remember in particular one day when he and grandpa were together by the fire, my mother at the table, busy making bread. 'It is a poor state that working men cannot get a fair wage,' he said. My ears alerted. So, coal no longer is the future I thought in joy. I shrunk back into the shadow, my eyes set on my Da, my ears attentive. I drunk in every word. 'Wages for colliers have been held for years,' my father said. 'If this goes on, people in this village will starve'.

'The Masters have invested heavily,' my grandfather replied. 'Look at that Guibal fan Booker is putting at the New Lan. State of the art, is that and will have cost him a pretty penny or two.'

'Father, from the Butes of Aberdare to the Crawshay's of Merthyr,' my father declared, 'from Blakemore to Booker, they are all the same. Invest they may do, but the riches they grow fat on come from the empty guts of working men and from the bowels of our country.'

'Then, you men must pull together, Abraham,' my grandfather said. 'I've said it all before. Unions, friendly societies. Men helping men.' Grandpa Shôn pulled hard on his old clay pipe, drew in the smoke and puffed. Leaning back in the chair, he stretched his legs before him, belly high. 'You always complain, boy,' he said with great superiority, 'but you work for the Masters, drink sometimes with Booker and will not unionise. You do nothing but philosophise and work. Join me in the Ivorite movement,' he declared, fists banging the table. 'Join me in the Friendly Society and you will see real change.' I remember how I watched the two of them, my father with arms on the table and Grandpa Shôn eating the steam about his mouth.

'The cooperative urge is strong amidst our men,' my father replied, leaning towards Granda Shôn. 'They all support each other anyway - their women help each other, too. Unions would bring them conflict, fear,' he said, his eyes wide. 'Getting food for their families must come before a fight for rights.' He banged his fist on the table to emphasize each word.

Grandpa Shôn dug in his pocket for more tobacco to stuff his pipe. 'The Masters live in their mansions,' he started.

'While my men only just survive down in the Level houses,' Da finished.

'Survive if they are lucky,' Grandpa agreed. 'Accident, injury and they are lost - belonging to the Ivorites would save them from dire poverty.'

'I know what you say, Shôn,' my father intervened, 'But a friendly society will get them nowhere. A bit of the Master's fortune is what they need.' Dada's voice rose loudly, his resonant syllables ricocheting around the stone walls of our cottage.

Hearing raised voices, my mother came from the table to the kitchen door, hands on her hips. 'Hisst, Abraham Phillips,' she said, 'Watch what you say. Mr Booker has been good to you. The job, the cottage .....'

Dada paused. *'Cariad anwl,'* he said, 'I respect Tom Booker as a man, know he has invested heavily in me. The Guibal fan down at the Lan is more than the mine deserves - its seams are spent, his business down there threatened.'

My mother was silent, face frozen. She had heard the worst. Business at the Lan failing meant poverty for everyone. Families would be destitute, thrown unto Parish Relief or the workhouse. She stood, listening, poised like a hawk, her bread dough in her hand.

My father got up abruptly, walked over to the window. He stood a moment silently. Then, spinning round to grandpa, said, 'You and your Ivorites are more about the language, Shôn. Your fancy handshakes, secret signs and passwords won't take a collier far.'

Surrounded now in steam, angry was Grandpa Shôn. Puffing violently, he coughed as my father spoke. 'I am not asking you for revolution, son,' he spat. 'The Ivorites are there for men, for collier to help collier, haulier and cutter, basketers, too. It doesn't have to be Scotch Cattle or a revolution. If the Lan is spent, even more you need the union of men.'

'Chartists, Unions, Ivorites, the aims are all the same,' murmured my mother. 'You get unions banding the colliers together and you'll have riot underground.' Dough on the table then, twisting her apron with anxious hands, she looked at my father, pleading almost, 'and if you don't join them, Abraham,' she said, plaintively, 'if you don't join

- or if they know that Booker has a special place for you, they will black-list you and we will all end up in Pontypridd. The workhouse is never far from the door, you know that, overman or collier.' With a huge sigh, and clearly near to tears, my mother rushed outside to the pump and started to fill the buckets with a frenzy.

'There's fiery your good woman is, son!' my Grandpa declared. 'My Deborah doesn't pump like that!' Grandpa Shôn laughed wryly. 'Hear me out, Abraham,' he said, extending an arm to my father who was keen to go to the pump to appease my mother. 'Listen to me now'. Like a child, my father stood looking at his father, obedient. 'Men don't have to band together just for the purpose of negotiation,' Grandpa said, 'or for complaints against the Masters. They unite in love for each other.'

Dada was impatient now. 'Love for each other, father? Love for each other? Have you seen them shouting and quarrelling outside the Colliers when they are tanked to courage? Do you not know Collier's law? Often times my men come up with cuts from settling scores, knuckles bleeding and not from falling coal. Elizabeth is right. We don't want torch light processions through the village every time their wage is cut.'

'And what in accident, Abraham?' my Grandfather shouted. 'What in accident? I remember when the furnace spilt - up at the iron works. I will never forget the screams of women and children as they fled, the injuries, the fathers burned - on straw for months with no-one to put food before their families. And think of those young hauliers down the Lan - when they have to stop a dram quickly, when they put in that sprag between the spokes - they are stuck there between the rail and the side of the level in total darkness. You know they frequently get crushed. And in the iron works, that continuous working, day and night. Children are there, Abraham, employed in all sorts of ways. It is not - '

'I know they are breaking lime-stone seven days week, Shôn,' Da cut in. 'The black and vitrifying mass stretches for hundreds of yard round here. I know it and I know about the sprigging. But the hauliers are agile and the tip-girls strong -'

'They work for a pennies, Abraham. Would you see Susannah at that job?' Shôn o'r Lan was scathing now, his old eyes rheumy, faded, fixed on my Da.

'I know about low pay - and accidents, too. I just don't see how your Ivorite love can stop it all.' My father's face was serious now. 'The people here are hungry. That I know.' I watched his mouth tighten, his eyes directly on his father's eyes. 'But you cannot fill their stomachs up with love.'

'Are you cold hearted, Abraham? Think of the under-puddlers, son. There are always boys around the puddling-furnace no older than your John - unprotected, they are opening furnace doors.' Grandpa Shôn waited for a response and getting none, continued, his old voice singing in high tenor as his anger rose. 'The boys and girls who do the pulling-up get no more than a pittance and they are breathing air at such high temperatures.'

'Aye, and the catchers, hooker-ons and pilers, too. It is the cruel way of industry. None of the children are adequately paid, I know. They should not work. I know that too. But all the Ivorites and unions or working men together could do nothing to alter the processes of industry. If these children could not work at straightening, iron-filling or being water carriers, their families would starve. The bit they make is that vital extra penny that keeps their family fed. No observation of Parliament's Ten Hour Rule has been enforced, so what, in God's name, could your Ivorites do? Many a little girl from the Hard Level works as a tip-girl and, yes, I know their labour is hard - but getting out the cinders is something they can do. It disgusts me that they have to work, Shôn o'r Lan, but I do not see the answer in the Ivorites. Nothing short of revolution will stop this exploitation.'

'But friendship and support in time of accident, son, that must help fill the gap,' Shôn said insistently.

'It is not enough. Children should be in school, not work. I have to say that constantly to John. He'd be underground now if he had the chance. Lucky he doesn't have to on my wage. There's time enough to work when they are men. But while the women are glad of the extra that a child can bring, while the Masters invest in this valley and there is chance to work, they will. It is the human condition, the evil costing of this industry. What can your Ivorites do? Women watch their little ones with such maternal love, but seem content that as soon as they can lift, as long as they are wrapped up warm, they can go to work with men. The industrial world insults them and they have no option but accept what comes.' My father was standing now. Pacing. Angry that Grandpa Shôn had pushed him into conflict.

Grandpa stood up and straightening his back slowly, walked over to my father's side. Hand on Da's shoulder, it was clear he would not stop now. 'A union of working men would provide help,' he persisted. 'A Friendly Society is more than a union, anyway. We speak of benefits as well as love. It is a good institution for the working class. Moral and social improvement for us all. Distinctly Welsh, too, are we Ivorites.'

'You mean the language, Shôn?' Da said, spinning on him. 'I'll work for that. Our tongue must never die. Now that the Irish flood the industry, working for less than women, and English men are brought down to manage us in our own pits, that push for the language is imperative.'

'You will not find the English in Wales hauling coal,' Shôn laughed, slumping down in the old wooden rocker, passion spent. 'Your new pit manager, Seymour does not graft.' Grandpa Shôn leaned back, rocking the oak chair quietly as he spoke. 'I agree with you, Abraham. Nothing is solved through violence. *Cyfeillgarwch, Cariad a Gwirionedd* - Friendship, Love and Truth - that is the motto of the Ivorites. We want to encourage the Welsh language and preserve our members from want. Simple aims, boy? Honourable?' The old man looked quizzically at my father, awaiting a reply.

Getting none, he muttered as he scrapped out his pipe, 'It all goes back to the Act of Union,' he said.

'Good God, Shôn,' my father exploded. 'I know the Acts of Union linked us tight to England, but that was centuries before the Masters claimed the wealth under our land. You can't just blame history and the English Parliament for the rape of our country. We are all responsible. They could not get the minerals out without our graft. And look how the village grows as willing families flood in to help. I fear that if we threaten their profits with unions or your friendly societies, working men will feel the Master's rage.'

'Like Elizabeth, you sound, Abraham.' My grandfather leaned forward in his chair. 'Son, in my life time I have seen children starve and parents die. The Taff is made of tears. Look at our valley. I have watched it laid waste by industry. Look at the little Garth - if you can see it through the smoke. The iron works have destroyed it. Look at the Lan where you are Overman, look at the other levels at our door. Is that wealth of coal savaged from our earth taken in the name of Wales or England?'

'The old Welsh gentry played their part,' my father said. He was calmer now, more measured. 'Dynevor owns the lands that Booker rents.' He bent forward to poke the reluctant fire into flame. 'This fire is as dead as the words we speak, Shôn o'r Lan. We had better get it going before Eliza sees.' As I hung back into the shadows, the two of them got on their haunches, blowing the embers into flame.

'You've let the fire out!' Mam declared as she burst in through the kitchen door, weighed down by water buckets, 'How can I bake the bread? Or make the tea? Are you two blind or stupid?' She flew across the room to the dying fire, quickly plying it with kindling John had cut. As she mended the fire, as I pretended to be reading, Grandpa Shôn stood up, paused to relight his pipe, and shrugging his shoulders, making eye contact with my Da, said with a wicked grin, 'I'll expect to see you at the next meeting in the Colliers', boy.'

Dada ignored him. Walking over to the buckets, he said, 'Ahh, Elizabeth, I see you have brought the water for the kettle. Tea now, is it?' My mother, peacemaker always, rubbed her hand to clear the coal, 'Aye, Abraham,' she smiled. 'Enough of talk.'

Cramped, I could scarcely feel my legs, but determined to stay invisible. As my mother cut *teisennau cri*- little Welsh cakes - from the mixture she had rolled, as she threw them to the bake stone, the sweet smell of cooking filled the kitchen. Soon, the old black kettle sang and Grandpa set to rocking in the chair. As my father leaned back looking to the sky, I thought this world of adults, life itself, impenetrable.

1864

Every person is proud of what they do well and I was no exception. School was a joy for me. Reading came like a spring breeze. I was there with Evan, and to my grandfather's disgust, reading in English alongside Welsh. Grandpa Shôn maintained that the downfall of the language started in the class rooms at Bethlehem, cursing and declaiming that English was not the language of scholars or Welsh a bar to moral and industrial prosperity.

John's heart was with the coal still. He was at school with us in body, though not in head. Daily, he picked father's brain about coal and mining, could quote all the technical stuff, had it all in his head. I remember that like a ripe seed, it would burst out like an explosion every chance he had. Off to school we'd go, pushed through the door with no due ceremony, our little round collared shirts as white as snow. Evan strode ahead, long legged and arrogant, alone, while Susannah stayed to clear the breakfast, help our mother, before running to catch up.

I smile as I remember I would go down the lane, singing, pitting my voice against the whistle of steam, bounding the grass tumps, making for Bethlehem and school. Behind me would be John, his big hands moving in insistent emphasis.

'Phillip, the Lan slopes down an incline before you reach the levels - do you know they used a clinometer to estimate the dip of the seam,' he gasped as we ran along, 'they use it with a compass. Phillip. Listen. Stop that noise.'

'Only a strike would stop that noise,' I ventured, clever, deliberately misunderstanding, while the rattle of trucks from the clay pit surged across the lane.

'I mean your singing, mun,' said John, puffing alongside me now and no escape. 'You never listen to me. Do you know, they have a long piece of wood several feet long,' he forced on my reluctant ears, 'they place it between the rock and edge of the clinometer - you're not listening, Phillip.' Insistent my brother now, his voice plaintive as the buzzard overhead. 'Do you know about metal tubbing, Phil? Do you know about walling?'

'All I know,' I said, 'is that we are lucky to be in school when children of our age from the Old Level and the village are working ventilation doors. Anyway,' I said, 'of course I know what they are and what brattice is, so please don't tell me,' I added quickly.

'And they use oak and larch for the sleepers,' he went on, 'and they bring in Norway fir - '

'And they cut it from the hillside and they rape the valley, John.' I chanted it to him with no deference to his passion. In truth, Grandpa Shôn had got through to me. A right revolutionary I would be if I had to go down underground.

Running now we were as the girl rang the hand bell, mud splashing in the rain which filled the ruts and crevices, John going on about galleries and headings, gate roads and trolley ways. Louder the hand bell, as our feet hit the yellow mud, breathless was John with his shaft pillars, packwalls, feet pounding, breath like Grandpa Shôn. Getting there at last, trousers splattered, hearing Evan tut and Susannah hissing under her breath that she would tell our Mam we must have dawdled. She shot daggers at John, who was still chorusing about hammers, hacks and slotters while he pulled- off his shoes. 'Phillip,' he whispered, through his effort, knees up to his face, 'They have swab sticks for drawing wet mud out of bore holes.'

'And Mr Madge has a tamping bar that he'll bring down on your backside if you don't shut it,' I hissed back.

I look out to the garden, down its long path to the small barred gate and understand how little we all knew. Our legs grew longer as the seasons changed. As we learned, the patchwork of our life enfolded us. We watched our father grimed with coal, our mother busy cooking, washing, scrubbing Dada's back and smiling. Time was subsumed by stark necessity. Strange how the years flew one to another. Soon it was time for Deborah to follow us to school. At three years old and she took my hand, her comforter in the other, and never once complained.

The next year had brought us Catherine, a quiet and lovely child. As she has grown to womanhood, her deep set eyes and coal black hair have haunted many a man. My father called her Kate - it suited her. Babies simply came to us from no-one-told me where. Evan aloof with his books declared he knew, refused to tell. John, swearing with the vigour of a puddler, knew only about the coal. Susannah, who by now was watching herself reflected in every darkening window, patting her hair, grown shapely like our Mam, just reddened when I asked and ran away. And then Elizabeth was born. Children are a gift from the Lord, my mother said. '*Happy is the man that hath his quiver full of them,*' my father agreed.

Strange how time passes when each day is eternity. Ominous how obsessive thoughts can dominate our time. I sit here at the window of the cottage, my ledger in front of me, my pen in hand, unwrapping the tissues of my life, layer by layer, rather than recording orders I have made. I write 1882 across the page, but look out at a valley where time stands still. Laid waste to poverty now, its people picking the last scraps from a failing industry. I called today at Evans' shop in Penygarn, saw a woman trade her family Bible for her debt. Men do not band together for they know authorities have soldiers and police to govern them. Turning to my work, I sigh and realise the colliers and the miners do not understand their worth. The interests of their Masters still comes first through obscene deference. Fine as my father was, he shared this arcane view. Inbred is their acceptance.

Light fades now, slanting across the desk, calling me to work, but the voices of my memory echo, haunting me. In the dark, in the darkest corners of this old front room, I hear still my sisters sing of *The rich man in his castle* - a pretty tune. I open my sample bag, check the numbers on the invoices against my lists. *'The poor man is at his gate,'* I mutter in disdain. 'The enactment of God's will is more than mystery.' The innocent voices of my sisters float through the extremes of wealth and poverty. I turn the pages of my order book. *God made them high or lowly*? I question to myself. Are these the Christian values we should teach our little ones in song? The room is shaded now, last vestiges of sunlight turn to dusk. Against the remembered hymning, against the rhythm of my accounting, I look out at the fine but broken men of this devastated valley, see their women scrapping through - see the tears of that poor woman in Will Evan's shop, caressing her family Book that one last time - and I cannot bear to think *He ordered their estate*. Who is this God to whom we make our children sing, I curse, and I consider my own weakness that led me to escape. I feel so humbled. I throw down my pen, the symbol of my success and failure, look at my ink stained hands and sigh. I move to fetch a candle as the darkness challenges sight. 'We are a people lost in subservience and in poverty,' I shout as I cross the empty room. 'No wonder it is argued venomously that we do not have the sense to vote.'

1866

I saw no apparition or death portent to give me warning, but I soon learned that one thing we are born with is a time to die. That, we all share, regardless of our state. Collier or Master, man and boy. Our days are numbered from our birth. Easy to say that as a man, but as a child, it was hard for me to think my mother would soon end her days. An oblivious, self centred boy, I did not notice how pale she had grown, how much she coughed, that she smiled less and often spent time lying on her bed. Grandfather Shôn had told me of *Lledrith,* the apparition that takes your hand when you are on the mountain or in the lane, that tells you when someone close to you will die. I did not meet the dreaded spectre, did not say her name or even notice as death came.

The Winter of 1865 my mother must have struggled to get through. In Swansea, there was an outbreak of yellow fever but it did not reach our village. Fifteen people died. The Cambrian was full of it, along with the opening of *Festiniog* rail. I remember now as I look back how little Catherine clung to my mother those days. I can still see her black curls tousled and unkempt, her little chubby hands clinging to my mother's skirts while baby Elizabeth, left alone, sat still and yowled. I know now that my mother was too tired, too ill to care for them.

Spring came, and with it the usual glorious display of white May blossom. While my mother struggled to keep going, I stood at the bottom of the garden, enjoyed the perfumed air and flowers hanging over our low gate, bewitched by its loveliness. But indoors life was changing faster than the blossom fell. Before long, down came the bed and *Mamgu* Deborah bustled in the kitchen, doing the cooking instead of Mam. I recall her banging the pans down hard and asking us for quiet while Grandpa Shôn, sitting by the stove, steamed like *y Ddraig Goch* but the red dragon brought no Merlin to do magic here. My heart beat to the rhythm of my father's anxious steps. As I watched him walk the kitchen flags, I heard my mother as she cried. When I think back to how she quietly wiped her tears into Elizabeth's curls, my heart could break. I never sat with her. I never told her that I cared. Susannah seldom spoke, but made the tea and kept herself busy at the bosh. 'When I am afraid, she said, 'I put my trust in God.' *Lord help my disbelief,* I thought, but did not speak.

Spring gave way to summer. Cold were those days I spent alone in fear. Then the rains came. All day, it rained - all day and every day. It was a summer where the rain rotted the vegetables, poured down the windows fast. I could not see the Gorge. Noisy the down pours in our silent house. Paths soaked and mud walked in to the kitchen floor. *Mamgu* mopped with tutts and banging; my father spent hours at my mother's bedside, taking us in to see her, but she did not smile. Then it was quiet. The rain stopped, the constant sweeping of my grandma stopped, my Dada stopped his pacing. And my mother stopped her breathing.

Grandma Morgan came to prepare her daughter for the grave. Susannah stood at the door with the little girls while I stood alone, watching, listening, afraid. When Grandma Morgan had done her work, when her tears stopped flowing, when my father took us in to say goodbye, I stood there petrified while Evan kissed my mother's cheek and John ruffled her hair. To my enduring shame, I did not find the courage to go in. I did not even say goodbye.

The house was full then. Villagers from the cottages up by the Colliers' Arms called in to see my mother dead. While I stood alone in deepest fear, Susannah held the little ones as Grandpa Shôn opened doors and *Mamgu* made the visitors tea. I heard the voices say how well my mother looked, how peaceful and how close to God. I stood bewildered while my father walked the garden, his face white and no time down the Lan for days.

Evan was silent still, his head in books but sad. John and I walked the garden hand in hand while Susannah took the little ones to her bed. Then the day came when they lifted Mam into the elm coffin, when I saw my father kiss her lips before the lid went down. As he stood up from kissing her, as the lid was closed for the last time, I realised for the first time that she would be with Deborah, not at home. I went to the window, looked out at the sky for Heaven but I saw no God. Then the horse and cart came to collect my mother for St Catwg's. My father had ordered a horse and farrier from the Lan, the cart borrowed from the farm nearby. Perhaps we had no money for a mourning coach, no money for the big black horses I had seen tamping the hard ground with fore-paws, plumes on heads, ribbons in their plated tails. Perhaps we had no money or perhaps my father had no will. It was August. The sun shone now, the garden white with Michaelmass daisies that our mother had planted there. Together, we picked them, placed them round her coffin in the cart. Bunch after bunch we gathered till we stripped the garden bare. I was glad to have involvement. Susannah was ever busy and the little girls, lost, just followed her. Though I was twelve, I took the hand of *Mamgu* Deborah, went with her as she opened the window so our mother's soul could leave. Dressed in black, she put us in starched shirts and brushed the dust from trousers while my father took out his black and mothballed suit. No one was crying now. The house silent, cleared of visitors, was hostile, cold. I went to the kitchen door, looked out at the waiting cart. Tears pricked my eyes.

Inevitably then, it rained. Violent was the downpour, its noise shattering.

Suddenly, sun shone through the rain and my eyes lifted to the rainbow beyond the hill. Grandma Morgan, watching with me from the kitchen, took my hand. At that moment, with a word from the farrier, we were off. A sad and disparate crew. My father and my Grandfathers walked ahead, the cart following, bumping over the rain-filled ruts, Susannah holding Elizabeth in her arms and Evan with little Kate. John and I strode out together trying to keep step. People bowed their heads as we went by and I saw some women cry. Slowly, we walked the hill to Penuel for Mam's Gathering and Farewell, and then on to St Catwg's, through the gate, half deafened by the bell. On the hard seats, sitting upright, *Mamgu* Deborah cried, dabbing her eyes with her lace handkerchief, but secure in her belief that my mother would go to Heaven and be judged righteous by a loving God. The Church, rebuilt ten years before, was grand. My father sat staring straight ahead and silent, his face immobile for Welsh men dare not cry.

'*I am the resurrection and the life, saith the Lord,*' the Reverend chanted. '*She that believeth in me, though she were dead, shall yet live.*' The words from the Book resounded in my brain. I tried to apply logic for I had no belief. My mother was dead and yet shall live? Evan was still, listening intently, John digging his ribs in bewilderment. '*Yet shall she live,*' intoned on the Reverend, '*and whosoever believeth in me shall never die.*' Susannah did not move, holding tight to the little ones on either side. I watched a fly crawl the stained glass. To the singing from John Robert's *Llyfr Tonau,* my head ran riot, for my mother had believed and she was dead. I stared up at the coloured glass, counting flies while John kept craning his neck to see the open window at the back, to watch the grave digger hew the rain drenched soil. My mother's coffin was there before the altar of her God. A sacrifice to illness and to poverty. Then, at last, I heard the Reverend intone the Blessing and we all trooped out into the church yard for Mam's committal to the earth.

I watched while my mother's coffin was lowered into the deep hole. I watched while my father threw a handful of soil unto her coffin. Overhead a pair of buzzards dipped and glided to the hill, their high pitched cry cutting the air. Suddenly a cloud burst and the rain fell in torrents. My father ushered us back then into the vestry where the Clerk had filled out the Parish Records and Dada paid the funeral dues. I remember that we stood there, drenched, rain glistening on my father's hair, my shirt sleeves sticking to my wrists and Evan complaining he was cold. The Reverend comforted us, saying that rain falling unto our mother's coffin would mean she went direct to Heaven.

It was all bustle now, all platitudes about her death. While John went to the window to watch the digger fill the grave, I looked to the Clerk's formal Record book. While my father talked to the Reverend, while he picked up Kate, I peered along the columns of neat manuscript, left open by my side. In good Welsh and in cursive pen it read, *'in memory of Deborah, daughter of Abraham and Eliza Phillips'* and then, *'also the aforesaid Eliza Phillips who died August 28th 1866, aged 41 years'*. I knew then that the Lord had taken my mother just as he once took Deborah and I wondered why the Reverend praised his name. A child I was, but suddenly became man.

It was quiet in our house now my mother was gone. Grandma Morgan in her black, sobbed quietly by the fire where Grandpa Shôn tapped out his pipe and slept. No more harp in the front room now, no singing from my father, no more laughter while he swept my mother in his arms. No busy footsteps on the stair to bed. Empty the bed now, cold her room. I knew the finality of death and I had not said goodbye. I crept out into the garden to find the space to think.

Beautiful were the clouds that night where my father stood staring at the mountain. Dreadful the noise of weeping that rang clear.

1866

Bright are the leaves of Autumn till they fall and wither underfoot. Dark are October nights, November worse. As the days passed, our house returned to living, Grandma Morgan calling more often, sitting with *Mamgu* Deborah to cry. Down in my mother's kitchen, their mourning crape rustling, those two aged women grieved their loss. '*Who breathes must suffer,*' Grandma Morgan said, '*And who thinks,*' *Mamgu* Deborah added, '*must mourn.*' I watched my two grandmother's nod together in agreement as they shared their grief. 'The responsibility for little ones hangs heavy on Abraham,' my Grandma Morgan said. Hearing the gate snap open, hearing steps on the path, they paused their conversation. Exchanging glances, they looked knowingly out together at my father, who walked in bent from work, black faced from coal and misery, John alongside him, carrying his tools. I moved quickly to the door to greet them, just as my mother used to do.

In through the door then, my father, managing half a smile for Elizabeth, who ran to him with her arms wide. Up he lifted her and carried her to Susannah's arms. 'A coal baby you will be if you stay in my arms,' he said.

'She's like her mother,' *Mamgu* murmured, standing up, 'that wanting to be lifted in the air. We did that to Elizabeth so often as she grew.' Wiping away a tear then, her daughter dead, she turned to the little ones, cajoling, smiling, singing, *'Jesus bids us shine with a pure clear light.'* Drawing them to her, she whispered, 'Come on you little girls, time for your prayers and bed. Come, Catherine, you come with *Mamgu.*' Little Kate, innocent and unaware yet of her mother's death, piped up in her childish treble, *'Like a little candle shining in the night ....'*

'I want to bath my Dada,' Deborah protested. Catherine, kept singing, *'In this world of darkness, Jesus bids us shine - .'* Deborah was arguing as Susannah dragged her to bed, protesting against every step they took. *'You in your small corner,'* sang Catherine. *'And I in mine,'* Grandma sang, laughing as she kissed her goodnight, but shaking her head in sadness at the little one's clear song. Then, she returned to her cooking while John dragged in the bath. Pots on the fire to boil the water then, Evan helping bring it in, struggling a bit with the weight of it. Giggles floated from upstairs with Susannah's gentle voice talking to the little ones as she pulled nightclothes on their wriggling bodies.

I remember that I passed the soap while *Mamgu* scrubbed my father's back. Food was cooking on the stove. There was bustle for a while, then food was eaten - then quiet, Grandma and *Mamgu* gone. So clearly I can see across the years my father as he went to the front room and stared out to the Gorge. I tread softly in his wake so he did not see me there. Death comes often to our valley and mining men don't cry. But I saw tears on my father's face that night as he stood there at the window, last light slanting on his face.

'Da,' I said bravely, 'Can I come in with you?'

'Aye, lad, it's cold enough alone.'

'Da,' I asked, 'Did Grandpa Shôn have a wife before *Mamgu*? Susannah said he did.'

'Gwenllian, lad. Why do you ask me that?' my father said, turning to look at me.

'Did the Lord take Gwenllian, too?' I asked him.

'Aye, lad. She was very sick.'

'Does the Lord just take the sick, Da?'

My father smiled, his lips tight from the cold. 'It's better when he takes the sick, Phillip. But there are accidents as well.'

'You mean underground?' Dreadful the shadow that passed over my father's face.

'Have I told you about Lan farm?' he asked, changing the subject clumsily. He smiled for himself alone - wryly remembering, before telling me that as a boy he had been so eager to leave the ancient parish of his birth, where the Rhondda Fawr and Rhondda Fach rivers ran.

Looking at me as I stood there beside him, he did not meet my gaze. 'I changed those country rivers for the Taff,' he said. 'For this smoke and industry, for the rape of a valley and its people. What makes a man so blind,' he asked bitterly. Then, pulling me towards him, he sat me down beside him. 'Granpa Shôn used to live with his parents in Ystrad Dyfodwg,' he said, telling the story as if I were a child. 'They were called Morgan and Gwenllian,' he continued, 'but I can't really remember them - *Tadcu* Morgan is just a vague memory now, and my *Mamgu* Gwenllian just a sound inside my head, an echo from my father's stories.' I sat listening, alert, as my father leaned back, struggling to remember. 'I never really knew them - I was just a baby then, Phillip,' he said, 'but their life story has grown inside me since your Mam has died. Memory is like that, son. It floods your consciousness when you grieve.' He closed his eyes a moment. 'When Grandpa Shôn was a young man, he married Gwenllian Llewellyn - it was 1820 when she died -just two years before I was born. It is recorded in the family Book.

'So, when his Gwenllian was taken by the Lord, Grandpa Shôn married *Mamgu* Deborah,' I murmured, 'and then you were born. Will you marry someone new now, Da,' I asked him tentatively.

My Dada wept.

With the safety of times' passage, I can understand and know that sometimes the child is older than the man. I know that as my father wept, I put my hand on his and felt a pride, a closeness and not fear. Time was somewhere else, not in the room. Someone had stopped the clock when Mama died. It was the custom in that day. Light was fading in the cottage as it fades around me now. I had never spoken with my father for so long - he usually talked to John. I loved him then and understood his grief, I thought him then an honourable man. Why do I doubt him now?

As the moon rose in the sky, as I sat with my father in the cold front room, he lit the old Brass lamp. Slowly, its wick licked into flame and its light danced through the etched glass globe. Walking from it, rubbing his hands, the smell of oil hanging in the air, he sat beside me and he talked again. 'We will miss your Mam, Phillip,' he said. 'If I don't talk of her, don't think that I forget. You children have your love and memories to share. *I thank my God upon every remembrance of you*, your Mama used to say over Deborah's little curl there in her box. We must be thankful for the memories we have.' My father looked thoughtful. Gradually, a smile of realisation spread over his face. 'Too many have trod this path before me, son. I will go on. Grandfather Shôn didn't mention his first wife much after she died and as you worked out, Phillip, he soon married again.' My face must have shown my deep anxiety at this for he put both hands on my shoulders and chuckling said, 'My father might have shut out all his words about his Gwenllian, but her children had plenty they could say. Your uncle John, your auntie Janet, Howell, Gwenllian and Morgan - they never stopped remembering! All happy things, though. I don't think they cried for long.' My father stretched then, flexed back his shoulders, made to leave, but sat down immediately again by the window there. 'I don't think men are made to live alone, Phillip. Grandfather Shôn married my Mam soon after his Gwenllian died. Deborah Thomas she was - and I don't need to tell you more for you know all about that good lady already!'

We laughed together.

'Morgan and Gwenllian.' My father intonated his grandparents' names, rolling each syllable fondly, letting them lie long upon his tongue. 'Good names, eh, Phillip? Gwenllian and Morgan.' He smiled to himself, shaking his head gently. 'I don't know what they would have made of the modern way we work. Sheep it was for them.'

'When did you come from Ystrad, Da,' I asked.

'How old was I when I left there?' he mused, rubbing his chin. 'Five or six, maybe.' My father pondered. 'It was after Queen Victoria married Albert. After the transportation of prisoners from Wales was stopped. 1841, I think it was, son. Around the that time, your Grandpa Shôn talked non-stop about industrial workers in the North of England who had started to riot - that's where all his Ivorite passions started, I suppose.' Da grinned. 'Grandpa Shôn was young then and learning to do the polka. I can still see him and my mother cavorting round the kitchen at Lan farm! And why I remember that when I have a problem recalling things that I should not forget, I'll never know!'

My father was relaxed and happy then as we stopped talking to hear clattering in the kitchen, Susannah shouting at Evan and the sound of the little ones running down the stairs. My father shrugged, eyes twinkling in his rugged face, unmoved by the chaos in the cottage, even when Susannah's feet stormed by, through the kitchen and up stairs, shouting.

He laughed opening his arms in a gesture of despair. 'Did you protest when you were a boy?' I asked.

'When I was a boy, Phillip, I was like John, head bursting just with coal. The Rhondda valley called out to me - it had become the very centre of the coal industry. Five hundred or so people living with the sheep in Ystrad didn't interest me. Those were the days of my father,' he mused, 'the olden days, as they say. Can you imagine it - even when I was born in the 1830s, there were only a thousand or so people living where we were. I wanted excitement, son. I wanted life not sheep. Then we left the Rhondda Valleys to come first to Lan farm and then to Pentyrch, to the top of the Garth. Because you have always lived here, you won't know how exciting that all seemed.'

I interrupted him but did not need to speak. 'Yes, son, I know. You have told me that you want to travel and I understand. This place was teeming with in-comers when we arrived - *Sy'n siarad Cymraeg* - Welsh speaking like our family - all coming here to work the coal, all industrial folk, no time for sheep.'

'You know that I want to move to a big city when I am a man, Dada. You know I do not want to work the coal.'

'You leave that to John, boy,' my father said. 'He's there in his head already. No keeping that one from the coal. But you - you and Evan - you are both clever with books. I've changed my mind about your future, boy. You listen to Thomas Madge and you'll earn more for your brains than you could winning coal.'

I remember feeling overwhelmed that my father had spoken to me like a man. No John to change the talk to coal, no more insistence that it was the future and the only future here. Upstairs we could hear the feet of the little girls, who were running rings around Susannah. 'Back to normal, eh Phillip?' My father said. 'I had better go to read the riot act or we will get no food.' We were both standing then.

'Your Mam was proud of you, Phillip.'

'Oh, Dada,' I cried out suddenly, 'why did the Lord take her so soon?'

'Come on, lad,' my father said, tousling my hair. 'Susannah will keep us all in order - and if she doesn't Grandma Morgan will have her say.' My father looked happier, more in control, as he ushered me back to the kitchen.

'Kettle on, eh, lad?' he said, dipping the old black kettle into the bucket as my mother did, but dripping water everywhere.

'You'll catch it from Susannah,' I warned, 'You've made a dreadful mess'

Picking me up, big as I was, he held me aloft in his work-strong arms and kissing me, he said, 'We'll get along without her somehow, Phillip. You help me and we'll get along.'

1865

I remember that Spring came early the year after my mother was taken by the Lord. The hawthorn, that whitened the starkness of our valley, reflected new hope around our garden gate. The ground dried quickly, the track to *Ty'n Coed* made easier, more beautiful. Purple violets nestled, hidden in the hedgerows and the yellow celandine glossed my way up to the Garth, where the gorse yellowed to the early sun.

Elizabeth was my constant shadow, looking up to me with her quick smile, grabbing my hand when I would let her, wanting me to swing her round until the ground spun and laughing she would sit while she was tipped to steadiness as the ground stopped tilting. My father was himself again, up at the Colliers' some evenings, down underground by day. Booker had given him more responsibility - he now watched other pits besides the Lan - coming home black but scrubbed and out with friends in Bedwas at weekends. Happy he seemed, full of voice, his resonant laughter again making this stark cottage home.

Susannah was sixteen then, out of school, shapely and dutiful, forever cutting bread for us. Easily she slipped into my mother's place - making sure Elizabeth was washed, the house was cleaned and us in school. Mornings would find her scolding Catherine, who had learned to shake her Celtic curls, stamp her foot and be rebellious as she grew. Every morning, she pulled-up the quilt when it was time for school. 'Slug-a-bed,' Susannah would shout in a maternal tone. '*Rydw i wedi blino* - I am tired,' Kate's perpetual reply.

Strange how my sister suddenly became a woman - how her legs grew longer, shapelier, how her waist got thinner, how her face lost all the childlike innocence. All breasts and modesty, Susannah now, all petticoats and blushing shy. When her chores at home were done, when the little girls were in their bed, she would go walking with boys on the mountain. I saw my sister grow to toss her hair seductively just as my mother had done when we passed the colliers on the mountain years before. I remember the day I looked at her as woman. Lovely she was, her eyes large as rock pools, her face a mirror of happiness, composed.

Summer was hot that year. A thrush sang in our garden and blackbirds pecked the grass for worms. Catherine and Elizabeth planted flowers and John, probably pretending to dig for coal, reluctantly tended the garden that our mother had made. He was a rebel, my brother John, arguing each point, quick tempered, strong but honourable. In those days, I would be up at dawn, when the sun burst into my room, always reading, ready always to head out for the Garth. Evan just turned 17, was quiet, deep, and always up before me. I knew that he was planning to go to England, intent on leaving home. He regularly declared that he wanted to leave Wales as we stood outside at the wash bench, our water taken from the water-butt, cold, green with algae and drowned flies. 'Life is too hard here,' he muttered as he took the cut-throat razor to his face. 'There is no sustenance in this poor soil. Poverty is everywhere and even sheep have to rummage on the stricken hills.' Through the towel one day, as he dried his face, he said, 'This is not for me, Phillip. I have no more patience with sheep or life underground.' I remember that he ran his fingers through his hair, trying out his reflection in the window glass as he said seriously, 'Dada comes home each night filthy and exhausted. I see children in their holed shoes and worn out clothes running to work. Have you seen their faces, Phillip? They haunt my nights with guilt that we go to our books while they go to their deaths. Wales is not for me. There is no future outside industry. With Queen Victoria on the throne of England, there is wealth. I see my future there.'

'A future, Evan? That's why Da came here,' I chipped in. 'He was looking for a better future.'

'No future here for me. I head for Liverpool - a rich and prosperous place.'

'I'd head for London, if it was me,' I said innocently. 'It is the capital of England.'

'Liverpool is the second most important city in the world,' Evan retorted scornfully, 'it thrives. Jobs are available - there are ninety six forwarding agents there against just sixty one in London. See? It is a thriving hub, Phillip, I have researched this well. Booker has a company there - I've seen his heading: Thomas William Booker and Co, it says, Liverpool and London and the Globe.' Looking at me directly, his deep set eyes shone as he said again, 'The Globe, Phillip. That is what attracts me most - the great Globe itself - the world.'

'What can you do in a big city, Evan?' I asked, ignoring his dreaminess for the very world itself. 'I know you are clever, but don't the Irish take the jobs? Dada says they work for nothing and pull wages down.'

Rubbing his hair dry with great vigour, my brother said, 'Liverpool has jobs for everyone,' I remember his confidence as he looked at me. He had his path well planned. 'I will work in cotton.,' he said. 'Strange really. Dada wins the coal in Wales - it goes down the Taff to the steamer in Port of Cardiff and subsequently up to Liverpool it goes.' He spoke between violent rubs of the towel till he glowed. Then combing down his hair, he added, 'and from Liverpool it gets transported to South America and cotton fills the hold for the return.'

'South America!' Suddenly, my eyes were opened to the wider world that dazzled Evan. 'Adventure it is you head for Evan!' I said in awe and jealousy. 'How will you find work?'

'There are many companies waiting - down here we have the Butes. In Liverpool, the Blarney family operate small boats that bring the cotton back. And then there is Fairwater and Jardine - they take out timber but run cotton in the winter months. It's exciting, Phillip. Part of the world I want to be, not stuck here in this death ridden valley listening to endless talk of coal, of poverty and strikes. Cotton from New Orleans to the Lancashire mills! The world! You can keep the Welsh Valleys, its subservient people and those dozy sheep. I will not return to this sad land.' Evan was in full flow, verbose, excited, positive. He was alive. His passion startled me.

'Don't let Shôn o'r Lan hear what you say, Evan,' was my reply. 'Grandpa is for Wales.'

'Grandpa Shôn o'r Lan won't hold me up. He has an independent mind. He'll understand why I must leave.' Evan was thoughtful, quiet then.

'He has an interest in the working man,' I said

'It's more for the Ivorites and the Cambrian way of life,' Evan intervened.

'You cannot be that sure you will not break his heart by denigrating Wales,' I said. 'Subservient people? Dozy sheep? Grandpa Shôn is highly regarded in our village a patriarch as well as patriot. His views are valued, his opinions sought. He will not tolerate your views on Wales.'

Evan shrugged.

'Where will you work, Evan? 'I asked, 'Can I visit you?'

'Newall and Clayton are a cotton merchant's there. They will have me and have sent me a travelling advance. It's a highly profitable industry, Phillip. Three hundred and twenty cotton brokers buying and selling cotton. So, it's settled, regardless of what the family say. The Dublin General Steamship company regularly runs packet boats from Cardiff along the coast to Liverpool. I have already found my lodging place - but I cannot promise you a visit yet. I go to be apprenticed to a cotton merchant and must work hard before I look to entertaining you.'

'Dada will miss you, Evan,' I said.

'He knows. He got me references from Booker. *Booker Thomas William* & Co. *Liverpool and London and Globe* - it's on the letter heading. Remember the Globe, Phillip! The world is there beyond our suffocating love of Wales.'

'Then I will miss you, Evan. Write to me.' My brother barely answered.

Formal was dinner the day that Evan said goodbye. Grandpa Shôn had come over to send him on his way. If he had strong views, he kept his counsel at that meal. *Mamgu* was a different matter. She made her opposition strong. There at the white cloth, at the table, at the family altar if you like, she banged plates, cut bread into thick chunks, which she almost threw at us. While Susannah cut the cheese methodically, Elizabeth chattered on to everyone who would listen, her sticky hands on my mother's best embroidered cloth. While Catherine and Deborah sparred for the best spoon, Dada sat at the head, master, his face looking from one to the next as his offspring vied for attention. Evan was rigid in his seat, John to his left, saying nothing, and me on his right, head full of new ideas. Tall was John now, disdainful. He ate continuously while we listened to Evan's plans, rugged from the sun, strong armed like our Da and dominant. Already man.

'Apprenticed to be a Clerk in England!' Grandma Morgan purred. '*Duwedd!* My Elizabeth would be proud of you!'

'Why England, boy?' my Grandpa said.

'Because this resource-rich country, Wales, is poor and still subservient.'

Grandpa Shôn choked, quenching whatever he wanted to say by swilling down a drink.

'Few words, our Evan. Clever words too,' *Mamgu* pitched in. 'You follow Grandpa Shôn with all those brains,' she added with a wink.

'Hidden in that city,' Grandpa Shôn preached, his finger wagging, not listening to his wife's twittering, 'you will find poverty, hardship - and subservience, too.' Knife and fork down. 'Big buildings, grand ones, maybe, modern - but the technology of trains and electricity they boast hide families in great hardship.' Grandpa Shôn drank from his glass, banging it down firmly before adding, They die of starvation and disease. Don't think, young Evan, that you leave it all behind in Wales.'

'I go to a rich industry and have a place to go,' Evan responded. 'And yes, I do know that the working man will face great danger everywhere. I will be in an office, Grandpa Shôn, do not afear for me.'

'The average life expectancy in the city is just thirty years,' Shôn whispered, leaning towards my father.

'We are well used to death in this small village, John Phillips. Do not fright the boy as he leaves home.' Dada stood now, moved over to Evan and put his hand upon his shoulder. 'Liverpool is a port,' he said quietly, 'a gateway to new worlds. Cardiff the same ..... and isn't that why we came,' he said severely to his father. 'A long way from Ystrad Dyfodowg, eh?' Turning again to Evan, he joked, 'And you will find more Irish there in Liverpool than we have here in Wales.'

'Children are working in the factories,' Grandpa Shôn rumbled on to no-one in particular. And you find them drunk in the streets.'

'Sounds like the road down from the Colliers after dark,' Grandma Morgan chuckled. 'Hush you too-clever-by-half old fool. Let the boy make his way.'

'They drink Gin because the water is so bad,' Grandpa went on. His pipe was out now and he was puffing violently. 'I read that it will cost you 1s 6d a week to stay there, Evan, that will be a big chunk out of a wage - and you can guarantee that your lodgings will be dark and dirty.'

Susannah jumped up from the table, moved quickly to the sink to wash up the dishes and avoid the conflict. 'There are trams there, too, and theatres showing dioramas, I hear,' she said quietly. Lovely she was. Gentle, her face flushed by the family argument. 'Bye, then, Evan,' was all that she could muster, with a quick smile. 'Send me one of those new picture cards from Liverpool if you can.'

While Grandpa Shôn worried on, sure that Evan would forget the language, while Dada shook Evan's hand for the twentieth time and the little girls ran out into the garden, while Grandma Morgan and *Mamgu* wiped tears from their old eyes, I said nothing, secretly longing for adventure to the city. I, too, had no time for sheep and coal.

The next morning we rose early, me yawning, Dada shaking hands over enthusiastically again and the girls in tears. Then, with the sun skirting the Garth to redness, books packed and scarcely a farewell, my brother was off alone from the Port of Cardiff bound for Liverpool.

1867

Human beings suffer - *It is not good that the man should be alone.* Nodding in wry agreement, I read from my mother's Book that still lies on the kitchen dresser, unopened now she does not live. Thumbing its pages, I find the lines, *He raises the poor from the dust and lifts the needy from the ash heap.* My lips tighten as I read the much turned pages by the kitchen lamp, my order book completed for the day. Times are hard for many in these villages. Not much sign of the poor being raised or the needy lifted from the ash heap of this broken place. William Evans up in Pen y Garn tells me that many of his customers need credit now, though he does good business with Cardiff Steam and Navigation. A comprehensive business has Will Evans - wheel spokes to thimbles, gun-powder to biscuits and a hot drink on the table while he looks at my samples.

As the oil nears the end, as the candle burns to nothing, invisible in the corner of the kitchen, I sit and contemplate my fate. This darkness is my hiding place. These are the hours of doubt. If *the destruction of the poor is their poverty,* the destruction of Phillip Phillips is his doubt. I sit here, transported to the kitchen of my youth, shrunk invisible by the failing light, remembering with despair my brother,

John, his head under the pump after a Colliers' night. *Am I my brother's keeper* that I feel disgust? Again I see that scene. By the dying fire, my father, head thrown back and half asleep while outside, hooting owls calling to their mates and the wind hollers down the front room chimney drawing down the spirits of the dead.

We are all created by our history, but I do not want to see again that door thrown wide. I do not want to hear that hollow whistling of the wind and with it, John. Disturbed from relaxation, my father jumped to his feet as John burst in, immediately alive. 'John, mun,' he cried, 'You look as if you've had a good night out. Soused you are. It's early shift in the morning, lad. Get up to bed. A collier needs his sleep. Drink is a demon when it dominates.'

'Sleep, Dada? That's for others. *D'w i'n feddw* - I am drunk. A pint looses my tongue. It makes me free. My head is buzzing, running wild with questions and no answers - or answers and the questions do not suit.' As I watched that night, as I pulled back into the shadow, silent, my brother John slumped down. His head was in his hands, his elbows on the kitchen table, his shoulders slumped.

'What is troubling you, lad,' my father questioned, now awake. 'Women is it?'

Shaking his mane of black hair till the damp sprayed the table like a shower of rain, my brother looked directly at my father. 'The men talk out again of Unions,' he said. 'Why have you not joined a union, Dada? Why don't you want it underground? Your men are not protected.' John picked up a knife left on the table and spinning it, said, 'You've seen the way your colliers live, you know the work of the young hauliers and the children on the ventilation doors. You know men smuggle down their little ones for extra hands - you've seen the women working, too, beyond the law. So why no unions in your pit, Da, why?' He spun the knife again, fixing it so the blade pointed only to our father.

'Survival, John, survival,' spat my Da. 'We have got to live. What use a dead collier to his wife and family?' He paused a bit, pulled back his chair to stretch his legs under the table, leaning back to think. Then, as if a wild dog bit him he declared, 'When I was young, lad, *Dic Pendryn* was the martyr on the name of every tongue. And all that I could think was he is dead.'

John looked up. Even in the half light I could see fire in his eyes. 'So, Dada, he was dead. Like all good men, he paid. Can you spell out to me just why he fought?'

'The Merthyr riots, boy. Do you know what that means?'

'Aye, Dada, aye. The Red Flag of revolution. 1831. I went to school - you saw to that. Crawshay's workers took to the streets. His men didn't get a living wage. And it is no different now.'

'I was no more than five then,' my father said. 'The times were ruthless, boy. Wage reduction, paying men in coin made by the Masters for their shops. 1831 and Tom Hepburn called the men together in the north of England. In those days, men only got paid if there was no stone in the dram. They were down for eighteen hour shifts - dark when they went down, dark when they came up. Worse than that, they were caught up by signing the Bond - had to work for the colliery for a year and if they broke their Bond, it could mean prison. We're not in that state now.'

'So you know the history of coal,' John sneered. 'Why do you not encourage men to unionise? To know the history and to shut your mind is bloody worse than ignorance.'

'It was strike after strike in the north of England, boy. 1831. 1832 - and that only achieved a twelve hour day for six year olds. 1844 and strike again for a fair rate -'

'And the Masters offered them a cut in wages,' John laughed in cruel disbelief at my father's attitude.

'They were ruining the country with the strikes - and worse, their families starved. It's that much better now,' my father said closing his eyes. From my dark corner I could see my father's eyes were weary in the flickering candle light, too tired for confrontation, but determined to let John have his say.

'The history of coal is blood and poverty,' John shouted, banging his hands down to the table. 'Coal miners wanted reform then,' he shouted. 'We want it now. Low wages and unemployment - little wonder whole communities rebelled. No wonder that the Merthyr riots spread.'

'They stormed Merthyr,' my Dada replied. 'Can violence ever pay? They ransacked the local debtors court, destroyed the books.'

'Aye, destroyed them, Da, 'but then paid back men's debts. *Caws a bara* - bread and cheese they chanted, *I lawr a'r Brenin* - down with King - as they marched from pit to pit to get the men to strike.'

'But the army was called in, boy,' my father said patiently, 'Order had to be restored or no one would get fed - and when the High Sherriff's meeting was disrupted by Lewsyn yr Heliwr with the appeal for more pay and cheaper bread, they brought the Highland Regiment in. Explosions, road blocks, guerrilla detachments - too many dead, John. Too many injured. It cannot be the way.'

'So you refute their banner - the loaf soaked in blood?' John scorned.

'Four hundred and fifty troops marched into Dowlais, boy,' Da said quietly. 'What price the insurrection of ordinary men?'

'You denigrate an armed uprising worked by men like me!' John shouted at him.

'Skilled men like you, the owners value,' Dada said.

John cut in, 'Oh, men like you Da. You're not much better than a scab. Overmen friendly with the Booker's of their world? Sick it makes me, Dada. Never me.' Drunk and virulent, my brother now. 'Your problem, Da, is that you are Booker loyal.' His head closer to my father then, aggressive. 'A Thomas William Booker Overman - and you don't want to form trade unions to help the working man because of that. He's bought your bloody soul.' Standing now, John shouted, 'He'd bring the soldiers in to keep you down - no question there. And if needs be, he'd hold the soldier's gun right to your head. In the pitch and toss of coal, you are not one of them. Your loyalty is misplaced, Da, don't you see?'

Over to the bosh now and water by the mug-full, gulped down before my brother turned again to Dada. 'Unions call for strikes,' John shouted. 'What other way, man, what other way?'

'Calm, John, calm. Within these walls we do not want such conflict. I want it better for the working man. But not through violence. Think of the Scotch Cattle - men crazed by power, breaking the legs of men who had to work without questioning why, demanding loyalty regardless of their deeds as they roamed the countryside burning and looting.' Hand on John's shoulder now. 'The ruthless become leaders, boy, they are not always right.'

John humped his shoulders angrily. My father's hand fell limply to his side. 'Horns and black faces do not make for good, John. I know we are all in hell. Right now, coal is going down in price, English men are brought in to make Overmen. No one is secure. World market prices have not held. Masters face that too. If Unions ask for more the pits will close. Already the Irish men will work for lower pay.'

'Bring in the troops again, I say,' cried John, 'but let those troops be colliers joined together for the fight.' My brother swilled yet another mug of water.

'I'm sick of fighting, son. We have to get the coal out. We need the Masters' money to invest in pits.' Weary now, my father slumped back into his chair. I thought how much like Shôn o'r Lan he looked. I noticed, too, how he had aged. Seeing him there, John fiery, strong and young, my father looked a spent man.

Still my brother would not give in. 'Colliers like you,' he spat, 'sit on their backsides, bleat about conditions down below, wring hands over starvation wages and shed tears about the children helping underground, but do nothing to promote the cause of working men. You make me sick, Dada, you make me sick.'

My father sat quietly, unmoved. 'You get the men on strike, boy, and you break the law. Troops will come in and shoot you down. Do you remember Newport? Death, boy, death and more death. What use are firebrands when they're dead.'

'Don't play with the word of death,' John screamed. 'How many men have died from winning coal for wealthy Masters? Aberaman, Blackband, Cwntillery - all count their coal in dead. What about Dyffryn the year that I was born? Sixty four dead. Cymmer in the Rhondda when I was six - I remember, Dada, a hundred and fourteen dead. You speak of Dic Penderyrn's martyrdom. Everyone knew he didn't stab that soldier, but the British Government were determined that at least one man would die. Eleven thousand signed a petition for his release, but still he hung in Cardiff's market place. Lewsyn yr Heliwr, too. What of these men, their families? Don't link your fear of unions with death. You speak of exploitation and let men die. Leave it others, Da. That's what you do.'

'I see another way, my son. I watch my men and keep them safe. A well run shift and happy men.'

'Incredible, man! Bloody incredible!' Scorn now covered John's face while Dada kept his calm.

'We have to work, John, and not fight. That is the contract of the working man. I don't want Unions; scores settled as men work. A safe pit mine and men work hard for coal. Get married, boy, your passions will be better spent in bed.'

'I'll never marry, Da, I told you that,' John spat. 'And as for bed and bringing children in to starve or bend their bones in work - not me. I want a better time for working men. If I make a step along that path, that will be my offspring, Abraham Phillips, not a kitchen full of children and a dead wife.' Rounding again on my father, his face just six inches away, his eyes held, John said scathingly, 'I know the history of this country even better than you. It's etched in my soul, Dada. Think on, father. Think of the iron masters - the Crawshays of Merthyr, the Butes of Aberdare, think of their men working for starvation wages. You bleat to me against unions. You fear torchlight meetings. I fear more the tommy shops of your lifetime, Masters like Crawshay paying miners in tokens for his shop. You have lived it all and still stay for the Masters. You tell me of the Chartist Riots in Newport and I remind you of the Union of Masters against men.

Your kind of selfishness costs progress, Da.' John hung over my father, his face fierce, hands shaking the shoulders of the older man.

I saw my father push his face away and weep. 'Son, I have lived through cholera in Dowlais and in Merthyr, have seen the poverty of working men. I understand the way you think,' he said through tears. 'You're fiery, John. If I agreed with you, I'd face your death. Violence against the establishment will never have good ends. They'll shoot you down and never mourn your loss. I seek another way......' My father was visibly exhausted, the flickering candle making him a ghoul. John slouched on the table, spent.

'We all question ourselves, son,' my father whispered quietly. 'We all ask did we make the grade. If you can't stomach me, look at my father, Shôn o'r Llan - you admire him. He's a free thinking man, an individual in every way. You're like him, son. Head-strong, maybe.' My father sighed and said, 'Our history has taught me to become a moderate man.'

John did not respond beyond a puff of his lips in sheer disgust.

My father stood now, walked from his chair across to John. 'You sleep now, son,' he said. 'I've heard you out.' Ruffling John's hair, he said quietly, Think hard before you set your life in coal. Think hard before you join the unions. Survival is the key to life and with your passions, you would die.' Aged and slow moving, my father rubbed his failing eyes. He noticed me in the shadows suddenly. He started then, and smiled.

'Gaunt shadows there are underground,' he whispered to me, hand on my head. 'You read your books, Phillip Phillips and be glad you are not obsessed by coal.'

John was asleep, head on the kitchen table now. As my father moved to the stairs, he roused a bit and said, 'I will not marry father - I feel that in my bones. But not because of Unions or a love or coal.' Tears flowed from his eyes, his young hand on the knurled hand of my father. I will not marry Da,' he said, letting his tears run free, 'I will not love and marry because I could not face your loss.'

1868

1868 was the year that Thomas William Booker had a daughter. Ribald comments rattled through the colliers' games of pitch and toss, as they downed their quarts trying to forget life underground. My father was officially out of mourning now, the black band gone from this sleeve. Booker had promoted him to a senior position answerable to the Directors. Overman and Under Agent, he was in charge of other collieries besides the Lan, was busier and oftentimes away. Change was afoot at *Ty'n y Coed*. Though Susannah was still diligently cooking food and getting Deborah, Catherine and Elizabeth to school, she was clearly tired of her responsibility. Twenty now, she was walking out with young John Thomas from the village - Joseph Thomas' son - and was keen to set up home with him. He had long since cut her a spoon, which I noticed she wore on a chain, slipped hidden behind her dress. Hannah Thomas from the Gwaelod was making eyes at me, but my love was for travel and excitement, not a girl to wed.

Love happens when you least expect it. It was a cold winter evening when my father first brought Jemima Jones to *Ty'n y Coed*. Evan had long since gone to Liverpool, and I was itching to be gone from Wales. John was a collier now and the house felt empty. I sat to my books alone while Susannah took to the hills for walking. Fast we had grown up after our mother's death.

Nearly fourteen I was when Jemima came with my father to our home. Back from a village walk, I found them one day, sitting there in the front room, fire blazing, laughing, my father young again. Small was Jemima Jones, hair tied back and neat behind her head. I have her image in my mind, I see her smiling in her reserved way - eyes deep set, kind and serious, forehead high, mouth firm, intent. It did not take me long to understand that my father had found himself a woman to replace our Mam, a faithful woman, not a passionate love. I could see from her demeanour she would scrub his back, cherish and care deeply for this man. I must confess here that my spirits lifted, all apprehensions gone. Now my father had found a new wife to mother him and care for the little girls, he did not need me home. Quietly, secretly, I wrote to Evan that I wanted Liverpool. He was in a position to help me now. His apprenticeship served, he was a qualified Clerk to the cotton merchant, established in his company and doing well.

In the June of 1870, my father, hired the pony and trap from William Evans in Penygarn and married Jemima Jones in style. The bride glowed, radiant in her pin-tucked dress, her gloved hands twisting the sprig of blossoms that my sister made for her. My father sat beside her, upright, smiling, proud as any man who takes a wife. Their happiness is well remembered. My country has a strong tradition of informal marriages, such an indifference to sacramental right, that I did not expect a wedding in this style.

After the ceremony, Jemima and my father jogged back home, all smiles. Tiny covered buttons down to her sturdy waist, Jemima's neat dress, all pin tucks, glowed in the hot June sun. Looking back, I can picture the group of us waiting by the gate to welcome them. Catherine and Elizabeth were waving flowers, Deborah opening the latch to let them in, Susannah beaming as my father helped his new-found wife alight. For days before the ceremony, my sister had scrubbed floors, turned beds, shook quilts and polished cutlery, in deference to Jemima, the new mistress of the house. Elizabeth had washed my mother's best crockery and hung it sparkling on the kitchen dresser to welcome her.

I remember standing there delighted only that this marriage paved the way to my escape. Days after my father and Jemima wed and she was sitting in our mother's chair, I announced with no due ceremony that I would leave. Evan had found a place for me in Liverpool. I was to join the staff of a provision merchant, apprenticed first and then a full time Clerk and I was overjoyed.

As I stand now, two decades on, in my father's house, looking out through the same window to the same garden where we sat to celebrate my father's marriage to Jemima Jones, I think, how callow, what a mean act, that I used this family celebration to announce that I was set for Liverpool. What could my father say? Another parting, another loss. Grandpa Shôn gave the same advice he gave to Evan, *Mamgu* and Grandma Morgan were tearful, reluctant for me to leave. Only Jemima shook my hand and wished me well.

I do not know what I expected to find in Liverpool but it was not the small dark houses built around the narrow courtyards, not the alley dwellings that I found. The city was thronging with people, who like me, were moving to the cities at this time. I found, too, that my status as a clerk would not bring in the wealth I had anticipated in my dreams - a working class cotton spinner could earn more. But I was happy to be in this busy city, happy to have left behind my country and its coal. I felt my social elevation in the manners of the men around me, felt my status in the clothes I wore. Sharing with Evan, I did not need to be a lodger with a family. As I walked the cobbled streets or sat on my high stool within the office, I felt secure and free.

Freedom is a tantalising state, security a gossamer of trust. Like happiness, they have invisible bounds. While I was in Liverpool, in the name of freedom, France invaded Prussia. Fears were rife this war would have a terrible impact on our trade, on the fortunes of the company, on our jobs. While office chat was focused on the war, my selfish heart beat faster at the thought my life in Liverpool could end. But the war was over quickly and global impact slow. Office gossip relaxed to local news - the fire in the Chapel of the Roman Church, the fifteen worshippers dead. Had I known then the crippling horror that this war would bring to Booker and his industry, I might have felt less secure. As it was, news of the signing of the Peace Treaty in 1871 coincided with a message from Elizabeth that Susannah was to marry and I was expected home.

*

My mother often said, *'The Lord will watch over your coming and going both now and forevermore.'* I must confess it felt like that as I returned. As I walked the track and up the path to *Ty'n y Coed*, I remember that I looked up at the mountain slope, that I walked past celandine and forget-me-nots, that I felt a sense of joy the cobbled streets of Liverpool were left behind. While I know nothing of my mother's God, there was something about Wales in May that hastened my step home - even though I had left Evan at his desk and could not tell my father he was ill.

Now, decades later, now I live again in *Ty'n y Coed*, I turn, look down through the Taff Gorge to the endless sky, see my desolate valley unusually still. And I see in the stasis, in the silence, in the poverty, the dreadful reverberations of that Franco Prussian war. Too long in England, I realise that I cannot settle, that I belong nowhere. As birds swoop and twitter with new life, as the Garth glows in the light of another spring, I think of my selfishness, my insecurity, my journey back from Liverpool. The packet was teaming with a myriad of travellers. Sun had sparkled on the coastal sea, carrying this restless Phillip Phillips home, but I am diminished now and fixed in doubt. I travel only in my head, my order book my destiny. I am a broken man. Is it the golden light over the Taff Gorge, its diamonds shimmering through the dense leaves of the beech, that haunts me so? For I am haunted. Is it the blue mist over the hill, the garden full of pecking birds, the shadows and light playing together on the earth that so unsettles me? For doubtless, I have no peace.

Strange how remembrance of Susannah's marriage makes me think of death, cruel the smell of death hangs on long after grief. I can only state that as I approached my father's house in 1871, the hawthorn blossom hanging heavy in the hedgerows, falling as usual in elegance over the cottage gate, that I could only think of death. A marriage I had come for. And there was a marriage. But it was death that filled my soul. I could not smile.

*

'Bore da'chi,' exclaimed Elizabeth, as I pushed open the door of *Ty'n y Coed* for Sussanah's wedding day. *'Cariad'* she murmured, then more lovingly, *'Cariad annwyl,'* as she flung her arms around me. As if I were never away, as if she had seen me yesterday, she asked no further questions, applied no more formality. 'Mind where you step,' she ordered, grown and dominant now. She did not ask of me, she did not ask of Evan, she did not ask of Liverpool. 'Watch where you put that bag,' she tutted. 'Oh, Phillip, do take care. This lavender fabric from William Evans stores cost us a pretty penny.' I knew that I was home. I knew, too, the loneliness of life in Liverpool.

The full onslaught of wedding preparations filled the kitchen. No time to think. 'Phillip, welcome back!' Susannah called out as she turned round in her petticoat, encompassing me with quick, shy smiles. At least Catherine, carrying ribbons and lace, rushed in with joy,shouting to Deborah, 'Phillip's home!'

Jemima bustled in and put the kettle on the fire to boil. 'So, Phillip.' she said, barely looking at me, 'So, you have come home! She was carrying sprays of ivy - symbols of fidelity, she said. As she leaned to place the sprays with care, I noticed how well she fitted into the kitchen with the girls. 'Your Dada is doing double shift so tomorrow he is free,' she said, turning to make the tea in the old brown pot I knew. Soon, there was the thump of mixing and Welsh cakes were on the bake stone. I should have felt at home, but I remember that I stood beside the fire in greatest awkwardness. Deborah was on her knees, her mouth full of pins, putting a tuck here and saying keep it off the ground there. Elizabeth was at the table, making the posy with no time for me. I watched as her quick fingers bound together lady smock, pansies and some early rose. 'We need a spray of golden gorse for luck,' she said as she wove in the ribbons she had brought. 'Perhaps we can find some on the hill.'

I knew I was redundant, that life had filled my place at *Ty'n y Coed*. As I watched, Elizabeth stepped back to look at the bridal dress. Susannah was smiling, Catherine fixing ribbons, and the Garth touching the sky outside the kitchen window. I saw their happiness, but my heart was back in Liverpool, heavy for my brother Evan.

'Why hasn't Evan come with you,' Susannah asked suddenly, as if reading my thoughts. 'Will he not see me wed?'

'Busy his office is, Susannah. He could not take the time. But he has sent you presents. Fumbling in my pockets, not daring to tell the truth, I brought out packages for them. 'For you, Susannah, the cards you asked him for,' I said. 'He went to Frith's shop specially. Elizabeth and Deborah, ribbons, Catherine too. And for Jemima Brussels Lace.' I pointed out the Liverpool I knew - the Foster Custom House, Queens Dock, the New Theatre Royal, the cobbled streets alive with industry. Then on the table, I placed tobacco for my Da. I did not tell them Evan's state was grave. I could not tell them all the gruesome facts I knew.

The sky was calm that night. I woke to village women chattering at the window, come to see Susannah wed. By now, the path in from the gate was spread with red clover to encourage the bride in industry, in shamrock to bring her light heartedness. My father, in his Sunday black, had cut a single straw to give his daughter. 'This will advise the bride to never differ with her man,' he chuckled, proud. Jemima, bent double from the waist, was polishing his boots while he craned his neck for comfort out of his starched collar, glowing in heat and happiness. I could see that he had aged, that he was worn, that the skin beneath his chin hung ragged, down. As I yawned and smiled and stretched my arms for wakening, he asked with over great formality, 'How is Liverpool, Phillip? Are the steamers bringing you Welsh coal?'

'Aye, Dada. You win it for the world these days,' I said.

'More like just for the iron works and Booker nowadays,' he added wryly. 'The price is so low that it makes me sore.'

'Abraham Phillips,' Jemima declared out loud, 'do you have to talk of coal while I shine your boots? Be joyous, man. Today Susannah weds.'

'And I will gain another Collier son, Jemima,' my Da replied.

'John Thomas will not trouble you as your John does,' Jemima smiled. 'He is not militant but hardworking - just like you.' Standing, she touched his back with tenderness. 'Come, Abraham and let me look at you.' Stepping back, mouth pouting, she declared he looked quite fine. Then, turning to me, she hustled, 'Phillip Phillips, you are not ready yet. Has Liverpool taken all your pride? Polish those boots and set your collar straight. You cannot go to chapel half asleep.'

Thus chastised, I washed quickly and put on my best. As I smoothed down my hair the wedding trap arrived, the horse bedecked with ribbons. Elizabeth, who had been up since dawn, rushed out to fill the front with flowers she had picked. 'A fine day for a wedding,' she declared, 'None of the old marriage by capture here. No locking up my sister or shutting tight the door, no horse-play, no searching for her by John. Dignified will Susannah Phillips go to the *Capel* with none of the traditional tom-foolery.'

'Don't you be too sure, Eliza! I just might seize her myself,' my father laughed. 'I'll take the farrier's horse and swoop her up - then you can all run behind us in the chase.'

'Abraham, we will have this ceremony in the modern manner,' Jemima said. 'It is time to go now. Are you all ready to depart?' With a final brush down of my father's clothes, a final straightening of his tie, he climbed into the flower strewn carriage beside Susannah.

Then to chapel and the place full. Village women in their tall hats, children with flowers in their bonnets, the organ playing *Merch Megan,* and everybody singing, the good Welsh descant raising the roof with happiness. In spite of my anxieties, I can look back with joy to see Susannah and John kneeling together, my father looking blissful, and the Reverend talking out about the glory of marriage. I noticed Hannah Thomas was staring straight at me. I turned my eyes immediately down. I was not for coupling, as she already knew. As I diverted my eye, everybody stood to leave the Chapel. The organist, sweating cobs, struck up *Men tra Gwen.* As he worked his feet and hands in a frenzy of extra notes, as the women of the village mopped their eyes, I rose to follow the mass of happy well wishers outside. It was all laughter, all rose petals, all smiles, all handshakes as I crept into the shade of Penuel.

It was home then, windows open, doors flung wide. The women and children gathered together in the best parlour with Susannah, all blushes, all petticoats and flounces, showing my mother's necklace as her something old and blue.

Looking back to Susannah's happiness, to Hannah Thomas's glances on that wedding day, I smile to myself, but recall that I was impatient with the romance of it all. John had long since retired to the kitchen, where he sat with Daniel Evans, talking unions, Grandpa Shôn intent on pressing them into his Ivorites.

'We want more than your secret handshakes, Shôn 'or Lan,' John was saying seriously.

'Fists it is we want,' cut in Dan Evans, 'Revolt against the Masters is the only way.'

'You cannot do it, Daniel Evans, you cannot do that openly.' Grandpa Shôn with an air of great conspiracy, whispered, 'It's a good institution for the working man you want ...'

'John Thomas,' called a guest to the bridegroom, cutting off Grandpa Shôn, 'no more of your politicking, Shôn 'or Lan. . Can we head off for the Colliers', John Thomas, now you're well and truly wed? I'm dry.' There was a chorus of approval from the men.

'Well, back by tea-time, then,' Jemima ruled. 'I've enough food here for Booker's entire workforce - don't keep us waiting, mind.'

Not wanting to join the wedding guests up at the Colliers' Arms, I walked the garden till the evening came, then watched as the guests, well tanked-up from the Colliers', reeled and danced. My father jigged with Catherine. He was clearly happy. Everyone was happy because I held from them the truth. Deborah was in the arms of a young collier from the village and Elizabeth stood smiling benignly, helping Jemima fill up mugs with more small beer. Dada was dancing still, sweating like a haulier, but I could only think of Evan. He had coughed for months now and was thin and weak. From the corner of the garden, I watched, inert and anxious as our Susannah hid and John Thomas was out looking for her in the old tradition. While they laughed together, I could hear my brother John and Dan Evans still seeking revolution. Suddenly, a voice jarred me from my reverie.

'Phillip ......'

It was Hannah Thomas standing there beside me.

'Are you home now in the village?'

She was young and lovely but I had no time for women. 'I return to Liverpool tomorrow,' I said immediately.

For a while, neither of us spoke. The music from the dancing filled the air. Hannah stood apart from me. Her slight figure, her serious face was silhouetted against the sinking sun, but I found no words to tell her she was beautiful.

'When I first saw you,' she said quietly, 'I fell in love with you. And you smiled, Phillip, you smiled because you knew.'

I remember that I only repeated, 'I leave tomorrow, Hannah. The packet is already booked.'

'Take me with you, Phillip,' she said. 'I want to see the world.'

1872

For dust thou art, and unto dust shalt thou return. Again, in the house of Abraham Phillips, I turn the pages of the Book. It moves my memory back to another June and home. Sad was that second journey back to Wales from Liverpool. Just a year had passed since Susannah and John wed. Evan was with me this time, dead and in his coffin. It had been a long year with my elder brother fading slowly by my side, and with me promising to take him home to Wales.

The sorrows of death compassed me. With Evan's body in the hold, I had time to think. As the steam packet skirted coast lines down from Liverpool to Wales, the sorrows of my life controlled me. I could see from this vantage point the exploitation of my country. I could see a landscape dotted with disfigurement, valleys of smoking chimneys and grim existence. I thought of John, of my father underground - a subterranean Wales, where fathers often perished with their sons. I thought of cholera in Merthyr, Dowlais and in Aberdare, of hardship and deep unrest as miners' wages fell. The world was too much with me. I thought of Evan and envied him his death. And a shame pervaded my whole being. Did the terrible interplay of my ambition, my ingenuity in leaving home, contribute to the desperate despair of my stark country? While John was raising hell to unionise men, what did I do but seek escape. Evan had sought it, too - and he had died. No God to call, I spat my agony to the roiling sea. *'So teach us to number our days,'* I whispered in anguish to the waves, *'that we may apply our hearts unto wisdom.'*

Busy was the Port of Cardiff when I disembarked that day. Overcrowded, dirty, bustling with working men, coal heaving, ship building, rope making, brewing and milling - all to the holds of waiting steamers. I had left behind the frenzy of activity in Liverpool, but found Cardiff just as busy now. As I sit here in the house of my father, I am overwhelmed by guilt and sadness that I did not bring Evan home to his father while he still lived. Instead I hired a cart to carry him to *Ty'n y Coed* that day. What a grim homecoming of any eldest son. Better to die side by side underground.

It is engraved on my mind: I see it page by page. Up the track to *Ty'n y Coed*, Dada opening the door, gasping with excitement as he held me close. Still grimy from his shift, his shirt thick with coal dust, he laughed, 'You should have warned me, Phillip. I'd have got scrubbed up.' His eyes shone happy, smaller now and rheumy, but white still against the black of coal. Rubbing his dusty stubble, he turned and called Jemima to the door.

'Look girl, a cart he has paid to bring him up from Cardiff!' he declared in joy.

'Rich is he now?' Jemima laughed, urging my father to the bosh to clean.

'Dada,' I said, 'before you move, I have to tell you Evan is with me ...'

'Evan with you, boy! What more joy could today bring! Jemima, call the girls. Evan is come home.' Then, seeing no son walking proudly to the door, 'Where is he then,' he asked. 'Surely one carriage was enough for two. Has Liverpool made you so rich that you both come separately?' Then, troubled, he asked beneath his breath, 'are there problems with you two boys that you both travel here alone?'

Taking my father's hand I told him Evan was dead.

The howl of pain I heard rang through the mountain air. A wounded animal could not howl so. He howled loud to the resounding air the one word - Evan.

'Dada,' I comforted, Jemima by his side, supporting him. He heard us not and screamed long in the gloom.

'EVAN............................'

Then shall the dust return to the earth as it was; and the spirit shall return unto God who gave it. I know the natural law and find no solace in the mystery, but a fine Welsh Chapel service Evan had. On borrowed money, the funeral trap was hired, black horses with plaited tails and plumes, their hooves pawing the ground outside the cottage. My father, John and I walked the way before the trap and villagers touched their hats or bowed their heads as we went by.

After the singing stopped, after the soil was turned, the digger paid, I walked away and up the Garth to be alone. The dawn breeze had turned to sultry summer and the air hung heavy on my soul. Birds overhead and grass beneath my feet gave me no comfort there. My father's howl hung, echoed through the dips and crevices. Turning, I could just see the funeral party heading home, Jemima upright, my father on her arm - a blinded man now, being led. Did tears roll down my cheeks or were my eyes caught by the gentle wind that suddenly blew? To this day, I do not know.

Footsteps I heard as I stood wondering and alone. Turning, I saw Hannah Thomas following me.

'Your Dada is a man stunned,' she said.

'Death he is used to,' I replied, 'but for his eldest son to die while safely sitting at an office desk? He cannot hold such grief and I cannot face his tears.' I looked at her directly, said in my father's defence, 'Hannah, he dies so young. Evan was but twenty four.'

'And you are crying too,' she murmured gently. And taking me in her arms she kissed me. 'I will keep you safe,' she whispered. 'Only take me to Liverpool to live with you.'

1875

In the March of 1875, I married Hannah Thomas, daughter of George and Mary from the village. Capel Bethlehem had opened again in 1872 and that made it easy for her family. Things had changed quickly after Evan died. Hannah had come to Liverpool with me and together we put my brother's affairs in order. So calm she was, the epitome of care and management. Gradually our friendship grew and I responded to her patient love. I remember those days in Liverpool, not from the smell of food in the stale passageways of our accommodation when I shared with Evan, but from the flowers that she put on every windowsill, not from the dirty cobbled streets and underworld of Liverpool, not from the ledgers and the documents I drew in careful pen across the vellum page, but from her hand in mine, her warmth and sustenance as I recovered from my care of Evan through the year. 'Be gentle with yourself,' she often said as she touched my lips with hers. 'Do not still grieve. You have given him back to the earth. And that is all.' Head on my shoulder, she would philosophise that from his ashes had sprung up our love.

I was a travelling salesman now, and marvel still at Hannah's independence as she learned the city on her own. She declared that she was glad to leave the village, but in the evenings, against the bustle of crime ridden streets, we often talked of home. As my father had said to Evan, Liverpool was full of Irish folk, prepared to work for a low wage - they could be seen begging on the corners of the street, in passages and alleyways. Hannah and I had once walked out to look at the new St Martin's tenements for the working poor and thought of the Level Houses in our village. People working for inadequate returns were everywhere, we decided sadly. It was the tragic history of our time.

'Do they not notice, Phillip,' Hannah asked me. 'Look at the fine middle-class houses adjacent to the workplace. Look at those horse-drawn trams for those who live in style. Could you take such a path while others starve?'

'I've done it, Hannah. Been to school while other children worked,' I muttered.

'But you have recognised the problem, Phillip. It is my fear that many do not notice, do not think these workmen as themselves. So many live in squalor.'

'Old Shôn o'r Lan warned that this city is insanitary,' I said, 'that cholera has broken out here at least three times,'

'And in our village,' Hannah mused, 'are we much better? The Hard Level houses back there have but one lavatory for all the cottages. I hope they don't see cholera ...' She put her hand in mine. 'The only time I went into a cottage there,' she added, 'was to visit a woman who was ill. Her cottage was very clean - and there was a Testament in Welsh upon her table.'

'A Testament in Welsh, Hannah! The Book! We speak of deprivation and always you take me back to the Book! Is a Testament on the table in the Level Houses worth your mention? That Book haunts me, Hannah. It's prophesy is damnation. Quotations fill my head like memories, so often did my mother make me learn. It keeps the poor subservient by promising a better life in Heaven! But I have no time for gods as well you know.' My wife opened her mouth to protest but changed her mind and smiled. 'I used to see the children from the Level Houses as I went to school,' I said, remembering my indolent past. 'I felt so guilty that they went to their work when I was dressed and starched, a bag of books under my arm.'

To change the subject quickly, Hannah turned to talk of coal. 'Father told me there was a Pentyrch mine that burned for years,' she said, 'that its smoke rose up from the ground and you could burn in its hot ash. ... Phillip, you laugh at me. Is it not true?'

'I think he saw the fire of *Y Tylwyth Teg,*' I teased, ruffling her long hair. 'Unless, perhaps, you are that fairy nymph yourself,' I murmured, 'you have her ethereal beauty and fair hair.' Hannah pushed me away a little, not used to such frivolity from me. 'Do you have a place, like her, where it is dangerous for me to tread?' I whispered.

'Serious, I am Phillip Phillips. Don't romance me with your grandfather's Celtic mythology! There are more important things' Hannah stared at me intently. 'Don't be angry with me Phillip. While you are at your desk,' she confessed, 'I spend my time in the library in Duke Street, where I read the journals. Yes, Phillip. I read English, too. You need not look so startled.' She leaned forward, away from my arms. 'Smaller unions are building up support again in the coal fields of South Wales - your brother, John - he does not stand alone.'

'Hannah,' I said, 'I have told you before that my brother John is wild. He will bring trouble to the men he leads. And anyway, in 1871 - just four years ago - working men left the Unions in disgust when support for their strike action did not live up to union promises. In Aberdare and the Rhondda men were ashamed they joined. If you remember, they were promised ten shillings a week, but they only got 2s 2d when they went on strike.'

'That union, the Amalgamated Association, was set up in Lancashire,' Hannah argued. 'Smaller District Unions have been set up in Wales since then.'

'They are little more than organisations set up by the coal owners to fix pay,' I said.

Hannah looked crestfallen. 'I know it is right that working men should band together,' she said. 'And I know the history of their efforts is peppered with death and violence. No one wants Scotch Cattle - but I know that working men together is the only way. My father, yours, your brother John, and Susannah's husband, too. What chance do they stand as individual colliers - except the chance they die?'

'Their life is cruel, Hannah.' I paused, pulling her closer to me. 'We both know the hazards of their work. The Friendly Societies of Grandfather Shôn and his like are noble, maybe, but they are toothless institutions and of little worth.' I spoke quietly, my wife now in my arms again. 'In spite of all the kneeling and swearing of allegiance to the Book, in spite of Orders that Members will work only with other Members and never undercut, they hold no sway. Still the Masters lock any union members out.'

'You are not militant, Phillip. It makes me sad.'

'I am indeed not militant, Hannah,' I said. 'You read me right, I am afraid that you have married a coward who just wants to survive.'

Hannah settled back in my arms. 'That old mine in Pentyrch,' she said, relaxing. 'My father told me that a Llantrisant Reverend's son fell into those burning ashes, that a long stick poked in it would suddenly go to flame ...'

'The Fair Tribe of fairies are more interesting than any Reverend's son,' I said lifting wisps of hair from her face, 'for they are immortal - shall we live forever my own *Tylwyth Teg* ?' I did not ever intend marriage, did not seek out love but I was so happy there with Hannah in my arms. We were quiet then. Outside, voices rang through the night air, the noise of feet on cobbled passage ways. Night was falling fast.

'Phillip,' Hannah interrupted the still air in our room, 'both our families have colliers in their midst. Did you never want to work underground?'

'John and my father were enough for me,' I said, 'John talked coal with every step he took - it's Unions now he speaks of and father disagrees. No, Hannah, the coal is not for me. When we lived on the mountain, I often walked down past the Colliers' Arms to where the men came off the shift each day at Coed Rhiw'r Ceiliog, just below our home. I saw their tired faces, etched in coal. I always knew that coal was not for me. St Cadoc carrying his live coals to Pentyrch has never had a chance to put them in my lap.'

'His church is beautiful, though,' Hannah intervened, 'St Catwg's with a spire that joins the clouds! I wonder why your Susannah didn't chose to marry there.'

'She loves the Gwaelod Capel. Anyway St Catwg's is the resting place for half our family - not the place for marriage. First Mother, then the baby Deborah and now my brother, Evan. For God's sake, Hannah, do we have to think of death and coal? I lived my childhood watching men and children go down pits. I looked to the hill towards the South and saw the lines of men, bent double, children reluctant, dragging feet to Coed-y-Bedw. I looked in the other direction and the same line of stick men and hungry boys walked up the hill to iron. Is this the country that we miss so much? It's sentiment we have, not sense. The Garth, the valley, that we yearn to love is gruesome in its stark reality. Why else are we in Liverpool?'

'Booker, maybe, Phillip,' Hannah said sarcastically. 'He gave you contacts and your references.'

'Too close for comfort, that,' I muttered bitterly. 'It divides my father's loyalties.' Hannah looked sad as I repeated staccato that I did not want a life in coal, I did not want to hear its cruel history from Master Miners to the Masters who took everything, including life and soul.

'There are good men too,' Hannah cajoled, 'Men like your grandfather, Shôn o'r Lan, who would have the working men unite.' She walked to the window and plucking me a flower from her arrangement there, said, 'Here's to the Ivorite chant of 'Friendship'

Then, walking to me, she said, as she put the flower in my hand, ' to Friendship, Truth and Love.' Kissing me, she whispered, 'The world really is too much with you, Phillip Phillips. There are good men working for better times and your brother John is one. I have heard him preach of unions to crowds of eager men ...'

'My brother is a firebrand,' I said. 'He would make riots, have the soldiers in. Have we not had enough of death without him calling loud for it? If he gave talks, what were you doing there? It is dangerous, Hannah. Unions are against the law as I am sure you know.'

'One day, my Phillip, you will understand their worth. I do. Think of the workhouse in Pontypridd. So many end there after accidents. Liverpool has got its workhouse, too. I have seen it while you worked. The poor, the working man, need unions. Without, the Masters rule and rape.'

I was dazed to hear Hannah in such voice again. My blood rose, but I could find no words to combat her. 'Do not follow John, Hannah,' I said pathetically. You make me so afraid.' Taking her in my arms, I found her strong, and caressing her soft cheek declared that we should sleep.

'Iron and coal from Cardiff rival Merthyr Tydfil now,' she said seriously, ignoring my attentions. 'And in both places women and children starve. Our home is under the wild, coal blackened Garth and still you do not see.'

'Because I look to the sky and hear the skylark rise,' I whispered in her ear. 'There is little else that we can do. Look skywards, Hannah, do not let your morality make you a victim. You speak to me of Merthyr. Do you know that in Merthyr there was a Welsh princess - her name was Tydfil - who was murdered for her beliefs?'

'Tydfil the Martyr was a Christian, Phillip. My beliefs are far less spiritual. I just want to see a union of working men.' Hannah was roused. 'Do you see Merthyr now?' she said. 'Full of mines to feed the voracious bellies of the furnaces. The Dowlais ironworks make it the most exploited town in Wales. They need to unionise.'

'It is against the law, Hannah,' I replied in exasperation. 'Survival, Hannah. We must survive. Do not be murdered for beliefs.'

'Come to bed, Phillip,' Hannah laughed. 'I have married a boring old pragmatist! The street light flickers and you have work to do tomorrow.'

'I cannot see a moon tonight,' I said with sadness.

'Because it only shines on your beautiful Garth,' she laughed.

1875

Morning and a smell of sleep in the tenement's passage ways. The sun had woken me early, a brilliant and unexpected winter beam directly to my face. I realised that I was happy for the first time since my mother died. I realised, too, that I had to stop thinking about the future, stop worrying about the past, and embrace the day. Our lodging house was a tenement on Garston Dock where we could watch the steamers loading coal for Lancaster. We had a splendid view of the activity. Garston took nearly half of the coal trade coming into Liverpool since the railway came, so spectacular tall masts and steam punctuated our skyline against the cold sky and ever restless sea.

'Warned me about Liverpool, did Grandpa Shôn,' I yawned as Hannah stirred. 'Didn't explain, though, how hard it is to get up in the morning when you're wed!' Sitting up, stretching, my foot towards the floor, the sound of ships' sirens echoing, the force of December cold held me in its grasp. I stared at the cold sky, shivering. I had never intended to take a wife, but here I was in a big city with my clever, argumentative Hannah and my life was full. I smiled contentedly.

'Come back to bed,' Hannah murmured, only half awake. 'Come and keep me warm, Phillip. Out in those dark cobbled streets,' she whispered as she held me, 'there are thieves to rob you, illegal drinking dens and tenements for the poor to worry you! Better to stay here, warm with me, in bed.'

I stifled another yawn and took her hand. 'It's time we headed down the stairs, woman. Don't you know it is your job to get me to work on time.' As we laughed together, I thought of how I had struggled to keep the past alive, how I had anguished over my future. I'll put all cares behind me, now, I thought, as we dressed together and went down to eat.

'These docklands really are littered with violence by night,' Hannah chattered as she put the kettle on. Busy cutting bread she smiled, 'Old Shôn o'r Lan was right. Glad I am to have a place that's safe. Do you know, Phillip,' she said, her hands moving to brush away the wisps of hair from her eyes, 'I have seen crowds of thugs hanging around doorways of the pubs and beer houses, intimidating passers-by.'

'The magistrate's court in Dale Street is forever busy,' I muttered between mouthfuls. 'Men rolling home happy from the Colliers' Arms don't have to fear the law. Nothing much happens in our village.' I looked up at Hannah, before the mirror now, tying her hair high behind her head, the winter sun back-lighting the wisps that danced, refusing to be bound. Putting down my spoon, I walked over to where she stood and put my arms around her waist. Kissing the top of her head I knew why I had come to Liverpool, knew why I had married her. It gave real meaning to my life, and I was glad.

A loud knocking at the door broke through my reverie. Breaking away quickly Hannah went to see who called. I stood, blissful, looking out at the empty sky, watching the seagulls dip and glide as men set about their work and ships' masts caught the sun. I had never intended to share my life with anyone, but I was happy to be with Hannah. Happy to be alive.

'It's a telegram, Phillip,' said Hannah slowly. 'From Elizabeth I see.' Hannah yawned, rubbing her eyes, still sleepy as she handed it to me.

'A big expense,' I said under my breath, tearing open the thin page. 'She can't be marrying already - maybe she has taken a position away and needs my reference urgently.' Hannah looked over my shoulder and read aloud.

So quickly it happened. Time stood still.

'Come Phillip. Dada dead. Pit explosion. E'

White I was, devoid of speech.

I could barely focus on the words.

'I cannot go to the office, Hannah. I must go directly to Elizabeth,' I said. My legs had turned to clay and my head swam.

'And I will come with you, Phillip.' Hannah put her hands on mine. 'But go to work today,' she said tenderly. 'We have to get a steamer place. It could take time.'

Long was my day. Ledger after ledger, account after account, the files at my desk mounting higher and my head blank, or deep in Wales. If we could not look back, our lives would be empty, but I had too much grief to welcome memory. Slowly the time passed, slowly the day grew tired. I could not concentrate, could only see the Garth as from my bedroom window, could only hear my father's howling while he mourned for Evan.

We should be used to death, but I could not weep nor book the passage home. Hours passed while I stared at blank walls, sat head in hands and did not speak. My memory compelled me to repeat traumas that I thought long gone. I faced again the room where baby Deborah died, heard Evan coughing his last breath, saw my mother fade to paleness while I played. The turned earth of their graves was in our room, their cold arms and their bitter lips transmuting me from happiness to pain. Like a statue of base metal, I was petrified by my past, could not reverse the passage of repeated time. How long I sat inert I could not say. Day turned to night and night fused to a new day. I do not think I slept. I did not eat the food that Hannah put before me.

'Phillip, come back to me.' Hannah spoke quietly, her voice cutting through my catatonic frame. 'I cannot stand this isolation. Your father is dead, but I am here with you. Does that not give you solace?' I looked at her pathetically and did not speak.

'I have booked the steerage down to Wales,' she said, touching my shoulder gently.' We can embark tomorrow. Please come now to our bed.'

*

Thus, late I came to the tragedy in our home. Elizabeth's telegram had chilled my blood, my father's death stopped time. So much had Jemima borne alone when I arrived. It was moving towards Christmas - I would have come back to *Ty'n y Coed* to celebrate that birth. Now death I found. Dark was the house of Abraham Phillips the day we came. Cold was the welcome.

Grief hung over my village like a mist that seeps into joints, into eyes, into the very soul. Dark it was, dark as coal dust. Light seemed to have deserted the ribbon of dwellings up the road, descended even on the cottages alongside the Colliers', where men drank silently.

We had walked, Hannah and I, up the lane to the cottage hand in hand, me like a child, a blind man, being led. She was my keeper and my hope. No windows glinted in late winter sun as we approached. We faced drawn curtains, the very house of my father, dead. Gloomy it looks when the lights of a cottage are dimmed and filtered through thick cloth, when the lamps at windows do not smile at you. I felt removed. Smoke there was as usual. It curled black into the winter sky, turning to grey gauze against the naked trees. Snow-blanked hollows of the Garth stared down at me, ominous, far distant now. How different it looked to the place we left in Spring after our wedding. How hostile, how remote. Quiet was the village we came through. People there were, but they moved, shoulders bent, head down against the snow. Hunger showed in their sunken eyes and sallow skin. Hardly people, little rows of moving shapes, run wild with grief, with shock, with poverty.

Arriving at the door of *Ty'n y Coed*, we could hear Elizabeth in the kitchen, her small voice quietly singing against the clatter of crockery. '*Neithiwr mi glywais lais angel fel hyn,*' came her plaintive voice - 'Last night an angel called with heaven's breath. *Dafydd, tyrd adref, a chwarae trwy'r glyn* - David, play and come through the gates of death'. I knew that she was crying as she sang. Jemima saw us at the window but did not come to open the door. Instead, we entered as if we had not left long months ago.

'Elizabeth,' I said, my sister at arm's length. 'I had your telegram. What can you tell me more?'

'Phillip,' she cried out, but her arms were by her sides, cold, immobile, drear. 'It is quite terrible here,' she said. 'First there was an agony of waiting at the pit head, then the wait for you. So glad I am that you have come.'

'You have suffered too much,' I said, but I could not yet move close to her. I could not take her in my arms. I felt so cold. And we were standing still, our baggage in our hands. No welcome here, no hospitality. The very air seemed cold.

'You look tired, Elizabeth,' Hannah interjected, putting down her bag and moving towards my sister, her arms outstretched. 'Can I help you now? Is there anything I can do?'

'The women at the pit head looked so frail,' Elizabeth suddenly burst out, 'they seemed oblivious against the driving snow. It was cruel weather, Hannah. They only wrapped in shawls. Babies cried, were held tighter to the breast. Feet stamped away the bitter cold. And old men gathered in union, remembering the pain of their long dead wives, facing now lost sons, lost workmates and lost friends.'

As Hannah went towards my sister, I moved further into the kitchen, taking off my outer coat. 'Those of us with loved ones underground will never learn to bear this agony,' Hannah said.

Elizabeth turned to me. 'Be glad you live in Liverpool,' she said bitterly. 'You did not have to face the pit. Hollow was the waiting, Phillip. Hard is life in this village. Harsh the industry that drives it. As I stood there waiting at the pit head - hoping Dada was safe - on the valley floor the distant sounds of machines we are so used to,' she paused, looking at me blankly. 'You know - the hammering, the clatter of the other industry - it vanished. The silence - it was terrible. Noise covers anguish. In that silence, hope aligned itself with fear.' Elizabeth slumped down beside the dying fire and wept. She could not look at me and still I could not touch her.

Jemima came into the kitchen quietly. She did not extend her arms in welcome but stood looking as if Hannah and I were ghosts.

'Jemima,' Hannah greeted her. 'Too much you have suffered. We have come at last.'

'And time, too,' Jemima said coldly, opening her arms to Hannah, but not her heart. 'Your journey to us could have been much sooner, Phillip.' I said nothing. Words charged around my head, words I assessed, but none came to my lips.

'As soon as word reached us, we booked the packet and came, Jemima,' Hannah said, holding the older woman tight. 'We have come here before we go to see my parents in the village, but I can stay with them if it would make it easier here.'

Jemima shrugged. 'You will not bother me,' she said, 'for I have much to do.' Turning to me, 'Your Dada is in there,' she said, cutting short Hannah's wasted words of explanation. 'I did the best I could with him, Phillip. He is badly marked and more it shows as days go on. The face is not his own. We have not shown the little ones today. Elizabeth went to touch him, but could not stretch out her hand, Catherine tried, but she, too, is distraught. Damaged he is, Phillip. He does not look at peace. We wait for Deborah yet.'

'And what of John.'

'John?' she said, 'What do I need of John?'

Elizabeth's eyes met mine with a freezing glance that made me understand I must not ask.

Confused, reluctant, Jemima's eyes on mine, I opened the door to the front room. Light filtered faintly through the vertical slot between drawn curtains. The smell of death was everywhere. I stood nauseated in the doorway. And I could not move.

'Will you not go in to see your father, Phillip Phillips?'

'I will go in immediately,' I said. 'But will you come to him with me, Jemima?'

'Your father - and you do not want to speak to him alone? Being in Liverpool has changed you then, for you always wanted him alone.' Taking my hand as if I were a child, this stoical woman who had come to us when our mother died, was trying to mother still, yet I could not call her by that name.

Cold was the front room where my father lay. Embers glowed within the grate, but its heat refused to spread. Yellow light from the vigil oil lamp flickered on his face, his once austere yet loving visage, inanimate now and crushed. Small he looked lying there in spite of buttoned suit and clean white shirt. Through the curtain crack, the last vestige of outside light filtered down, dancing with dust mites in the slanted beam. His injuries blackening, diminished my father looked, and frail. I could not move the cloth that covered him.

'And the accident?' I asked without meeting Jemima's eyes.

'Crushed,' she said, 'crushed against the wall. A truck exploded in his path as he moved towards the heading where the colliers worked.'

'Is he cleared now for burial,' I asked.

'Phillip, Phillip, some five minutes you have been here in my house and already you want to know when you can move him.' Jemima looked distraught. 'The coroner will come tomorrow, filling my house with his great-coated, idle men. They have never been below, have never opened eyes to absolute dark or had the coal dust scraped from daily scars.' Jemima moved towards the window. 'There were sixteen deaths, Phillip, and others wounded. Too many families will go hungry now their man has gone. Buried on the parish they will be. Such shame for them to bear on top of loss. I hear that some will have to go to Pontypridd - the workhouse is the only place there is.'

I stood before the corpse of my father, searched for words that I could say. Jemima stood beside me, her hands beneath her apron. Waiting. Waiting for sorrow that I could not show.

'How well you have laid my father out,' I said lamely. 'Shall I get flowers for him, too?'

Jemima shook her head. 'Outward display from us would not be right. So many are so poor, too many dead. We had the wages of an Overman but must not show it now.'

'The poverty of the colliers has always haunted me,' I muttered. 'I went to school and opened books while other children opened ventilation doors. I can still remember other eyes watching me as I walked past the furnaces.'

'Your father was proud that he sent all of you to school,' Jemima interrupted. 'How can you talk this idle and self-centred guilt before his body is interred?'

Her anger caught my breath. 'How well you have prepared the room for saying our goodbyes,' I mumbled, unable to find words to explain, or enough emotion yet to cry. 'Will you open the house for neighbours now?'

'I cannot, Phillip. Too many deaths within these villages for that. And many will have paupers graves.'

'And for my father? What is planned?'

'After Penuel for your grandparents' sake, you will walk with him to St Catwg's. You will make a four to carry him. Richard and Phillip Thomas will carry their brother with you and John - '

'So my brother John will walk with me,' I said, relieved.

'John Phillips is not welcomed to the funeral,' Jemima said harshly. 'Susannah's husband John will make the four with you. A good bass voice he has.' Jemima's face became less stern. 'I remember many a Chapel when his voice rang out so clear,' she said. 'Sing for your father, he will, sing up the hill, sing for him past cottages in the old tradition.' Noticing my reticence, Jemima put her hand on my arm. 'You will do it, Phillip,' she said. 'And you will do it without your brother, John. You have worked too long away, but proud of you your father was. He was joyous at your wedding back in Spring. He loved you all. Broken he was when Evan died.' She looked at me and read my fear. 'Carried by his nearest and dearest Abraham must be,' she said firmly. 'You will do it, Phillip. You owe him that.' Jemima stood upright, eyes directly on me. 'I loved your father,' she said, 'and he was good to me. Now I must return him to his real and only love, Elizabeth, your mother. Together they will be in Pentyrch church.'

There was quiet then, uneasy peace. We had stood long in the cold sitting room, my father lying there in the last light. I had done all this before, for my mother, for baby Deborah and then for Evan. I looked at Jemima, aged but stoical. And I thought of her words about my father's love and searched my mind for words of comfort. None could I say. I stood in silence in death's gloom, death's stench. Jemima did not call me to her and I could not outstretch arms to her.

'I will do it,' I said.

Jemima nodded and the first semblance of a smile lit her careworn face.

'I can help with the burial fee,' I said quietly.

Jemima bristled. 'It is a nominal charge. I am prepared for that. Just be sure you have the *arian y rhaw* - the silver coin - ready in the churchyard for the gravedigger's spade. I like this old tradition. You do that for me and that alone. The Minister will meet you at the gate and we will wait to kneel around the coffin at the altar of the church.'

'You have it well in mind, Jemima.'

'I will throw the soil into the grave. I give my man back willingly to the earth and to Elizabeth. He was my one and only love, but he loved her still, I know.'

The sounds of Hannah and Elizabeth in the kitchen forced our interlude to end. Elizabeth opened the door a fraction, saying tea was made. Smoothing back her hair, Jemima turned and left me with my father. 'Say your goodbye, now, alone, she said.

The silence in the room was overwhelming. The smell of death. My damaged father lying there alone in the big bed. And I thought how terrible to die already underground, what a disgusting and unnecessary death. I thought of progress and cursed the human cost of coal. I railed against the God my mother loved. I fought against the shadows of this death till I was breathless in my agony.

'The Lord giveth and the Lord taketh away,' I muttered to myself with bitterness as I headed for the door. As my hand held the worn cast iron latch, as I felt the warmth there from Jemima's hand, I hesitated, turned and walking to the bed, I took my father's ice-cold hand and wept.

1875

Night fell and with it shadows that encompassed all hostility. Hannah was with Jemima in the cold front room, keeping vigil where my father lay. Silent the kitchen now, flames from the fire danced oblivious. At last I found a peace beside Elizabeth, understood her anger that I lived away.

'Phillip,' she said, 'I must tell you about John.'

'He was not underground with Da?' I scarcely dared to ask.

My sister shook her head. 'Look out of the window, Phillip. See the snow. Soft is the night when the moon shines through the trees and snow lights the room. But harsh the sound of doors burst open, dreadful the sound of raucous singing when your father lies dead before the embers of the day. Such things filled our house, Phillip. I can barely tell what I have seen.'

'I am listening, Elizabeth,' I said, bewildered but aware of her distress.

'Susannah and I were in the kitchen,' Elizabeth went on. 'The night was quiet like this. Exhausted by crying, we were watching the moon through the branches of the beech. You see that tree, Phillip? Large now it has grown since you have been away.'

'It is imposing in this night-time glow,' I said impatiently.

'But it is not lovely in our house. Oh, Phillip. Why did you leave us for the city? We needed you here so desperately. I do not know how to tell what has happened in this house.'

Moving across to my sister, I stood, taking her hand. 'Elizabeth, be peaceful,' I urged, sitting down by her side. 'Tell me what it is that I must know.'

'We must whisper, Phillip. Jemima must not hear. You have seen Father laid out in the front room. Much marked, he is. I do not know that face. His eyes were open when they brought him home. The stare was horrible. Jemima closed them, Phillip. She is composed but she must be in anguish. She says so little but her heart must break.'

'We must look after her. I am to blame. I simply cannot see her in our mother's place. I know she suffers. We have lost a father, she a husband, provider and a friend.'

'But there is worse to tell you - if things can be worse than father lying there the way he is. John is outlawed, Phillip.'

'John? Outlawed?' I exclaimed. 'What has he done? Is it his politics? Has he tried to form a union against the law? Where is he now, Elizabeth? I need to talk with him.'

'He does not live here now. He is cast out. Late it was, and dark - and he came bellowing in, shouting terrible things that I can barely say.'

'Tell me, Elizabeth.'

'I will start with what he said, Phillip. Drunk John was, so I do not know the truth. He was at the Colliers and the talk was all of needing unions and strike, that Da was not for this in spite of Shôn o'r Lan and his Society. But worse, Phillip. He says there is a rumour that Dada sent men into the pit to die. They say that Dada knew that there was gas - '

'No. Elizabeth, that cannot be. Abraham Phillips was a careful man.'

'John was screaming out about it all with Dada lying there. Names he called him. Dreadful names. I cannot say it here. Says he can no longer work with colliers after this. Says the shame is overwhelming him. In agony he was, Phillip, spent and hoarse. The shouting was terrible. Catherine and Deborah woke, came unto the stairs and listened. How they wept, Phillip. Weak with it they were. And Jemima stood there listening. She was so calm, Phillip. So upright and still.'

'What did he say?'

'Murderer,' John shouted to the door where Dada lay and 'Bastard Master's man.' Jemima stood before him. Then asked him to leave. Quietly she spoke, Phillip. She simply said, 'Go, John. I know your father. So do you. Go now and leave this house to mourn.'

'John almost spat at her as he stormed through the door. He shouted Bastard Master's man again, slamming the door behind him as he left. I think he now resides with Daniel Evan's wife in Tongwynlais. Her Dan lies dead, John keeps her company, plays with her little boy. He was in anguish, Phillip, but I could not comfort him. What he told could not be true. It was only whispered in the Colliers' Arms with drink.'

'Stop, Elizabeth. I cannot hear this more.' I sat in the kitchen of my father's house as patriarch now. My brother John outcast and Evan dead, I had to mediate. Da was my brother's hero. He clung to my father in the way some people cling to God. The love he felt gave him security. 'He is not himself,' I said. 'It will take him time to grieve. We cannot think on this. This dreadful rumour will be quashed. When is the Inquest, when will the evidence be given?'

'You are too easy on him, Phillip. I was here and tell you now that he was terrible. We all must face the powerful emotions that death brings.' Elizabeth sat rigid. 'But such words, Phillip. How can you excuse him? How could John cause such pain?'

'His immaturity has been exploited,' I said. 'That story will be no more than drunken scape-goating. Sharing this grief may help us bear our pain.'

At last I felt in control. Putting my arms around my sister, I held her while she cried. But my soul was deeply troubled and in my hand, I felt the seraphim's burning coal.

1875

'You know that they opened the Coroner's Inquest on the day of the accident?' Elizabeth asked. 'I wished so much that you were here. It was too much for me to do alone.' She was sitting beside me now, leaning on my shoulder as the evening fell, once more the little sister that I loved. 'After they brought Da's body home, Jemima did not want me there, so I went down to the Junction Hotel to see the coroner,' she whispered. 'I couldn't settle in the house. After the long wait at the pit-head, I wanted to find out more. Little groups of men were there already. Words were not flowing, but I heard one say, 'Old collier Evans will have to get here and tell all'. 'Poor bugger', chipped in another miner, who sat with a slumped back, hands on the table. 'Can't think he'll want to go through that again. All too close, I should think. He's got the guilt of the survivor, anyway. A real state he is in apart from his burns. And I'll not forget that scene in a hurry. Ask me about hell and I'll say Lan.' He threw back his head, Phillip, stared at the ceiling of the room, then without another word, he left, moving like a wraith across the floor. 'He's taken it bad', said one of the Colliers to me. 'He'll be back in when he has had a breath of air'. He told me that this man got down there first with Seymour. Henry Sant from up the Gwaelod was a friend of his, too - now he lies dead in his poor cottage.

'I nodded, standing up to leave - but one of the older colliers spoke to me. 'We don't see you often in the village now, Elizabeth Phillips', he said. 'I remember you as a little girl. A good man was your father, Abraham Phillips. Sorry I am that he is dead'.

'He said that, Elizabeth? So father is still held high. Maybe the drink affected John. Maybe he heard a spiteful drunken comment - there is always that need to find someone to blame.'

'We must hope that.' Elizabeth paused then went back to her recounting of the day. 'I thanked the collier and then looked towards the door, saying that I must go through to the other room, by way of an excuse, a way not to engage him in further conversation - afraid what I might hear. 'Coroner Reece, will already have arrived,' I explained, 'and I must speak with him.'

'As I entered the Inquest room, the Coroner was scanning the names of the jury. Hovering behind him was a young man - I was told he was William Galloway. The Coroner introduced him as the Regional Inspector of the Mines. Turning to the colliers waiting there, he said, 'The Police have picked the jury and today, I will make the formal opening of this Inquest'. Then he explained that there would be a delay for he wanted the twelve men to accompany him to view the bodies of the dead before the Inquest could proceed. 'I have to certify a cause of death before I hear the evidence', he said. He told us that he would reconvene the following day, saying, 'There is no point in you assembling here today'. Against the shuffle of miners deciding whether to stay, against their complaining voices, some deciding to follow the Coroner on his walk through the villages, others more than ready to go home, I stood there in a dream. It was hard to believe that what I saw was happening, that I, barely a woman, was there alone. Reece turned to William Galloway, saying, 'Will you tell the jurors to assemble at the front. Tell them to put on their outdoor wear. We head off now into the villages'.

'As everyone moved slowly to the door, as the Coroner stuffed papers to his leather bag, William Galloway asked permission to survey the scene of the explosion at the Lan. He said that from what he had heard, the flames had spread and caught men far from the explosion. 'I need to go in there to see for myself', he said.

'The coroner replied, 'Aye, man, you do that now.' He was deep into the official papers that he held. Barely looking up, he said that he would listen to the survivors' statements when he had assessed the dead. 'No doubt I will hear your evidence at a later point when we reconvene', he added to Mr Galloway.'

Elizabeth paused. 'It all seemed too hasty, Phillip. The accident had happened just hours before.'

'Women like to bury their men quickly,' I replied, 'and some men will not work with dead bodies above ground.'

Elizabeth nodded. 'Some of the men who had walked down from the Colliers' Arms sat down,' she said, barely taking a breath, 'others leaned against the door ready to move. I was the only woman there.' She was looking directly at me, her tired eyes red from crying. 'It took great courage and I felt ashamed of my intrusion there. Do you understand that, Phillip? I was there because I had to know.'

My sister clearly needed to talk, to expiate the suffering she had seen. I sat attentive, she distraught. Her words tumbled out in long awaited grief. 'Reece stood up at his table, cleared his throat,' she said. 'He brought down his hand to summon quiet. 'I formally open this Inquest into the explosion at Thomas William Booker's drift mine, the New Lan, on December 6th. 1875', he read out quickly. 'We go first to the homes of the injured and dead'. He turned to the jury, who had been sworn-in, 'I have a local man to guide me', he said. I saw old Mr Gedrych waiting there, Phillip. Do you remember him?'

I nodded, though I did not know.

'The Coroner turned to the little group of village men,' Elizabeth continued, 'I therefore adjourn proceedings until tomorrow, when I trust we will have concluded this investigation', he said. Men shuffled in the aisles, not sure what they should do. Reece asked old Gedrych how far they would have to go.

'The old man thought for a while,' Elizabeth said with half a smile. 'Good legs you will need, Mr Reece', Gedrych explained, as we know well, Phillip, for the walk would be some fourteen miles and up-hill, too, to get to the mountain villages. Some of the jurors looked aghast, but Coroner Reece nodded and gathered his outdoor clothes against the cold. Snow was no longer falling, but it lay there underfoot and the air was bitter still.

'Standing alongside Gedrych, I plucked up courage and asked the Coroner if I could accompany them. 'I am Abraham Phillips' daughter', I said, extending my hand. 'For his sake, I would like to see the families of the dead'.

'Right', Reece agreed, his eyes scanning his official page. 'But only to observe. I must inspect the bodies, these jury men my witness. You must not speak and no one must confer. Tongwynlais first', he announced addressing the jury men, who had assembled at the door. Consulting his list, he said, 'a death from fire damp there, I understand'.

'In little groups, silently, the motley crowd stepped out, followed by a group of villagers and me. A sight we must have looked, incongruous, Reece in his formal clothes, cloak dragging around his legs in the harsh wind, the scrubbed jurors in their great coats, the colliers still grimed. Slamming shut the door to the Inquest room, Reece had a quick word with the proprietor, then we walked along the riverside road and round to Tongwynlais. The cottages stood in silence, grey, while sympathetic neighbours of the humble place where Daniel Evans lived stood whispering together, women openly distressed, men dragging their clay pipes against the wind. A slight woman, her eyes red with sleeplessness and tears, opened the door and curtsied slightly as Coroner Reece walked in. The body of her husband, Daniel Evans, lay there on the table as if asleep. He had no injuries. I did not see John there, Phillip, though I hoped I might.'

I shook my head and wondered where my brother lay.

'Quickly, methodically, Coroner Reece made his inspection. I stood by Daniel Evan's wife as she said quietly, 'Peaceful he looks, my man'. Looking up at me, she murmured, 'Calm he looks - but the afterdamp has taken him from me, suffocated him'. I was not allowed to answer her. It was heartbreaking, Phillip. Her child clung to her skirt, sucking a sleeve on the limp garment that he wore. They looked so poor. Her braveness broke my heart. 'Wanted to change the world, did my Dan', she said. 'Just last Saturday, a relative of mine died in the New Tredegar accident. It was the gas again. Dan was upset, so angry that the men went down to gas. He says that roof falls get ignored. The Masters just want coal out at any cost. The men need unions, he said. I do not know. We were going to New Tredegar after my Dan's morning shift. And now - he's dead'. She picked up her young child and wept into his hair.

See what the love of God has bestowed on us, I thought bitterly.

Elizabeth continued speaking, her story well fixed in her memory. 'The Coroner wrote methane poisoning in his notes,' she said. 'He touched his hat and the little group moved on, me following just a pace behind.' Looking directly at me, her face afraid, she murmured, 'How I wished that you were there, Phillip.' Her fingers were tight around my hand. 'Through ploughed fields we went,' she said, 'their furrows hard with the frost. We cut across to Morganstown, to the home of young Moses Llewellyn. The day was beautiful now. Sun glinted on the remains of snow, but it was dark in the cottage where the tiny body of the twelve-year-old lay on the table, washed and tidied by his silent mother. 'He was a good boy', the mother said into the empty air as the coroner pulled back the covering sheet. 'Stood on this very table where he now lies dead, stood here with such patience while I cut down his da's trousers to fit. Look at the child. Beautiful he looks. And dead'. Her eyes stared into the distance, lost. Elizabeth was white faced. She paused to look out at the night. The moon was fading now and darkness blanketed us as we sat there.

The Lord giveth and the Lord taketh away, I thought, grimly.

'I'll miss young Moses', came the breath of one of the collier's walking with us, his voice crackling to silence. 'So proud he was to be working on the ventilation doors', he said. 'Always wanting to help that Mam of his, the poor woman'. Reece was a man of few words. He turned to look at the collier and bid him to be quiet with his eyes. While the jurors stood around him, spilling from the room to the open door, I took the mother's hand as Reece recorded, Child. Aged twelve. Death by methane. He said the words aloud mechanically, as he wrote.

'As the crowd of us backed out into the air, as the mother wept, I looked at the tiny frame dead on the table. Did not our mother comfort us and say of the sparrows that not one of them is forgotten by God? How then could any God allow this child to die?' Elizabeth was distraught. I took her hand in mine to comfort her. From the sitting room, I could hear Jemima singing quietly, and was glad that Hannah sat with her.

'Still we went silently,' Elizabeth cried, eyes wide drawn red in tears. She let the brimming grief flow down her face, un-wiped. 'I could not move the face of Moses from my mind. Still the wind blew,' she whispered. 'Coroner Reece's cloak was wet now, flapping loudly round his legs. He showed no emotion, strode out determined, and the jurors, cold. Down the road we trailed, turning to the hill of Penygarn. The steep hill's gradient was hard going. Muscles were aching, feet slipping as the mountain glistened to our side. I looked into the slanting light. It painted the Garth in blood.'

'I remember how I ran there joyous, as a boy,' I said. 'A different journey you faced on that day.' My sister nodded.

'I watched as the sun silhouetted the sad band of men,' she said, 'Reece with his flapping wings like a hovering bird of prey. The jury men were dragging their feet. It was a grim task, Phillip. Their figures stooped with stress and effort as they followed old William Gedrych up and along to the house of young John Thomas.'

'Another young man given to the earth by coal before he had the chance to live?' I asked.

'Yes,' said Elizabeth. 'Once in their tiny home, Reece quickly lifted the covering cloth, assessed the injury, listed again the name and age as if he tabulated stock. Without apparent concern, he got identification from a distraught father before continuing with his party to make his way to the next cottage to identify and tabulate another lad, David Rees. Why did I follow, Phillip? Why did I need to face this human suffering?'

'You have recorded it for me, Elizabeth. Remember what the Psalmist wrote? *My tongue is the pen of a ready writer* - your words will help me understand.'

My sister smiled wanly. 'There is much to tell yet, Phillip. As we approached, a man called out to us. He was pale, gaunt, himself a collier, recovering from an explosion at Llantwit Faerdre. He moved over to the group with Reece at its head and touched his cap. 'Strangers, you are', he said. 'Lost are you?'

'Reece,' said the coroner, without extending a hand. 'Coroner Reece. Taking evidence for the Inquest. Were you down there this Monday morning?'

'Not me, sir', the man declared, old bruises yellowing on his sallow skin. 'Caught mine at another pit. Same story, though. Explosion. Coal should stay where it is if the Masters can't make it safer. Borrowed time we work on. Borrowed time. Could happen any day, see'.

'We must move on', said Reece, clearing his throat, uncomfortable, not one to be involved in interchange. 'We seek the cottage of one David Rees'.

'Indicating the cottage, the miner said, 'Horrible injuries that boy got. Back of his head smashed in. His mam is in there still, cleaning him. Washing him like a babe, she is. Singing to him, too. Face hardly bruised mind. Strange that. Makes it harder for his mam'.

'He was right, Phillip. It was eerie. In the cottage, father and mother stood with their son, his mam singing quietly as she washed the boy's body, '*Cysga di fy mhlentyn tlws,*' - go to sleep, lad, she sang. '*Cei gysgu tan y bore* - you can sleep until morning *Wedi cau a chloi y drws*

- the door is closed and locked'. She was not in her right mind, Phillip. 'Can we lock the door now, Dada?' she asked. 'There are too many here, man. They will wake our David'.

'I thought the Book promised *The Lord God will destroy death forever,*' I spat sarcastically. Elizabeth pressed her lips together, did not answer me. Instead, as if I had not intervened, she continued to relate to me the tragedies she had seen.

'Excuse my woman', Mr Reece, the father said, 'I know you have to do your work ... but ... well ... this is a small place - and there's quite a lot of you'. Looking over at his wife, cradling their son, he said to the coroner, 'We share a name, man. Will you take lunch with me at the Pentyrch Inn? Not far extra to walk, and you look as if you could do with some bread and cheese - and a quart of beer'. Gesturing towards his wife, he said to me under his breath, 'She needs a bit of time. Taking it bad she is'. I went to comfort him, but froze and held my ground.

'Coroner Reece looked embarrassed. It was clear that this man was poor and there were twelve in the party apart from him, but I think he understood the needs of pride. 'A fine and thoughtful man you are', he said to the father of David Rees, 'we gratefully accept your hospitality. Then we must move on to the dwelling of William Llewellyn, who I see here leaves a wife and three children'.

'I did not enter with them at the public house, but could see the uncomfortable attempts at conversation, hear the scuffling of muddied boots on the scrapping iron. While they ate, I leaned against the wall assessing what I had witnessed of the accident in which our father died. These people, I thought in despair, the colliers of this valley and this hill, they need the unions of which John speaks. What do you think, Phillip? Is there another way to protect these colliers from sheer poverty and violent death?'

'They walk in *the land of darkness and the shadow of death,*' I quoted. 'Dada would say it is the price of progress and of coal. If you work underground, you have to live with it and die for it.'

'They die for it, alright,' Elizabeth said, 'above and underground. We saw William Hughes walking out as we left the Inn. That poor man, Phillip! David Rees' father said to me that he was not long for this life. He has afterdamp and the fever that goes with it. He won't last much longer. I didn't speak to him - he just waved - well, hardly a wave. When he saw the coroner's party he disappeared back into his home. There is more, Phillip. Can we sit longer here?'

'While Hannah is with Jemima, we have the time,' I said.

'When Will Hughes went indoors, the coroner shrugged. 'We press on', he said and the group followed him as he strode out up the Garth Mountain to a little thatched cottage on the rise. I had hung behind a little, the silence of the party difficult to join. But I caught up with them at the cottage, heard Reece knock to no avail. As he let himself in, I heard him gasp. There, laid out on the bed together were Thomas Llewellyn father and Thomas Llewellyn son. Mrs Llewellyn stood silently at the bed corner, her hands twisting the apron that covered her old dress. 'Burnt my son is', she said quietly. 'Look at that face. Where is my son, Mr Reece, where are the eyes that once shone? And his Dada there... friends they were. Always teaching the boy, was Dada. Finished now. What peace will he have after that?'

'Reece cleared his throat. Phillip, I could scarcely look. The boy was so badly deformed by burning the coroner had to ask his mother for identity. 'Are you sure it is your son', he said, 'I have to ask'.

'Look at that face ...' she said. 'The shape is gone. Where is his smile, where are those pitch black curls of his?' She sobbed silently while the coroner again asked her to identify the dead. 'Thomas is the older one, Thomas is the younger one', she said. 'My husband. My son. I do not need the face to tell you that. Now will you go, please, and leave me with my men'. She turned her back on the sombre group before her. I was ashamed of inquisitive humanity, ashamed that I was there. 'Go now', she repeated. 'Leave me in peace'.

'I suppose Reece had his job to do', I muttered. 'The men could not be buried without his certificate'.

'But it was just hours after the explosion, Phillip. It was too soon for any to feel peace. Heads down, the coroner and jury men shuffled from Llewellyn's cottage, muttering embarrassed thanks, spiritless condolences. Mrs Llewellyn neither cared nor heard their steps retreating down her neat swept path. I wanted to comfort her, but had to leave.'

'Blessed are the dead which die in the Lord,' I said. *Grind the faces of the poor,* I thought.

Elizabeth knew my mood and did not censure me. 'We moved then to our house,' she said. 'Our father had to be certified dead along with all the men.'

My sister paused to gather her thoughts. I looked at her, almost afraid of what she would tell me next. I supposed the track down the hill to *Ty'n y Coed* was cold and hazardous. I was sure the wind blew and the winter sun dazzled their eyes. I was sure the task of Coroner Reece was arduous, the jurors silent and intent -

'When we got to *Ty'n y Coed,*' Elizabeth said, her eyes now wet with tears, 'Jemima stood at the gate, waiting. News had come down from the Inn that the coroner was doing his round. She would not have expected to see me there, but made no sign of her surprise. Silent she stood, a small and solitary figure in her bombazine black.'

'Well acquainted with grief, this woman,' I said, remembering how she came to us after our mother died.

'I think she helped Grandma Morgan prepare mother for the grave,' Elizabeth said. 'She has helped others in the village in this way. Silent in the snow, Jemima was, her eyes sore from the cold and wind. I have her image etched into my soul - her eyes rimmed red, her face so pale. She is so brave, Phillip. She stood there, isolated, upright and waiting. Old William Gedrych waved to her as the party rounded the track's bend to our cottage, but like a fixed statue, she stood, watching, ignoring me. As the party approached, she pulled herself even more erect.

'House of Abraham Phillips,' Gedrych announced. 'Mrs Jemima Phillips'.

'Extending her hand to the coroner, Jemima said without emotion, 'Mr Reece'. Turning directly to him, she added, 'I knew you were coming. Abraham is ready for you'.

'One by one, the jurors followed Reece past the widow, to the door. 'Will you please be mindful', Jemima said, 'Susannah's children are here. They cannot see their grandfather as he is. I know you will need to remove the sheet. I could not get the shirt from him. It is too deeply sunken in. He is too badly crushed - no sight yet for the children. I will get him clean before he leaves us'.

'Susannah peered through the kitchen window, gaunt with grief, as the line of men filed into the door of the front room where our father lay, Jemima, like an automaton, leading the way.

'She has not cried yet', Susannah whispered, catching my arm. 'She would have no one help her through the grim task she had in washing Dada. Oh, Phillip, I am so glad you are here.' Elizabeth was weeping now. 'I am so afraid, Phillip. I need you here.'

'You want me to take the place of Dada?' I asked. 'Elizabeth, you know I cannot stay. My work place is Liverpool.' Elizabeth sobbed, putting her head on my shoulder.

Close to my neck, so I could feel her very breath, my sister whispered, 'In the front room, where Jemima now sits with Hannah, she stood quietly at the corner of the bed. Light from the small-paned window slanted down to where Dada's body lay. Cold was the room. The fire, lit early when father would have set off on his early shift, was untended, no more now than smouldering ash. The high pitched voices of Susannah's children were floating through on the winter sunlight. Moats of dust danced in the light, the only life in that cold room until Coroner Reece and his retinue walked through.' Elizabeth could barely speak now. 'Too many black clad men crowded the room,' she whispered, 'too many faces stared through open doors. Coroner Reece moved quickly, methodically to father's bed.

'Jemima lifted the sheet.

'I heard the Jurors gasp as they saw the body of a man crushed to his sudden death. I looked at him, Phillip. Saw his body with the bones pierced through.'

'I will soak off that shirt yet,' Jemima said, eyes to the coroner. 'Embedded it is. In too deep to move'.

'Reece surveyed the body quickly, then turning to Jemima, said, 'Can you confirm this is your husband, Overman Abraham Phillips?'

'I can', Jemima said quietly. After a long pause, she looked up at those crowding her small front room. 'Do you need more from me,' she said, 'for this man needs to be washed again'.

'Embarrassed by their intrusion, jurors shuffled one foot to the other. 'Age, Mrs Phillips. I need to ask his age', the coroner said mechanically. 'My notes are incomplete'.

'Abraham is fifty-three,' she said perfunctorily.

'Children?' asked the coroner.

'There are six.' Jemima said. 'Elizabeth, fourteen, Catherine, fifteen, Deborah sixteen, John is twenty-five - and Phillip, who is away, is twenty-eight'.

'You said six, Mrs Phillips.....'

'Susannah is married with children of her own,' Jemima said curtly. 'Evan died these three years back; Phillip is newly-wed and will bring Hannah to us for Christmas - there was a baby, too - Deborah - died many years ago. Their deaths are recorded in the Parish Register. She spoke like an automaton. 'Is that all?' she said, 'Must you know everything?' Jemima stared at them. Like a sculpture, she stood, waiting.

'Tense was the atmosphere. Cold.

'And Mrs Elizabeth Phillips?' Reece asked, his finger running down his notes.

'I am Jemima Phillips, Abraham's second wife. Elizabeth Phillips is long dead - and why you need to know that is past my understanding', Jemima declared. 'Elizabeth the daughter stands here by me. Now will you all please leave to give my Abraham some peace'.

'Reece signalled that they should move on. As he turned to the door, he said to Jemima, 'We go next to Taffs Well, to the houses of Robert Taylor and of William Peters. I understand your husband saved Peters' life', he said. 'An act of bravery, I have heard'.

'But he did not save his own life, Mr Reece', Jemima said mechanically. 'I did not go to the pit head this morning when the accident was told - but waited here for him to come back home ... and they brought him here under a brattice cloth, his eyes still wide'. She stared at the coroner, immobile. Her eyes met his, but he redirected his gaze.

'I am sorry, Mrs Phillips,' Reece said perfunctorily, retreating backwards to the door and into the comfort of December cold.

'Are you?' Jemima asked him quietly.

'Hurriedly, the jurors and the coroner left. I did not join the last part of their walk. They were heading to the house of Henry Sant up in the village. He has left a wife and five young children - and I could not face their grief. Then they were heading for Taffs Well to authorise the burials there. Did you know William Peters? A newly married man about your age and dead.'

I shook my head. 'I have been too long away, Elizabeth.'

'Did you know Robert Taylor? He was twenty one. I think that he is single and a friend of John.'

Again, I shook my head. Elizabeth stopped speaking as Hannah led Jemima from her vigil in the best front room. '*Lord, make me to know mine end, and the measure of my days, what it is; that I may know how frail I am.*' I heard her say.

I could picture the band of men, led by the coroner, going up to the village then down the hill. I could visualize them in my mind's eye, distant on the zig-zag path, down to the river, where they would whistle for the ferry. I could see the ferry woman pull the boat hand over hand towards Taffs Well and I hoped she would say that Abraham Phillips was an honourable man.

I could not face my step mother or wife. Instead I walked alone into the cold evening light. Furnaces lit the sky and the usual cacophony of sound echoed around my ears. My father dead, so many dead, yet industry crashed on as if they never were. What value the life of man, I pondered with each step. Slumping down outside the window where my father lay, I sang out to the putrid sky against the furnaces, I raised my fists in anger at the valley floor. The stars were bright, puncturing the sky against the hell of stagnant smoke. '*We have made a covenant with death, and with hell are we at agreement*' I cried.

What other honest prayer could I have offered then?

1875

There was a thaw in the villages as we woke up to the final Inquest day. Elizabeth's relating of the horrors of the Lan dominated my thought, precluded peaceful sleep. My father still lay dead in the front room, awaiting burial, Jemima stoic, sitting vigil, while the smell of death was everywhere. I thought of the grief in other houses - William Morgan, just eighteen - escaped from underground, only to face death from fire damp lying at home with his father, acutely ill and dying too. Unable to sleep, I watched the light dawn slowly over the Taff Gorge. While Hannah slept, her hair spread across the pillow, I watched the usual morning web of moving lines - spider men already heading for their work, their tools projecting extra arms and legs. Trudging like ants in obedient rows, one following the other, struggling through slush to get to work. Tracks brown with ochre, squelched underfoot, hanging heavy on thick, poor shoes. At the levels in our village - at the Garth Drift, at Booker's Cym Dews, Rock Level and the Garth itself, I knew that men and boys would be preparing for their shift. While I sat listening to my wife's deep sleep, at levels through the valleys, picks and mandrels were assembled, spades counted, men counted as they headed underground. As I bemoaned my lack of sleep, my torrid dreams, the smoke of industry called less fortunate men as it rose now into the scant daylight.

I dressed, stared out of my window. The smell of work, of poverty, the stench of death, hung visible in the early mist. And I cursed the God of the Revival, felt ashamed that I had left my home to work with paper and pen in Liverpool. While I stood, full bellied, self pitying, looking out, I knew that children were waking, crying hungry, bellowing cold. I knew that in the little ribbons of miners' cottages along the road of Gwaelod, on the mountain near the Colliers', in the terraces of Ffynnon Taf, new widows would be putting on their best to go to the final hearing of the Inquest. In Tongwynlais, in the farmstead of Ty'r Ffynon, others would be pushing gruel at tired children who had to head for the furnaces or underground. I knew, too, that Jemima would face poverty without my father to provide.

I noticed then that Hannah looked at me. No longer sleeping, her face distressed, she said, 'Phillip. I know your mood - you ponder poverty and death.'

'Look out over those coke ovens, the chimneys, over the sound of hammers banging,' I said to her. 'What do you think of when you see that valley floor?'

'We have to live, Phillip. I hear only the sound of feet running - Susannah's little ones, of Catherine and Deborah, the room of your father echoing with the quiet voice of Jemima singing,' she said. 'The strength of ordinary people supports me. Gives me hope. It is time to be more practical, Phillip. How will they manage now?'

'The Coroner has seen the Llewellyns, father and son together on their bed in death. He has seen the crushed frame of my father. Ask him, Hannah. He has seen it all.'

'And you can know that he is used to it,' Hannah said. 'It is not his work to think of what comes next.'

'Is he not human, then? Does he not feel?' I said sarcastically. 'And what do you think of Hannah? Unions?' She turned from me and sighed.

Hearing Jemima in the kitchen, I sought escape and slunk down the stairs to her. Already she had stoked the fire, already she had sat beside my father. 'Is the Inquest keeping you from sleep,' I asked.

'What is sleep, Phillip Phillips?' Jemima asked. 'The dark of the pit has stolen sleep.' I watched her smooth her long hair, fading now to grey, tie it to a roll, pinned tight. Pushing it quickly under her hat, she took her shawl. 'I am going early, Phillip. The ground underfoot is treacherous from the thaw.'

'Wait while I get my jacket from our room. I will accompany you.'

'Stay,' Phillip. 'Stay with your wife. I want to do this alone for Abraham.'

I watched her as she walked out of the gate, saw her descend the track and head towards Taffs Well. I had to follow her. Without a word to Hannah, I grabbed my coat and walked behind. At the Portobello, ropes were being shaken, checked, the paths made ready for the men to cross. Down by the river, I could see old Saunders yawn as he rubbed his hands against the cold and ambled to the ferry, the stepping stones too hazardous for use.

My breath condensing on the still cold air, fingers red with cold, I paused outside the Junction Hotel. Jemima had already entered. I could hear tables and chairs being dragged into position. Through the window, against the scraping, I could see that Coroner Reece was already shuffling his papers impatiently. As chairs were put in line, as ordered rows replaced the chaos of arrangement, he paced the floor, deeply intent. His mouth moved as if rehearsing what he had to say. I watched him go to the tall window, stare out at the valley, his eyes scanning the hell my people call their home.

Jemima sat alone on the front row of chairs. The Coroner turned and noticed her, recognition dawning on his face. As I watched from the shadows, he walked to her; his hand extended as an offering. I could just hear him say that this would be the final assembling of the Inquest, that the papers were in order, the men released for burial. He was formal, reserved and looked uncomfortable. Jemima looked at him defiant but extended her hand politely, as we all do face to face with those in charge.

'Mrs Phillips, I am ready to hear the evidence,' he said, 'all the dead and injured have been named and seen. We just await the arrival of the Mines Inspector now, then we may proceed. I trust I will not keep you long.' In the dark, in the darkest corner, I listened reluctantly, unobserved. My head thumped to the methodical smashing, clanking of machinery, my heart jumped to the rhythm and counter rhythm. As the room filled, I noted that Jemima still sat alone. Against the engines whistling, hammers beating, against the racket of the furnaces, I caught my breath, hung back while little huddles of men arrived together, sat silently, their waiting faces inert, ignoring others who leaned heavily against the doors whispering together.

Time passed. Time that was full of silence or of grief. Men coughed from rasping lungs. Women pulled shawls tighter around themselves, their worn torn hands twisting together round the knot. Jemima did not move, her gaze directed to the fore.

Wet was the floor now, wet with the sludge brought in on worn shoes. William Williams, haulier, down the pits since he was a child, sat beside John Thomas, down from Pentyrch. '*Bore da i chwi*,' he whispered. 'I just called in to see Mrs Llewellyn. She won't be coming here today. Taking it bad, she is.' He waved across at William Thomas, fellow haulier, 'Squeezed by a tram he was when we were boys.'

Voices rose and fell as stories of other events were recounted and mulled over. Jemima spoke to no one, did not turn. Solitary, quietly composed, rigid, she sat formally alongside Thomas Madge, who touched his forehead to her as he took his chair.

Over at the top table, the coroner cleared his throat, pulling his great coat to him, clearly cold in spite of the thaw. In from the back room then, the twelve good men and true, Booker employees all, well-dressed and out of place in this god-forsaken valley. Straightening waistcoats, smoothing hair, they stretched their legs before them, gloved hands resting on corpulent bellies. In the corner, thumbing through pages of his notes, a young man sat apart. As quietly I slipped into the Inquest room, I saw Coroner Reece glance at him, and mutter, 'If anyone can get to the bottom of what happened at the Lan it will be you, Galloway. We're lucky that you moved to Wales.'

The young man, lean, pale and serious, allowed himself to smile. 'What will Erington Wales think,' he murmured back, 'what will the colliers think of me, the eldest son of a Coal Master, Iron Master and Justice of the Peace, being so involved? It will not be William Galloway, paisley shawl maker, that they think upon. Me'be I'm a bit close to the Masters in some minds!'

'The Chief Inspector chooses his assistants with care,' Reece whispered. 'The colliers know that well.' Snippets of their conversation reached my vantage point. I listened intently as the assembled group of people stared ahead, waiting impatiently for the Mines Chief Inspector to arrive.

'Educated, you are, William Galloway, experienced, compassionate,' came the words of Reece to my intruding ears, 'And I have heard that your declared life mission is to make the lives of miners safe. What could be better, man? The colliers will know that Tom Wales has chosen you - and chosen well. And the Chief Inspector has some status here.' Galloway looked doubtful. He made no answer, but turned at the sound of a door banging shut. The Chief Mines Inspector, Thomas Errington Wales, had arrived.

Immediately, the Chief Inspector took his seat alongside Galloway, with a cursory nod in the direction of the Coroner. With a quick look at his pocket watch, he leaned over to Galloway muttering, 'Good to see you here.' He beamed. 'You are not new to investigations of this kind. You will bring new light to this, I'm sure. I hear you've done a fair number in Scotland,' he added, shaking Galloway's hand. 'I read your paper on the connection between colliery explosions and the weather. Can't recall, though, what you said about snow.'

'I d'na go into snow. More explosions in dry weather than wet in these shallow mines,' Galloway said without looking up.

At the door, I listened unobserved.

'Not much dry weather in Wales, Galloway, but we get the explosions,' the Chief Inspector said dryly.

'Different rules must apply up in the North!', muttered a member of the jury who had come over to them.

'A poor joke,' the young Scot cut in, looking directly at Booker's man. 'We speak of death, man. Have you nay been underground?'

Reece stretched out a conciliatory arm towards Galloway. 'A bad business,' he said formally.

'Aye,' replied the young Scot, 'so are they all.' Taciturn, he went back to his findings, marking his pages, ignoring the hovering figure of Reece.

The Inspector of Mines nodded to his assistant, handing him back his notes. He pulled out his watch and stared at the Coroner, willing him to start proceedings.

By now, many of the seats were taken by relatives, shawled, silent women, old men and boys, colliers who had no thought of work that day, survivors, injured, interested villagers. The place was full. Dai Evans, from Cefn Colstyn, had left his farm for the day, and Thomas Madge had left his desk to come over from Bethlehem, accompanied by one of his teachers. They sat, prominent, in the front row beside Jemima. At the door, a huddle of listeners who did not want to enter paid no heed to me.

Reece tapped his table and brought the jury to attention. Like crows on a linen line, the twelve of them sat, blankly stiff, perched on upright chairs, the podium behind them. Booker men all, I thought, assessing their healthy skin, their well-cut black attire. They sat waiting, far from patient, as Galloway and Wales conferred quietly. I moved as close as I could, saw Errington Wales pull out his pocket watch and signal the coroner to begin. Hands on portly bellies then the jury leaned back to a man, waited, eyes to the ceiling, while the coroner went through the formal introduction, first in English and then in Welsh.

I watched from my vantage point through the open door. A room full of gaunt faces stared up at the podium. Reece introduced the jury, said they were sworn in; then gave the background of Will Galloway. Indicating Thomas Wales, he announced that the Government Inspector had been at the scene within a few hours of the explosion. No one moved in the hall. No one murmured. Just the persistent coughing of an ailing man disturbed the silence there.

'I have personally visited each house of the injured and the dead,' Reece said, and I now formally confirm that the bereaved have consent for burial.' Reading then, he said methodically, 'The seams being worked were Hard Vein, Forked Vein, Wing Vein and Brass Vein. I can confirm that the explosion took place in Brass Vein.'

Head down to his papers then, Reece promised that his Clerk would read the names of all the injured and the dead. He looked up at the rows of villagers from time to time as he made a rapid summary of the date, the time, the numbers of men employed below and above ground at the Lan.

'There are already many stories around the explosion in the Lan,' he said. 'I can confirm that the men were working with naked lights.' Against murmurs from the floor, he added, 'I must confirm also, that this practice is permitted other than in the Forked Vein, which is fiery. It is correct to say that workings had been driven in to make contact with broken coal adjacent to the windway. It is also correct to say that a hole had been pierced some days before and had been blocked with straw to prevent cross ventilation.' Little surges of voice rose and fell as the coroner spoke. 'There was very little damage to the pit,' he went on, 'and the rescuers found no serious obstruction to their work. It is important to stress that men from other local pits were on the scene immediately, offering their help, as is the custom in Welsh mines.' Nods of approval moved the stagnant air. Feet, frozen from the unaccustomed stillness, shuffled against the shushing of the clerk. 'The injured men and the deceased were all brought out within four to five hours,' concluded the Coroner. 'I defer you to my Clerk,' he said, taking his seat. 'He has the list of the injured and the dead.'

The Clerk stood, a small figure, bent. As he read, staccatto, my eyes were fixed on Jemima. 'The list of dead and injured,' the Clerk began, moving his page to find his focus for the words. 'I will first name the deceased,' he muttered. Clearing his throat then, one hand on the table to steady him, he read, 'Abraham Phillips, fifty three. He leaves a wife and six children, Mr Reece.' I saw Jemima wince visibly. Reece waved him on.

'Thomas Llewellyn Senior, forty five married, from Pentyrch - leaves a widow and four children,' the Clerk read, 'Thomas Llewellyn Junior sixteen, same address; William Llewellyn twenty-nine, married, also from Pentyrch - he leaves a widow and four children. David Rees, Pentyrch - just a boy - ' The Clerk, a local man, cleared his throat again as sounds of sobbing reached him from the gathering there. He paused respectfully. Then, a quick glance at Reece, carefully looking at his papers, he continued: 'Henry Sant from Gwaelod y Garth, fifty-one and married - leaves a widow and five children; likewise a Pentyrch man, William Peters thirty-three and married - he leaves a wife and two children - babes they are, Mr Reece,' he added.

'A Pentyrch man? And where was William Peters domiciled,' Reece cut in abruptly.

'Taffs Well, Coroner,' the Clerk added. 'I would have come to that.' Eyes misted now, he continued his grim task, methodically reading out: 'From Taffs Well - Robert Taylor, twenty-one and single; Moses Llewellyn, aged twelve, from Morganstown, Radyr.' The Clerk paused and consulted the Coroner. 'Should that read Taffs Well?' he asked. Reece shook his head.

'Daniel Evans, twenty-eight, married, Tongwynlais,' the Clerk droned on. 'He leaves a young widow and one infant; John Thomas, eighteen, single. From Pentyrch; John Pritchard, sixteen, also a single man from the same village.' The Clerk moved to sit down.

'And the injured?'

Taking a deep breath and with a sigh, the Clerk read on: 'Shadrach Davies, married, from Gwaelod y Garth, John Flyn single, the same; Evan Howell, married and living in the Old Level Houses; William Harding, single, Pen y garn, Pentyrch; likewise Charles Mills, single.' He broke off, saying, 'No ages given for the injured, Mr Reece.' Again Reece nodded, waving him to progress.

'Morgan Morgan, married, and William Morgan, married, both of Pen-y-garn, Pentrych; Evan Davies, also of Pen y garn. Abraham Williams and Samuel Evans, both domiciled in Tongwynlais.' The Clerk folded his pages, picking up a note passed to him by a juror. 'I have to add,' the Clerk read out, 'That within this week of the disaster, William Morgan, eighteen, and his father, Morgan Morgan, forty-eight, both have succumbed to chokedamp and have died. A few days later, Evan Howell and William Harding both came to the end of their lives. Total number of dead is sixteen.'

The sound of each name brought a breath from the watching survivors.

'Do you have the causes of death listed there,' Reece asked the Clerk, who rustled through more documents. From his seat, he read, 'All were burnt and suffocated. The boy, David Reece, was killed by a ventilation door being blown on him, causing massive head injuries.'

'And Abraham Phillips? At the mention of my father, my blood ran cold.

'The Overman was blown against the wall in the second blast, Mr Coroner,' read the Clerk. 'Crushed by a dram. Extensive injuries.'

Jemima's face was white as she sat there, upright and outwardly unmoved.

'A further note, if I may, Mr Reece,' cut-in a juror, 'Four other workmen who reached the surface have been reported dead, but their names are not yet on record.'

Reece paused a moment, nodded, and then took into his hand the Order papers for the Inquest. 'It is recorded here,' he said without lifting his gaze, 'that none of the above men were in the Miners'

Union. This being the case, the pension of nine shillings a week will not apply.' Silence fell over the listeners as the Coroner referred to his Order Sheet, eyes down. Then, lifting his gaunt face, he indicated to William Galloway that he should now give his evidence.

From his seat, Galloway, the young Scot, started to read from his Report. Reece called him to the top table. I noted that Thomas Wales watched him intently.

Galloway pitched straight in. 'Two exploration levels had been driven. They were abandoned, the coal quality being poor. When this was done, the roof began to fall away and the airway which took air to the faces was neglected and became so bad that air could not be travelled. As a result, no air reached this face. The ventilation was so defective that the quality of air reaching the faces was of the worst possible kind.' Looking at the jury, he explained, 'Instead of conveying fresh air to the lowest point and allowing it to ascend in the heat of the mine, it was taken to the workings at the highest point. This forced the gas downhill. Such a system of ventilation always leads to accumulations of gas - especially in the elevated parts of the colliery.' Scribble of pencils, nods, as the jurors took in what Galloway was telling them. At the back of the hall, I noticed hacks from the Western Mail were also making notes.

Reece intervened. 'As I understand it,' he said, 'Firedamp has a low flash-point. When that first blast is past, there is a second - an aftermath that is every bit as deadly. Is this so?' Wales nodded. 'Experts at the scene of this explosion,' Reece went on, 'thought that the Lan explosion was a blow-out of gas from the seam, or a build-up from old workings, ignited by a naked flame.' He looked up at the assorted crowd of villagers watching him.

'Aye, this is often the cause of explosion underground,' Galloway agreed, 'but it is my view that this was not the case in Brass Vein at the Lan.' Mutterings of translation provoked the Coroner to tap the table for greater quiet. 'In the weeks since the explosion,' Galloway continued, 'I have been regularly to the site and my findings are different.'

Chairs scuffed the floor as colliers leaned forward to hear more acutely. 'I have long been interested,' Galloway said, 'in the place of coal dust in accidents like this.' Some slight chuckling interrupted his flow. 'Ye must take it seriously,' he declared. 'Ye know from the Coroner's report that the miners far from the explosion were badly burned? Well, if you didn't know, let me re-iterate it here - those men who were burned most badly were furthest from the explosion site. The explanation is simple. The Lan mine was too dry.'

I watched as men looked one to another, some shaking heads, others more curious.

'I have done experiments,' Galloway explained, 'experiments that prove even low levels of gas become explosive when mixed with coal dust in the air thrown up by an explosion. Believe me, it propagates over a considerable distance.' His soft Scots lilt drifted across the cold room. 'The coal dust feeds it, you see,' he said intently, 'and if the dust is fine enough, and concentrated enough, it can be ignited even without the presence of methane.'

Again the murmur of translation passed along rows of watching colliers. Scorn showed on many of their faces. Some voices of dissent openly expressed disbelief.

Reece interrupted. 'Will you give us your findings at the Lan, Mr Galloway. Time is of the essence.'

'The timber in the heading was coated with coal dust, coked with it,' Galloway said quickly. 'It will have also encrusted the support timbers, most of which are now demolished or fired by the explosion. The worst charring of timbers was far from the site of the initial explosion. I maintain the problem at the Lan pit was exacerbated by dry mining.' Galloway stared at the colliers before him. 'I recommend damping when work is resumed again.'

Nods of interest spread along the rows like a breaking wave. In the general whispering, Seymour was called. 'That is all news to me, Mr Galloway,' he said dismissively. Standing before them then, Pit Manager from England, proud, he explained that the Brass Vein workings had been driven to make contact with broken coal adjacent to the return airway.

'Why did you not inspect this return airway as required of a Manager under the Mines Act?' Thomas Errington Wales asked.

'I've been here but five months, Mr Wales,' Seymour protested.

'And for how long were you a Mines Surveyor before that, Mr Seymour?'

'Nine years.' Seymour hung his head. Then bullishly defiant, he looked at Errington Wales. 'Abraham Phillips checked the airways,' Seymour spat, 'He's Booker's Agent now, and he is over me.'

The Inspector of Mines stared out at Seymour. His lips tight, he made a scribbled note as the manager stepped down. A murmur from the assembled company shivered my spine. I changed my posture, moved closer to the door, eyes on the woman who needed most to know. Jemima Phillips remained impassive, staring, eyes directly ahead.

As I listened from the vestibule door, various survivors were called to give their evidence. The coroner heard first hand that on at least one occasion before the accident, the pillar had been pierced through to the old workings and had been patched with straw to stop short circuiting.

Collier Evans was then called to give his account of the disaster. Coroner Reece explained to people who already knew, that Evans had witnessed the explosion, but had miraculously escaped. 'This man,' the Coroner told the jury, 'was first up to give notice of the accident.' It was clear to see that Evans was badly burned and traumatised. Cruel it seemed to have him standing there.

'Mr Evans,' announced the Clerk as the miner's disfigured face looked up for all to see. 'Will you give your evidence now,' he urged as the miner stood there silently.

The room was silent, yet the miner did not speak.

'Have you forgotten what you came to say,' Reece pressed.

'The times I would remember are past recounting,' Evans breathed, 'and this I would forget, but it will always live with me.'

'I pray you, then, get started. We have but little time.' Reece opened his hands in a gesture of despair.

'Someone had clayed a candle to the hole,' Evans said then. 'I was sitting alongside it, smoking my pipe when - '

'He is allowed to do that,' Reece muttered to the jurors.

'When I heard the gas rush out,' Evans said. 'The flame went straight across my face -.' As he stood there giving evidence, dreadfully misshapen, the old collier was visibly shaken, his swollen, burn-scarred face broken with his pain. 'Do you know what blackness is?' he challenged the Coroner. 'Do you know what flame can do? Do you know what fear is, what experience can tell? I knew that it was gas. All I could do was shout and run'. Tears fell down the old man's face. 'I could not stay…. all I could do was run'.

I stood there silent while the Coroner heard the sad tales of survivors, destined to tell their stories over and over to all that would listen. They had already been echoed through the villages, imbibed with pints at the Colliers' Arms. I heard of young Moses Llewellyn, who had died while playing hide and seek, leaving his ventilation door to run into Brass Vein. Another said that Daniel Evans shouldn't have been in work that day - he had planned to visit his wife's family in New Tredegar, where loved ones had been lost three days before - and now he was returned to his wife, a victim of the Lan. The words of my father were recounted, his absolute calm was praised.

As the evidence was given, as personal stories were retold, the listening villagers touched hands, one with another. The jury men remained aloof, barely exchanging glances, devoid of outward emotion. And what of Phillip Phillips? Secret observer at the Inquest, I stood watching, filled with foreboding, filled with fear.

'I call William John, fireman.' The voice of Reece again cut through the chatter of the assembly. John ambled to the podium, a tall and sturdy man. Legs at ease, he stood before the Coroner, unafraid. 'William John. I understand you were on duty on the shift in question. Tell us of the procedures you followed on that day.'

'At 4.30 a.m.,' the fireman said, 'we went as usual down to inspect the veins.' He carried his Report book in his hand. 'We found gas again,' he said. 'We had found it several times of late, Mr Reece.'

'And did you report it?'

'Report it? Course I reported it. When the Overman arrived, I was clear to him about it. Told him there was gas. Showed him the book.'

'And was the Overman Mr Abraham Phillips,' the Coroner asked him.

'Yes. He is Overman and Under Agent at the Lan.'

The Coroner looked quizzically at William John. 'Are you sure you entered gas in the Record Book? It is not there, Mr John. I have inspected it myself.'

'I did enter it in the book.'

'It is not there, Mr John. It is not recorded there. Do you know that is against the law?'

The fireman did not speak.

'And what did the Overman advise you, Mr John?' the Coroner prompted.

'He said we should brush it out - brush out the gas that is - and remove the reference in the book.'

A murmur spread like burning gas around the listeners there. My blood froze, cold.

'And what is this practice of brushing out, Mr John? Will you clarify it for the Inspector and the Jury?'

'Well, Mr Reece, we flaps our jackets about. That moves it on.'

Again, an upsurge of muttering. Jury members made notes, tutted, conferred one to the other.

'Let me get this straight, Mr Williams. The Overman, Mr Abraham Phillips, knew there was gas and still sent the colliers down to work as usual?'

'Yes, Mr Reece.'

There was a ghastly pause. Coroner Reece stared at the fireman, challenging. He was grey faced, serious.

'This is most irregular, Mr John. It is illegal practice to brush out the gas. It is illegal not to make accurate record in the book. You say the Overman gave you this advice?'

William John nodded.

'Faint I felt. Fast beat my heart. But Jemima sat impassive as the eyes of the room fixed on her. Woman whispered to woman, man crossed eyes with man. The Overman had sent their boys down into gas. After the wave of disbelief, the scorn, a long silence fell over the room. Jury men made notes, William Galloway shook his head and Thomas Errington Wales and Coroner Reece stared straight ahead.

The atmosphere was palpable. Eventually, after what seemed a life-time, Reece cleared his throat, anxious to bring proceedings to their end. He conferred quickly with the jurors some of whom nodded in agreement all too quickly, while others looked bemused.

'From evidence given us during our investigation,' Reece concluded, 'We have to tell this assembly that, as to how the explosion occurred, we are not agreed, but the deficiency in the ventilation has been clearly demonstrated. The exact cause of the explosion cannot be identified. It is possible that it was the naked candle flame. We are clear, however, that there were deficiencies in the ventilation system. The maintenance of the airways was below standard. We recommend greater vigilance in future. We also accept the findings of Mr William Galloway, and suggest that his method of damping be adopted in the Lan workings.'

As he sat down, shuffling papers, Thomas Errington Wales stood up. 'This,' he declared, hovering on the word, 'this accident in your local mine is the most serious explosion this year. I conclude,' he said 'that this explosion and the consequent loss of life is fairly attributable to poor ventilation.'

Heads nodded in the jury. Papers were gathered together. But Thomas Errington Wales, Inspector of Mines, had more to add. 'The presence of small coal in the gob was a factor in fuelling the blast away from the initial fire,' he declared. Then, as he stood to leave with the jurors, he turned to the miners, the colliers, the people from the villages. 'One thing more,' he said. 'I find your Overman, Abraham Phillips, guilty of negligence, for allowing men to work with naked lights in a badly ventilated chamber when he knew that there was methane present at the face.'

The assembled villagers, colliers and wives, gasped. As the wave of disgust rose again and swamped the faces of the survivors, many of whom stood up in anger, Reece led the Jurors out to the back-room, followed by Galloway and Wales.

My father was found guilty of negligence. John was right. As I shrank into the shadows, heart beating fast, as I took in the Inspector's final blow, I saw that Jemima Phillips had retained her seat, that she sat there alone, proud, head up and looking straight ahead.

As everyone filed past, ignoring her, I should have given comfort, but I could not move. Instead, I shrank back to the shadows of the vestibule and hid my face in shame.

1875

Well accustomed to grief, my family. My father lay in the front room awaiting burial; depression filled the air. Silent we sat together round his bed. Silent we ate together at the table. Silent were the days in *Ty'n y Coed*. But at night, Jemima's sobs shook the house, echoed round the furniture, hung in the dust of coal on neglected windowsills. Strange how much settles when no one moves the air. Strange how unimportant it all seems. The woman who organised the house, scrubbed floors, prepared our food, sat lonely in the family group. No one had words to resolve her agony.

'Negligent, your father? I cannot believe it. Somebody has lied,' Jemima said bitterly - almost to herself, as she got up to clear the table after food. 'Abraham watched the Lan pit with his very soul,' she breathed. Moving to the wash bowl, she muttered, 'He could not have told the men to work if there was danger from the gas. Would not have done.' Shaking her head in disbelief, she put the kettle on the fire and stared at flames that licked around the coal.

Hannah stood up directly and went to her. Stroking her shoulders gently, she said quietly, 'Jemima, will you talk with me?' Jemima did not move. Her face impassive, her eyes blank, she stood, a woman dazed before the coal. Hannah looked at me, gesturing with her eyes that I should break the impasse, speak. Scraping my chair back noisily, I went to Jemima, who stood there like a woman lost. 'We must organise father's funeral,' I said. 'Dada cannot lie much longer in that bed.'

Jemima did not look at me. Instead, she sank down to her knees to better tend the fire. She did not speak. The atmosphere was terrible. Elizabeth hung her head and Deborah cried, while Catherine moved in haste to leave the kitchen table. Hannah caught her white hand as she passed, encompassing the girl with open arms. Still, Jemima sat staring as flames licked round the coal, her face aged, lined deep and dreadful in the flickering glare. Her very stillness dared the waiting room. Catherine pulled away from Hannah, sank down beside Jemima on the old rag mat. Sobs shook her body as she put her head against her step-mother's rigid frame. Gradually, Jemima's hand moved, slowly caressing Catherine's head. I saw the mother in this woman that I could not accept. I saw that my sister loved her and I felt my shame.

Jemima's stupor lifted. She at last stood up, in full control again, erect, composed. 'The funeral will be tomorrow,' she said to me. 'I have ordered the funeral carriage already. Abraham shall have a horse as Evan did.'

'Jemima, is that wise?' Elizabeth burst out. 'So many will have pauper funerals - you said yourself that there should be no show. There are so many dead. And we have not paid-off Evan's funeral yet.' Jemima froze Elizabeth with tightened lips. Undaunted, Elizabeth spoke on, 'We have no income now. It will be hard - unless, of course, Phillip can pay.' Elizabeth had said the worst.

Jemima pulled herself to her full height and glared at Elizabeth. 'I have changed my mind about a quiet funeral. It is my duty to bury him and I will do it in the Welsh tradition. A black horse and carriage it will be. Phillip pay, indeed!' Turning to me, she added coldly, 'You left the family here when Evan died. You were then my Abraham's eldest son, the carrier of his name and you chose Liverpool instead of home. What kind of man are you? Are you a son?' She looked broken for a minute, then added sorrowfully, 'Your Dada needed you here. Why did you stay away?'

Hannah moved to my side. 'It is grief that talks, Phillip, do not heed her words. Do not let tragedy give birth to tragedy,' she said gently, turning to Jemima. 'Dada had John.'

'Aye, he had John, but does not have him now.' Jemima said.

'His hero fell, Jemima. He will learn,' I said. Seeing her unmoved, I added, 'We will do the funeral as you chose. You have lost a husband to the coal. It is your right to chose his ceremony.'

'My right, Phillip,' Jemima said tartly. 'It is my obligation and I will do it with full pride. Abraham Phillips was an honourable man. We will inter him with all due respect. The carriage and the horse are paid for. I have saved.' Jemima sat now in Dada's old oak chair. 'The horse will take him to Penuel,' she said, and you will walk with him to his final resting place. We women of the family will all go, too. No time to sit indoors and weep. United, proudly we will go - you hear that Catherine? You will stop these tears. We will hold our heads up to the sky and know it is the burial of an honourable man.'

'Another Memorial at St Catwg's church,' I heard Catherine whisper, 'another Phillips at that resting place. Why can we Phillips not survive?' Deborah held Catherine who was sobbing quietly. Grief and doubt make fertile sobbing ground.

In spite of cold, the next day brought us sun. Well used to death and burial, our family, but different was the bleak journey that we took to Dada's funeral. It was not for lack of singing and due ceremony. Jemima looked regal in her Bombazine, my sisters all walked upright and the horse was glorious with its plumes and ribbons, its black back glowing against remains of snow. The carriage sides shone brightly in the winter's sun and the harmony was there. My uncles sang out loud and resonant, Elizabeth's brave descant floating over their bass voice. It should have been magnificent, a worthy end, but as we walked the narrow road from Penuel, cottagers went indoors rather than bow their heads as usual when a funeral passed. I saw that curtains twitched from darkened rooms, but noticed no-one touched their cap or shed a tear.

At St Catwg's, the Reverend waited at the gate, the death knell tolling loud. His voice called on the Lord in good, loud Welsh to welcome Abraham Phillips to his House. Throbbing was my head, weak my knees from the walk down from Penuel. Heavy was the coffin, heavy my heart as door after door shut in our face. As I kneeled at the coffin, my sisters all around me, Hannah by my side, I felt heavy of heart. When the prayers were done and it was time to move my father outdoors to the cold and into the wet earth, a wave of nausea drenched my face with sweat. Dizzy, I stood on the edge of that stark hole to throw in earth. White were my shameful hands, white were my sisters at the graveside, bent and stained with tears. Jemima stood alone, a tiny woman against the open sky, proud, as she threw in her hand of soil.

Out of the corner of my eyes, I saw my brother, John. Grimed from his shift, face gaunt, he watched from the shadows as our father's grave was filled. I went to him with open heart, my hand extended. 'So you have come, John. Glad I am to see you here.'

'You went to the Inquest?' he asked, declining to take my hand.

'I did. John. Will you come home now?

'Jemima?' he asked.

'I will walk in with you. She will not bar you now.'

'A sad business, Phillip. I feel such shame.'

As I gave the gravedigger his silver coin, my brother stood with me. As I turned to walk down the hill back to the house, my brother walked alone. I thought how bent he looked, how destroyed. And I remembered the boy who had followed Dada everywhere. The figure slouched before me was not he.

Back at the house Jemima was all bustle, food to the table and half a smile to John. He sat in the corner drinking on his own while Grandpa, serious but splendid in his Sunday black, put out his pipe to read his poem. Strange is the gathering after a funeral. Strange is the isolation that it brings. No-one had much to say. My father had no mention and no one wanted food. I felt displaced, that I belonged nowhere. I longed for Liverpool away from *Ty'n y Coed*.

While the grandmothers sat almost asleep beside the fire, while Jemima busied round, Grandpa Shôn stuffed the pages he had written into his pocket and walking over to speak to John, he said, 'I am glad to see you boy, but you are troubled lad.'

'We are not the only ones to bury dead today, Shôn o'r Lan,' John mumbled. 'The explosion took the lives of others too. Because of Da their children will go hungry.'

'Your father took a risk, and paid for it with his life. We do not know the pressures of that day.' The old man put his hand on John's arm. 'Be easy boy. And try hard not to judge.'

'He was a Master's man,' said John, under his breath. 'Grandpa, I cannot live with that.' Huge eyes my brother had that day. Eyes as deep at caverns, black as coal. He stared at nothing in particular as he spoke.

'Your father had a place for every man and boy,' said Shôn o'r Lan. 'Master or Collier,' he saw the humanity in everyone. The men respected him. It's grief that turns the villagers away.'

I saw tears run down my collier brother's face.

'Don't light the corpse candle with those tears,' Grandfather Shôn declared. 'We have lost enough in grief. You will heal, John. Time is more powerful than you. One day you will be an Overman yourself and understand the clutches he was in.'

John stared at the old man, caught to listen there. Intent. Quiet the room apart from Grandpa Shôn. Hannah and Jemima had left to sit in the front room, Deborah and Catherine had gone upstairs. Only Elizabeth remained. Silent, invisible, we listened in the flickering gloom, fire dying, embers blackening, John drinking, Grandpa Shôn puffing his pipe. Elizabeth put out her hand and touched my face. 'Today cannot be memorable,' she whispered. 'We are too troubled. Will we ever understand?'

I could not answer her. Instead, I listened to the voices in the room. 'The villain, if you need one, John,' I heard Shôn say, 'the villain is progress and the natural wealth of Wales. We can damn the Masters, but they risk their fortunes too. We need investment to make work.' As John opened his mouth to protest, Shôn o'r Lan held him with his eye. 'True they exploit our land and men,' he said intently, 'true they live fat and happy while the workmen's families starve. The balance is not there - we need a moderator, John. We need the friendly union of men.'

'And how can men fight Masters without a change of law?' John asked, alerted now. 'Four together is an illegal meeting. Your friendly societies are mild compared to what we need to combat the evils of this industry. Strikes are against the law. Men die for lack of safety, women and children work or starve. And I had a father who was a Master's man. Do you not see the problem, Grandfather, do you not see his guilt?'

'John, John, do not put the whole world's grief at your father's door.' Dragging hard on the pipe, Grandpa Shôn leaned back in his chair. 'I have grown more benevolent as I age,' he said. 'Learn not to judge, John, learn to praise without the flattery that makes men cringe. Your father was a diligent worker, boy, a skilled and knowledgeable man who wanted good for everyone. Let that be his memorial today.' He chuckled then. 'He had no place for God's existence, that I know.' Looking sadder then, he added, 'John, your father was my son. I know a father's love. I loved him just as he loved you.'

I watched as the old man embraced my brother John. Together, they sat as the evening fell.

'Will you men let the fire go cold! Abraham must be turning in his grave already.' Jemima was back with us, her passion spent. 'John,' she said sharply, 'fill the bucket with coal and mend the fire.' Smiling then in her way, she called in the girls saying, 'There is food enough here to feed the village. Come and eat with me. We will celebrate your father as he sleeps.'

Weary now, uneasy with the family, I whispered to Hannah that we would soon leave *Ty'n y Coed* for Liverpool.

1875

Y Nadolig - Christmas, and Jemima in full mourning, her black dress rustling over kitchen chores. Catherine and Deborah had collected holly which they hung over the doors. Hannah helped Jemima as I went about the business of probate. The letters of Administration would be in Jemima's name.

'You need plenty of mistletoe,' Elizabeth shouted from the kitchen, 'we need to protect this home from more bad things happening.'

'I thought it brought eternal life,' Catherine rejoined.

'You need more insurance for that than mistletoe,' John muttered as he tended the fire. While Jemima rubbed her hands against the cold, while Hannah cut the bread, from Capel Bethlehem the sound of carols drifted up to us, their four-part harmony warming the cold air.

'Christmas? There will be no carolling, no feasting here,' Jemima said. 'We live with not-long dead.'

'There will be little feasting in this entire village,' John butted in, yawning, head heavy from the Colliers'. 'No-one has the money. I heard a family from the Level Houses heads for the workhouse today. Some bloody *Nadolig*. And Dan Evan's wife has nothing for her boy.' Jemima shot him a glance, daring him to speak against his father. She knew the pattern of his thinking when drink loosed his tongue. John caught her eyes and tightening lips, went outside to the cold.

Christmas Day came and left us empty. Hannah and I walked together on the hill. She was my refuge and my strength these days. We said little. There were no birds, no distant song to cheer our way, only the hooting of the owls as evening fell.

Gwyl San Steffan came and went. No boys holming ventured to our door. If they beat holly round the village, they did not come to *Ty'n y Coed*. Catherine and Deborah sat together quietly in the front room. A sad and silent house that Boxing Day. Slowly, painfully the long day passed. Fires were lit as usual, food cooked and put before us on the table, but conversation flagged. Hannah sat close to me, her eyes saying what she could not say. Instead of celebration, there was too much sleeping, too much whispering, too much guilt and grief. Elizabeth sat to her books while Jemima, hands folded on her lap, sat erect and quiet by the fire. The clock ticked the minutes through the silent room. With all the persistence of a death-watch beetle, it echoed, ominous, as slowly, the day settled down to evening.

The week passed with the usual display of family chores. As we walked through the *valley of the shadow of death*, John filled the coal bucket, cut the logs, went to his shift, and slept his drink away. My sisters huddled together in their distress while Jemima kept her distance, folding my father's clothes and putting his work implements away.

'Phillip, when can we go from here,' Hannah whispered as we waited for *Nos Galan*. 'This dark and tortured family breaks my soul. New Year it will be soon, but here the time has stopped.' Taking her hand I showed her the steerage passes back to Liverpool. She smiled.

'I will enter at the New Year's strike and you will open the door for me,' she said under her breath. 'That way we will bring better grace to *Ty'n y Coed*.' I saw the sorrow in her face. She had tried so hard to keep all spirits high. Now she was near to tears. I took my young wife in my arms to comfort her.

As the night darkened, as Jemima slept, as Catherine and Deborah chattered with Elizabeth in the best front room, I held my Hannah to me. 'Do you think my father was negligent?' I asked her in anguish. I had never intended to take a wife, never intended to allow myself to feel this love, this exquisite pain, but now I felt dependence. Whispering quietly in my ear, she said, 'No greater man was there than your father, Phillip. I have heard such good spoken of him. This hostility around you all will cease.'

Silently we sat together. And I realised that I could again be happy. So lovely was the room then, warm from the day, moon high, shining through the darkness onto Hannah's face. Such peace our love had brought. *Nos Galan* was transformed.

Our closeness was halted by a noise outside, by sudden shuffling and footsteps on the frozen flags. 'Visitors Hannah?' I questioned breaking from her embrace. 'I'll see who is there.'

As I stood to leave the kitchen, as I leaned to Hannah for another kiss, our peace was shattered by the sound of breaking glass.

And then Elizabeth screamed.

I rushed towards the hall where my sister stood, white-faced and terrified.

Through the window hung a horse's skeletal head stuck on an ugly pole, its ghastly eyes black, staring and manmade. My heart froze but I wanted to calm my sister. 'The Mari Lwyd,' I called out to Elizabeth, 'it's just the Mari Lwyd.'

But there were no ribbons and no reins or bells, no decorated sheet, no poems of joy. There was no laughter as the bringers knocked the door. This was the gruesome message of an insult won. A harbinger of evil, not of joy.

'*Blwyddyn Newydd Dda,*' I lamely shouted out to everyone. 'They have brought to us the *Mari Lwya* to wish us a Happy New Year! You see, they do not leave us out of the *Nos Galan* celebration! As I looked at the skull nodding there, as I looked into those gruesome holes that once held eyes, I saw that rotting flesh clung to its bone. This was no token of *Nos Galan* joy. My father's negligence had fuelled this venomous revenge. I pushed the offensive token to the path and turning, quickly swept the broken glass. As my face froze in the winter blast, as the unsealed window let in fear, my head was full of deep anxiety and my heavy heart was dark and cold.

1876

On New Year's Day, Jemima rose early, put on her best bonnet, shawl and boots, and set out alone. She did not tell us where she was going and no one dared questioned her. Hannah and I watched from the window as she walked with great purpose on the frozen road. As a shaft of weak sun hung a shadow to her heels, we saw her reach the road and head for Cardiff, the black of mourning prominent, her tiny upright figure brave and heartbreaking.

'How fast she walks,' Hannah said to me. 'She should not be alone. She is broken by her grief.'

'Jemima is independent,' I replied. 'I wonder where she goes on New Year's Day with such determination.'

The sun shone that New Year's day, the skies were clear. Frost was heavy on the grass and the trees dark. Hannah sat with Catherine and Elizabeth, while Deborah busied round the cottage intent on clearing last year's dust. For me, it was back to my accounting, getting my books to tally, ready for the return to Liverpool.

It was evening when my step mother returned - did it take my father's death for me to name her so? She had about her a confidence, an assurance I had seen first when she came to us after my mother died. Without sitting down, without pulling off her boots, Jemima stood at the table, in full control, smoothing a sheet of paper that she had held in her small pouch.

'I have met with Thomas William Booker,' she declared. 'He sends you his good wishes and has agreed that I can pass on the tenancy of Abraham's house to George Thomas of Pentyrch. I saw George Thomas in the village in the days before Christmas. He is a roller at Booker's Melingriffith works and needs a place - you know that I cannot stay here, I am sure.'

I had just accepted her as mother, just allowed my heart to care. Now, we stood around the kitchen table as she told us she would go. Pointing with her still gloved finger, she directed our stunned gaze to the bottom of the page.

'I have followed the old custom,' she said, 'See, all my existing debts are cleared. I have settled the account of Abraham Phillips. I have paid my debts to Booker - £1. 0s 11d ground rent was owed and now is paid.'

'You met with Booker today, Jemima?' I asked in great surprise.

'He saw me at the office in his house - invited me to enter, I feel so proud. He praised your father, Phillip.' She glared at my disbelief. 'See there, his hand? And see the crossings out? It frees me from my obligation, lets George Thomas in. See there? His name instead of Abraham's. He wrote it while he spoke with me. Do you see his signature? It is so strong.'

'That is hasty, Jemima Phillips,' said Elizabeth angrily. 'Da fixed that we could have this place for a hundred years. It was our family security and you have renounced it without a word to anyone - '

'I cannot stay here in these cold stone walls,' Jemina cut-in bitterly. 'They are too full of memories. We still will hold the Freehold Lease. Anyway, your father made this cottage for Elizabeth, your mother. She was his eternal love, not I.'

Silence fell in the cottage. No one tried to comfort poor Jemima who had borne so much, who had taken over from our mother, who had washed the body of Abraham Phillips with such care.

I looked at Jemima standing there in the kitchen, still dressed for outside. I saw how small she was, how vulnerable. How ridiculous almost in her pride. Her boots were sodden, caked with mud, her shawl, tied tight, was thin. And I realised she had aged. I realised that she was traumatised by grief. I realised too, how cold I was to her. 'My father loved you too,' I said with halting words and great embarrassment, while Hannah put her hand out to appease.

Stoical, Jemima said, 'No matter now. I will go to my parent's house in Bedwas. They will have me there. Susannah will have the girls and you, Phillip, to Liverpool, away.'

'And John?' I asked.

'He will be happier away from me. Some collier will give him lodging, I am sure.'

Stunned were my family then. 'Well, not the workhouse, anyway,' Elizabeth declared, as she moved over to mend the fire. 'We will do well with Susannah and her John.'

'When must we leave,' Deborah and Catherine asked, speaking in unison.

'Our tenancy here is ended. We must go immediately. We still retain the freehold rights, but I cannot pay the ground-rent now Abraham is dead.'

Tradition says that our behaviour on a New Year's Day will indicate behaviour for the year ahead. Bad were the omens for our family, then, as morose and irritable we stood around that kitchen in my father's house, Jemima diminutive and proud, the rest of us in shock.

Ghosts of the dead haunt the twisting paths of the Garth. While the women packed belongings, I walked out alone, heard names, saw wisps of men that turned to a low mist. Names of the dead - young Moses, Tom Llewellyn and his Da, Shadrach Davies from higher-up the village, young John Flynn and Evan Howell - John's friend, Daniel Evans from the Ton. Names of the men I knew, and others who had died. The face of my dead father hung from every tree, blowing in the bitter wind, buffeted by the dreadful echoes of his voice, resonating, singing with long dead leaves, 'Brush it out, boys, brush it out.' I wanted to cry out but was devoid of words.

I heard footsteps then, echoing behind me, quickening. My blood froze as I recalled the *Marie Lhwyd*. I felt threatened. Was I so threatened? Strange how guilt and grief combine to haunt the tired mind. I walked faster, broke into a run. My breath came in quick sharp bursts. As I ran, the steps behind me ran. I could not look around, could not control my fear. I heard a voice call out my name. I ran faster, but my chest ached with the exertion in the frosty air. Breath came in painful gasps. And then a hand fixed on my shoulder.

I turned reluctantly, expecting settlement by collier's law.

'John,' I gasped. 'You frightened me.'

My brother grinned. Tall he was now and big. 'Is it the sins of the father that worry you, Phillip?'

'Fathers shall not be put to death for their sons, nor shall sons be put to death for their fathers; everyone shall be put to death for his own sin,' I quoted at him.

John shrugged.

'You heard what I called him, I suppose? He was a Master's man, Phillip. Our name is stained because of him.'

'You called him Murderer, John.'

'Murderer. Master's man.' John laughed. 'What difference is there? It all accounts the same. Look to the West, Phillip, to the Lower Garth. That hill is emptied and diminished by centuries of iron workings; look to the East to Forest Fawr, its woodland cut from serving industry. And to the North, the Coed y Bedw coal bringing lines of ravaged men to harness black gold from within its guts - this valley's floor is abused, interspersed with exploited men and industry that fills my heart with desperation.'

Standing beside me, he took my hands in his. I saw how big and strong his were and mine so thin, so white. 'I look out at the tributaries of the dividing flow,' my brother said, 'Industry everywhere. From east to west, the Taff draws for my eye a line to mark the outcrop of the coal. It feeds the Masters' greed, Phillip, but scarcely feeds the villagers' mouths. Lives are shorter here, brutal. Hard labour ennobles no man.' Up to the edge of the track now, John pointed to the paths down to the Lan. 'When I look there, Phillip, all I see are lines of bent, worn faces, meandering like a powerless tributary themselves.' He looked directly at me. 'All these worn tracks lead to work,' he said, 'and men come heavy and worn back home, smiling as their waiting child grasps their hand at the end of a long shift. This valley is made of strong minded people, Phillip. I admire them but they accept this tyranny of work without protection. They will not band together.'

'Unions are illegal, John,' I said.

'That is your usual chorus, Phillip. So, you are an honourable, law-abiding man just like your father,' John spat. 'You sit there in your clean-arsed job while other men wield picks. If I could motivate a powerful union of working men, we could re-shape this industry. We could make Rebecca look like a childish game.' My brother's eyes shone with the vigour of revolution.

'In the name of God, John, do not ask for death.'

My brother laughed scornfully. 'Do you see the Taff? I don't know about God, but that river is a mighty power. See how dark it is? How swift? It runs through this valley, fast emptying, cutting through the rim of the coalfield of South Wales, shaping the Gorge, much as the picks and mandrels plied by colliers cut through the seams of these black and hollowed hills.'

We had walked to the point where the mountain road would take us to the Colliers' Arms. Turning to look over the valley, I said, 'I see its dark brown body snake easing through our midst; I see the Gorge it has cut through - but it is the work of man,' I declared, 'that has made the river dark. It cannot reflect the sun, so great is its pollution.'

'You blame the work of men?' John spat. 'We're just cogs in some almighty machine. It is the greed of the industrialists who seize our guts regardless of the outcome. 'It's all out there for them. Men to work for next to nothing - and, look. There's sandstone to the north,' he indicated. 'See? Building blocks for settlements, for furnaces and store sheds. It is all here for the Masters' taking. They have no regard for future, no regard for men. Do you see how it is ravaged, Phillip? Grimed by the burning of resources better left untouched.' I did not answer him. Tired now, I leaned against a tree. 'Look to the West,' John said insistently, 'Look to the Garth hill. Listen to its clank of industry.' Hands in his pockets now, head thrown back, like a preacher my brother John cried out to the cold air. 'It has heard the cries of men and children, echoed to the sobs of wives whose tears merge with those draining streams. It makes me miserable, Phillip. I know this valley floor - it is just a few hundred yards across but in its microcosm I see the rape of Wales.'

'Look, John,' I said,' It is time I went back to the cottage. Hannah will be looking out for me.'

'In this place, within these homes and furnaces,' he said ignoring me, 'The Masters of industry have all they need. Even the mighty Taff works for those men as it carries coal and iron to the docks. It is all here, Phillip, all here for them. They don't look at the mountains and wonder at the beauty you and Hannah see. Look down the valley, boyo, look west to Cwm Llwydrew, the hoar frost valley is a place where winter ice holds frosts that the sun can't lick away until late. You remember how we ran there as boys through all the industry in search of joy? All I remember are outcasts of iron disfiguring the hill. As they take limestone for the flux, those Masters of Industry rub their hands, their eyes bright as they build their ever bigger mansions with the wealth torn from this valley. Look at me. Look. I feel it in my heart. Those trees there. They are beautiful. But they do not grow for us. Masters will crop the woodlands for the fuel of industry. Take the sandstone, build. And of course, they take the coal oblivious of the men the coal has taken.'

By now I was exhausted by my brother's preaching, but he clearly was not spent. 'John, I ventured,' 'Where will you live now Jemima has given up the lease?'

'As far from her as I can,' John muttered. 'She is not my mother.'

'You saw Jemima, John. She is broken by her grief. But it is not simply bitterness that makes her move away. It is this very valley, what it means. While you see the need for revolution, she only sees death. Me, too. I cannot tolerate this place. We shall soon go back to Liverpool.'

'At least you do not work with colliers who you father took underground to die,' John muttered bitterly. 'I'm up to the Colliers' now. I won't be sober when I get home.'

I watched him amble up the steep track to the Colliers' Arms and turned back down to *Ty'n y Coed*.

'Phillip, where are you? Why do you walk alone?' Turning I saw Hannah barely shawled against the cold, her long hair blowing in the haunting wind.

Quickly I regained demeanour, quickly slowed my step. 'Look, Hannah,' I said as she approached, holding her against me, 'See how dark the Taff? How dark and clear the night? I did not expect you here. Look at the stars. How bright they are tonight.'

'I expect those same stars shone when your father walked your mother on the Garth,' she smiled.

'It is so long since I ran there as a child,' I said, 'but I still see the buzzard, hear the owl -'

Heads down, we walked together along the main road of the village.

'Do you remember those streams we ran though, children on a summer day,' Hannah said seriously. 'They mean water power today, not beauty. The Master's eyes assess the value as they estimate iron on the west bank, grist there on the east.'

'You sound like John,' I whispered in her ear.

'But he is right, Phillip,' she said firmly back to me. 'The men here do need unions. Exploitation shows everywhere.

'Hannah, Hannah. Do not be so serious.'

'Think of Jemima, Phillip,' Hannah said, 'She struggles there alone. Her husband is dead, she has no money to live in his house and we leave her this night alone.'

'Hannah, *cariad,* you shame me. We must go back there now.' Taking her in my arms, I murmured, '*dw i'n dy garu di.* I love you.' She smiled at me, her serious, happy smile. 'I used to wait for my father to come home from the pit,' I said, putting my arm round her waist. 'He always told me that it lighted his way home. Now you have come to meet me and I walk happy, home with you.'

Hannah smiled and taking me closer, ran her fingers through my wind-swept hair. Then quietly, we stood together, looking out across the vale.

'*The Valley of the shadow of death,*' I said with resignation. Hannah squeezed my hand tightly. 'But it is sometimes lovely here, my Hannah,' I added. 'We have run with rabbits, seen the moon through trees and counted stars ………'

She did not speak.

'This village is the well scrubbed cottages,' I said, 'the little gardens, hedgerows neatly kept and the sky which is ever there above the grime.' Putting my lips close, I whispered in her ear, 'it is the love of man to woman, the laughter and song, the Eisteddfodau - those things resonate through our valley regardless of the devastation and the smoke filled days.'

'The people here are stoical and strong,' she replied. 'They cling to each other and to God.'

'I don't know that they cling to God,' I laughed. 'But there is something special here. Call it humanity if you will, my love; call it family, if you like.' Then kissing her in the cold and moonlit night I breathed, 'Just call it Wales.'

'I understand. Now will you come back to *Ty'n y Coed,*' she replied with a quick peck on my cheek. 'Your family are held here by something more than coal. Come now. Jemima will be waiting - she will never go to bed till all of you are counted in. Elizabeth and

Deborah will be watching for us through the window - they have been so unnerved by that dreadful skull - and poor Catherine will be asleep waiting for us beside the fire.'

Hannah slipped her hand out of mine and ran ahead of me, looking back over her shoulder, daring me to catch her with her smile. I watched her, legs flying, hair flying, her face catching the light of stars. I heard her joyous laughter and saw in her exuberance my father and my mother when we first came to *Ty'n y Coed*. And realised fully just how young and happy they had been.

1881

To every thing there is a season, and a time to every purpose under the heaven. A commercial traveller now, I did not need to remain living in the city. The land of my father's called me, and we left Liverpool to return to Wales. Hannah had always predicted that I would return. I was well aware that the kitchen flags, the old stone walls of *Ty'n y Coed* held grief tightly in their grasp, but in 1881 I decided to go back home. The house was empty now. The Melingriffith had shed workers and George Thomas had to move. The freehold of the lease my father signed with Booker allowed me to take residence, but I walked again to the house of my childhood with no exuberance. Sunlight flickered through the trees as I strode with Hannah up the incline to what was to be our home, holding within my grasp not the small hand of my wife, but the burning coal of memory.

It was five years since my father died when I took over my uneasy heritage of *Ty'n y Coed*. Much had happened. My Hannah, concerned with poverty, intent on learning, had not wanted children and I, haunted by my family's history, was happy to agree. *Write ye this man childless*, Jeremiah wrote, for *no man of his seed shall prosper* - and I thought that likely to be true. Susannah had a family now. She had moved from Maesaraul to live up on the Garth. Deborah had left her job in service and was married, too. She and Tom Francis, a Newport boy, had made me an uncle three times over and she was now heavy waiting for her fourth. Our little Kate, our Catherine - a milliner now - had gone to Ystradyfodwg, to our father's childhood home. That left Elizabeth, still a scholar at the local school. Susannah's house was full of little ones, so we agreed, Hannah and I, that Elizabeth should live with us at *Ty'n y Coed*.

'I hear the men have been on strike against reduction in their wage,' Hannah had said, breathing heavily she walked beside me up to *Ty'n y Coed*. 'It must be the only strike ever around here,' she added, 'The people have been too subservient. Your brother John must be jubilant at this show of militancy.'

'They say John's changed a bit,' I laughed as we approached the gate and walked the steps. 'He is less of a firebrand now.' As we moved along the straight path to the cottage, my heart beat fast with apprehension, not with joy. I knew the risk. Moving back to Wales was motivated by my need to know. We made the last few steps to *Ty'n y Coed* in silence. Quickly, I unlocked the door, the heavy well-used mortise, responsive to my key. Taking off my coat, I helped Hannah remove hers too. 'John is an Overman himself, now,' I said to her. 'He will be more understanding of all needs, the Masters and the men - but yes, I heard from Elizabeth that it pleased him to see militancy.' I looked at Hannah, looked round the kitchen and tried to feel well pleased. 'It was only a short strike,' I added dismissively as we took in our bags.

'A short strike, Phillip,' Hannah declared, without pausing to look at her new home. 'How can you be so casual about weeks that caused so many such distress to no avail. My parents told me there were soup kitchens in the villages and bread was needed for the children in the school. It was all too desperate to dismiss it so.' Not waiting for an answer, looking around her now, Hannah declared, 'How well George Thomas has left the garden! Flowers, Phillip! And see, there is fruit and vegetables in ordered rows just as your mother had it years ago!

'I wonder that they grow in this sad soil,' I said. 'You know George Thomas lost his job and had to leave this place. He had no money to pay the rent. It was not planned. These vegetables and flowers mark his shattered dreams.'

'Don't spoil my pleasure, Phillip.'

We were at the door of the front room now. I opened it with great reluctance, saw the same slanting light through those same little panes that had fallen on my dead father's damaged face.

'Thank goodness he has left the place tidy,' Hannah declared. Her voice was lost to a background of my own distress. As I walked through the door to that front room, as I took a step into that space, memories were handed to me like Isaiah's burning coal.

'Time has been gentle with the house,' Hannah chatted, looking at the more mellowed stone. 'It is warmer, Phillip, warmer than I recall.' Smiling happily at me, glad to have left the city, she opened her arms wide and said, 'Welcome home, Phillip Phillips. Welcome back to the house of Abraham Phillips.'

I could not respond to her. Instead, I looked out through the window, looked out over the valley floor. *I have seen the travail, which God hath given to the sons of men to be exercised in* I thought, but now, where once I had watched rows of men crawl early to their work, to the pit or iron works, little workless groups of men gathered in postures of abject despair. No sound of furnaces, no endless rhythm of picks and mandrels. The silence of Poverty hung over the valley of my childhood like a cloud.

I stood in the house of my father, encompassed by my wife's gentle arms, but all that I could think of was the vagaries of history. How small the world in spite of distance, I reflected, how insignificant in spite of passing time. When I was in Liverpool first, a decade ago, we all feared the effects of the Franco Prussian war. Now it was clear to me just what war had done. Trade was depressed in the whole of Europe and the effects could be seen even in my valley now. While my Hannah looked to setting up house, my thoughts were full of what calamity that war had brought for Europe, what poverty it still was causing here with Booker's empire squeezed.

I saw sadness on the face of Hannah through her determined smile. Pulling myself together for her sake, I muttered, 'Am I far away, again?'

She nodded. 'Can we ever be happy here?' she asked. 'I thought you would put the Phillips' history behind you and find peace,' she said sadly. 'It seems that I was wrong. Will you always be so locked in misery.'

'It is not the family but the 'great globe itself' which saddens me,' I answered. 'Look at this valley now. This poverty is the calamity the Franco Prussian war - its tendrils stretch out everywhere.'

Hannah shrugged her shoulders, pulled away.

'A mess, isn't it,' I said to her as we looked out and up to the silent hill. 'Everything is closed down. World prices were against Booker,' I took Hannah's hand in mine. 'He tried to renovate but failed,' I said. 'Have you heard the company is to liquidate?'

Hannah shook her head. 'A fine homecoming, Phillip Phillips. You and your politics. Must you always concentrate on grief? You think too much and I am shut outside.'

'A new company runs the Melingriffith now,' was my obsessed reply. I did not listen to my wife's distress, did not recognise her infinite need. 'The demand for its massive output of sheet iron and tin plate has been replaced by calls for steel.' I said to her un-listening soul. 'I hear Booker is in such conflict over money and inheritance that he took his dead brother's wife to Chancery to prevent her selling her share before the company crash. So many of his cottages have been sold-off - we are lucky to still be here.'

My wife stood back and looked at me, head to one side. 'I am tired of it all, Phillip. We are impotent and cannot change what is history. But, I suppose to hear you worrying over Booker is a new event. Phillip, I read the papers, I know that to add to his troubles, the West of England Bank called in its debts and this very year Booker has had to put his undertakings up for sale. As the valley fades, Booker's empire crumbles and no one wants to buy. I hear they will lease out to the Cardiff Iron and Tin Plate company.'

'The Pentyrch section is already closed down,' I said, immediately enlivened by her interest. 'It has brought this village abject poverty.'

'Yes - and the Melingrifith works have closed,' she fired at me, 'the brick works just behind us in crisis, too. On top of that, the decline and closure of Booker's iron works and the closure of the Lan. Booker's empire is in pieces and the valley swamped in a mist of need. I know, Phillip. I know. Are you satisfied that I am well informed? Each day in Liverpool I went to the public library just to read. What do you do about it, Phillip? What do you do about anything other than recount a history that we know?'

I opened my mouth to protest.

'The workhouses are busy,' Hannah chanted, 'the collieries, quarries, foundries and furnaces all slowly falling silent. Thomas William Booker made brave efforts to save the industry, but he has failed,' she said. 'We are all impotent, Phillip. At least its quieter here now.'

'Quieter it may be,' I spat with great hostility. 'But it is dirtier now with poverty and dejection.'

My wife did not reply. Deliberately ignoring my mood, she moved from room to room. 'George Thomas certainly has cleaned well,' she called.

'Pulling myself from my destructive and obsessive words, I called back, 'I will go upstairs to see the bedrooms. Elizabeth will join us soon and she must have her pick.' I went up the stairs, stopping half way to see the Garth. It was glowing in the sun, red against the sky. As usual, buzzards in their pairs soared high above the peak and a skylark shot upwards to translucent day. Then up the final five stairs, past the small room on my right, and ahead to the room where all we boys lay down together, its tiny panes the windows of my memory. I wanted happiness as I surveyed the other rooms but saw only ghosts of those I knew, wanted to hear the sound of laughter but heard still that resonant and distraught pitch of my father's voice crying out for Evan. And worse, I heard with every step I took my father's words that last day down the pit: Brush it out, boys, brush it out. This was the burning coal I had to carry. My need to know exceeded happiness.

Down the stairs again and back into the front room where my dead father would lie forever in my mind. I stood almost afraid where once his bed had stood, and stupefied, I could not move.

'What is it Phillip?' Hannah paused in work to look at me. 'Are you not feeling well?'

'*Woe is me for I am undone, because I am a man of unclean lips and I dwell in the midst of people with unclean lips.* Do you remember the words of Isaiah?' I said automatically. 'They come to me as I open this door again - *Then flew one of the seraphim's unto me,*' I quoted, '*having a live coal in his hand, which he had taken with tongs from off the altar.* I carry it now, Hannah. Can you see the stain.' I opened my white hand out to her. 'I have been given that live coal to hold.'

Hannah stared at me as if I had lost sense. I stood there in the memory of my father's sin, hypnotised by my thoughts, more of shadow than of a man.

'*And he said Go and tell the people,*' I muttered, '*and he laid it on my mouth and said, Lo, this hath touched thy lips and thy iniquity is taken away and thy sin purged.* But it has not touched my lips, Hannah. I carry my father's sin here in my hand. Returning to this place - it frightens me.'

Hannah looked bewildered. She took a step to me. 'What is it, Phillip. I do not understand. You wanted to come home from Liverpool - .'

'It is my father's guilt, Hannah. I carry it in shame.' We stood there, two isolated people in a house full of ghosts.

Elizabeth disturbed our silent misery. On tip toes, she had crept into the front room, moved over to the window where we stood. 'Phillip,' she whispered. 'Hannah. How good that you are here.' Hannah kissed Elizabeth and went into the kitchen to make tea.

I took my sister in my arms with genuine gratitude. 'And you, Elizabeth - I am so glad that you will live with us. Do you see that tree?' I pointed as I let her go, 'that oak there on the corner? I first sat in it the day that you were born - the Phillips' tree to heaven I called it then. Of course I am back. Hannah and I are here to stay and you will live with us. Since I sat in that tree alone while mother struggled to give you life, you have been my sustenance. After little Deborah, I was afraid when you were born.' I paused, looking at my sister, remembering her birth. 'Baby Deborah,' I said aloud, 'such darkness her birth brought and such joy yours.'

Elizabeth pulled me away from the window. I looked at her and realised how much I had missed. She had grown into a woman while I worked away.

'Our Deborah who lives is settled now,' she said. 'How many years is it since Thomas Francis cut her a spoon? He is a good man, Phillip - and their little ones do them credit. I hope she is happy with her lot.'

'A sight better than being a maid,' Hannah said, coming in with steaming mugs. 'Welcome to your home, Elizabeth. I am so glad that you will live with us in *Ty'n y Coed*.'

'It's just what father planned,' Elizabeth laughed, 'generations of Phillips living in the house he made. I am happy, too.' She took the tray from Hannah. 'It will be easier for me to study here. Susannah's little ones were everywhere!'

'You are not here to be our maid,' I smiled at her. 'You go to your books as often as you wish.'

'Oh, I would never be a maid to anyone,' laughed Elizabeth. 'Deborah has told me enough about life in service to stand my hair on end!' Her face clouded. 'A strange burden she has carried all her life getting the same name as our lost baby,' she said.

'Thank God she is healthy,' Hannah cut in. 'She is like Susannah - she and her John make a good family - though why she chose to wed a collier I'll never know.'

'They thrive up there on the Garth,' Elizabeth declared. 'John Thomas works hard. But yes, I wish he were not a collier with the risks it involves. It gets into their blood at birth, I think! Look at our John. He learned to speak with Da's vocabulary as a babe. He always lived and breathed for coal.'

'A sound way to bring in the money to survive, I suppose,' chattered Hannah. 'My father was a collier, too, remember. Phillip, drink your tea. Susannah will be here. How fast time goes. Little Gwen is five already, young Evan two.'

'And Joseph,' Elizabeth smiled, 'he arrived the year Dada died - I saw him yesterday, trotting down mountain road with Susannah, a little man already. Have you looked at him, Phillip? He is so lovely. Exactly like his grandfather Joseph, or so they say. God bless his memory.'

'Stop, Elizabeth. For God's sake, stop,' I shouted. 'Stop this ceaseless chatter. Can't you two women stop prattling for even a minute? My head aches.' Hannah and Elizabeth looked at me, amazed. 'Are you not bothered by hostility since Dada died?' I asked. 'Is this family forgiven for what he did? Do we not still bear the stain?'

'Can you not think on family, Phillip?' Hannah said quickly, clearly irritated by my mood. 'There are thriving children all around us in this family. Your father would be proud. Why do you always turn to grief? Think of the little ones, Phillip, think of this family happy and be glad.' Turning to Elizabeth again, she said, 'Gwenllian always makes me laugh! She certainly doesn't resemble her stern Great Grandmother from what I have heard, except in name!'

I remained silent, listening in anguish as the women prattled on. The burning coal I carried seethed within my mind. Their continuous chatter floated around, disoriented me. Had they forgotten that the valley starved?

'Susannah follows mother,' Elizabeth laughed, 'Always full with child! And it was she who had to bear the nursing at Mam's end. She is a born mother. She was when I was little, too.'

'You see, Phillip, your family thrives in spite of everything. Deborah is settled, Susannah happy on Garth Hill. They manage in spite of the poverty here. They are not bothered by the mindless chatter that you say is all around.' Hannah's voice was stern. 'I think no-one is against you. You imagine this hostility.'

'Susannah is strong in belief of both God and our father,' I said bitterly. 'She questions nothing, does not have my doubts. I am haunted by spectres. How much of this poverty we see is because my father erred?'

'Phillip. What is the matter? You look so serious and pale. You look now at the tree you showed to me,' Elizabeth said quietly. She had finally noticed how morose I was. 'Stars shone behind that tree as we started to live, and they still shine now. They are so beautiful. I know we have faced great sadness, have lost many to the earth in death, but the stars, at least, are beautiful and they are perpetual.'

'Who said beauty lives?' I asked sarcastically. 'Everyone in our family dies horribly, the valley dies horribly and the dead go on living to haunt us.'

Elizabeth suddenly became the adult, creating me as child. She put her hand on mine. The warmth of her small hand made me aware how cold I was. 'See, Phillip? See, now?' she murmured quietly, 'Stars shine there in spite of Booker - the iron masters, the coal masters that tore the hill apart. Stars still shine after all this household has been through. See how strong the trunk of that sapling becomes? It will live here long after us together with stars and moons, joy and sadness.'

'You mean,' I responded harshly, 'that all the history of this house, the poverty of this valley, will gradually dissolve from us, free us now? Are you sure of that? You are too innocent. I hold Isaiah's burning coal.'

Elizabeth squeezed my hand but looked confused. Hannah stood silent, watching us.

'Black are the nights, Elizabeth.' I said. 'Black is the soul of the industry that haunts us. But blacker still this valley without its work.'

'Phillip Phillips. Stop.' Hannah stepped between us, wife dividing brother and sister, but her hand fondly touched my shoulder. 'This land was here before the Phillips,' she said firmly, 'and the house will stand facing this industrial devastation for many a life-time more. I know the village is in the grips of poverty but I know also how strong, how resolute these people are.' Looking directly at me, she said, ' We have only just come home, Phillip, but you make me think it is time to go. This place has a macabre hold on you. You carry your anxiety too high.'

'For better or for worse, our names will be etched here for generations,' I said. 'The name of Abraham Phillips has seen to that.' As I continued to stare out of the window. Hannah raised her eyes to Elizabeth, grimaced and the two of them left me there, a solitary silhouette against the squared panes of the dark front room. I ignored their absence, rubbed the glass where my breath had obliterated the outside. My back ached as I leaned against the reveals, watching the oak bend slightly, its leaves moving in defiance of the still world round it. I should be the strongest branch of this family, I thought grimly, but I am weak and broken by my doubt.

The room was over warm, the pressure great. My head ached. 'I must walk, Hannah,' I said, moving to the kitchen. 'I need to clear my head.' My wife looked-up at me but did not answer.

Silent it was outside. I looked intently at the southern rim of the South Wales coalfield, looked at the Taff that had long ago cut through the narrow Gorge. The valley floor which I had carried in my mind, diminished. I had thought it vast, but could see now it was a bare few hundred yards. My childhood world shrank as I looked at it. As my head throbbed, I could still see an everlasting image of the bent shapes of men filing through the valley to the coal face, to the brick works, to the hill. They are the ghosts of history that invade my dreams.

*

Days passed, months passed, years passed as we made our lives in *Ty'n y Coed*. I was not in good health. Obsessed by my anxieties, I grew thinner. As the dark beneath my eyes became perpetual, as my dark thoughts dominated me, as I sank further into isolation, Hannah and Elizabeth grew close. Each evening I would watch from my despair as they leaned together over books, laughing a little, arguing over topics that they read. Elizabeth continued her work in the school, Hannah kept house, and I travelled reluctantly as my services were required. My order books occupied me in the evenings but I sat alone, my company no longer good. My head ached often and my back was in continual pain. Still I struggled with my father's guilt. Still I could not accept or understand my inheritance. People moved from me as I approached, speaking groups went silent as I passed. I found the village hostile and my family cold.

Autumn turned to winter. Sudden winds shook the timbers of the cottage. Fierce was the weather now. Rain fell in torrents. The Taff, like my heart, was still filling fast, flowing fast and still black with waste, emptying in the vastness of the sea. My eyes scanned the spaces between the branches of the oak towards the Western ridge. The noise of the iron workers had abated, the shunting of engines, an occasional metallic thud. On the East, the hollow valley drained by streams, looked down on Fforest Fawr. There, sleeping on the west bank of the Taff, was the booty of nature which had brought Booker and his ilk into my valley. I heard my own sigh as I looked down to the Valley of the Hoar Frost. At Cwm Llwydrew, all would be frozen soon and cold. Out of my father's ashes, out of the suffering of men and families like ours, fortunes have been amassed. Hannah was right. Nature had provided free an ideal situation, an obvious draw for exploitation. Men harvesting coal. Men harvesting iron. Now, men struggling for survival.

The words of the Book that I had learned so thoroughly at my mother's knee haunted me -*That which hath been is now; and that which is to be hath already been* - what is happening now, I thought, has happened before, and what will happen in the future and has already happened because the Lord makes the same thing happen over and over again. I decided it was time to challenge this circle of memory with truth. I had to know if my father was guilty and could no longer say *in mine heart, God shall judge the righteous and the wicked: for there is a time there for every purpose and for every work.* I was more concerned with the judgment of local men.

Call me weak. I am. Call me the son of Abraham Phillips and I cannot say his name. The weight of anxiety crushed my chest, my nerve was failing, my temper, short and Hannah clearly disturbed. The closeness that we had in Liverpool had gone. All I could think of was my father's guilt. I made a decision to clear my head, and with determination, made a plan to head for the cottage of Collier Evans. His name had come to me as I retired one night. Knowing he had escaped the Lan that day, I had to speak with him but knew that Hannah would not approve, so I went my way to his cottage secretly.

Maybe I would have walked directly past his door, but old Collier Evans called me in. His cottage was neat, clock hanging on the wall, the small room clean, well ordered with a flitch of bacon on the side, and a good Welsh Testament on his table there.

'I have long expected you, Phillip Phillips,' he greeted me. 'When I heard you had returned to *Ty'n y Coed*, I knew you would come. No need for words from you. Sit down, Mr Phillips, please, and I will tell you all you need to know.' Evans sat down in his rocking chair, urging me to take the other seat. I could hear his wife working in the kitchen. She did not heed my entry so I sat down with him beside his fire.

'1875. December six?' he asked. As I nodded, he said, 'That date is carved deep on my brain.' I unbuttoned my coat but sat upright in the chair.

'You know I live away,' I mumbled. 'There are things I need to hear - '

'Morning of the accident?' he asked. I nodded. 'Snowing hard, it was.' He started, his story, well practised syllables rolling from his tongue. As he spoke, I took-in his scarred hands, his coal imprinted face. I knew the story's provenance from his disfigurement, from his burns, now falling with creased wrinkles as he aged.

'When I set out for work that morning,' he continued, 'Abraham Philips stood alongside his garden spring. His stubble was spiked with snow. I remember he smiled a bit. Flakes settled on his hair, his lashes, those serious eyes of his bright with it - you have his eyes, Phillip Phillips, but not his stature.' Again I nodded, as he relived that day.

'I said *Shw mae* and he said, *Bore da i'chwi*. Formal he was, your father. Told me Jemima had coughed all night, keeping him alert. Apart from that, he had difficult seams to work that day. Booker's man had tied his mind in knots with news that money was tight, production down, and survival of the New Lan more than a bit unsure. Brass Vein will have to be worked harder, he said to me. I knew that there was good coal there, but we had nearly finished it - and the air there wasn't good. While we talked, your father was clearing snow from round the pump, filling the buckets energetically. A strong man, your father. He never really stopped.'

The old collier paused and looked at me. Having made sure that I was attentive, he grinned widely. 'Your father said early morning always made him think of Ystrad Dyfodwg - though in those days, he said, he ran the mountains like a sheep rather than heading underground. He said December with Christmas approaching always brought memories of his father's home - you know, Phillip Phillips, sheep down from the mountains, grass - a rural scene.

I smiled falsely, wanting to hear directly about the accident, but knowing I had to let old Evans take his time.

'Well, your father looked at the sky, watching the snow twirling. Lost in his memories, he was. Was he religious, Mr Phillips? As he worked that pump, he kept looking up at the sky as if he was looking at Heaven! 'Feathered' he called that snow and 'determined' - I often think of it. A bit of poet, your father, eh? Like your grandpa, Shôn o'r Lan - he always had a few lines going.' The old man grinned. 'I was a haulier when I was a boy. Knew a bit about heaven! Well, my heaven, anyway. Not the one that God lives in - that one's for the future, if I'm lucky.' Collier Evans smiled. 'I loved to get the horses on the hill, under the sky,' he said. 'Fast we would go, galloping between the Garth and heaven. Those horses knew me. Responded to my call.' He paused in recollection. 'I wasn't religious, Mr Phillips. Didn't go to capel. But working underground makes you prone to prayer.' He raised his eyes to mine. 'Your father's life can't have been easy with all little ones.' I nodded in agreement, wondering where this tale would lead.

Sitting back in his chair, thoughtful, Evans continued, 'Your father was talkative that day. He said he hoped he was providing well, but at fifty three, he would like to bid the pit farewell. Men are working underground till they are eighty, I reminded him. That's if they survive at all,' Evans grimaced, leaning forward to poke his fire to activity.

'Your father said he was stressed that day,' he added, 'You could sense it as he hit the clog of embers hard. Said his head ached. The snow, maybe. Cold it was for sure that winter of '75. But it could have been anxiety. Old Pit in Tredegar had exploded three days before. That must have been on his mind. It focuses your thought, young Phillip. Did you know about that accident?' he asked looking up, 'given you live away and what happened in the Lan, you just might not have heard.'

I quickly assured him that I had been told and that my brother's friend had family killed there. 'Dan Evans of Tongwynlais,' I offered.

'Oh, Dan. Yes. Left a young wife and a child little more than a babe. He was a rebel like your brother John. A collier's life is always precarious without their line of politics,' Evans commented, adding, 'Twenty men and boys dead at Tredegar. His wife's brother at Tredegar, wasn't it?'

I nodded.

As the flames licked round the coal, Evans continued, 'As we talked, your Da and me,' he said, 'Morgan Llewellyn from *Maes Gwyn* struggled down the lane, heading for his early shift. '*Bore da,* Abraham

Phillips,' he called. 'Brass monkey weather, eh?' '*Shw mae*, Brass Vein weather for me!' your father replied. 'Hot down there it will be when we get working!' 'Bad business up at Old Pit, Mr Phillips,' Morgan Llewellyn said. 'The colliers went in against the Overman's instruction,' your father replied quickly. Protective he was of Overmen.'

My head still ached. It was over-hot in the Evan's small front room. I could feel sweat forming on my face, but had to stay. I had to listen to the story this old collier had to tell.

'Eight o'clock in the morning it was, down at Old Pit - a massive explosion, too,' Morgan Llewellyn grunted. None of us spoke for a while. Just stood there, thinking. Will Strong was on fire duty there, Llewellyn said, and he had told John Morris all was well. He stared at your father, Mr Phillips, sort of challenging him. In the top Ras Las seam it was, Llewellyn said, all the doors were blown out. There might have been an explosion the day before as well, he told us. He had it from John Lloyd, the timber man, who was with the rescue team. They found John Jones first, John Lloyd told me. He picked up Jones' lamp - well that poor sod had no more use for it - and he gave it to Sam Thomas. Apparently, they found several bodies. Your Dada didn't speak. Silence hung in the air then, as it only can between us miners - we all know the odds. 'Too many deaths, Morgan,' your father muttered to him after a while. More would die, he said. Firedamp would take its time. He had seen it before. I suppose we all had, if it be said. Men escape but fade. More misery, more hunger for the families. 'There's too much cutting corners everywhere these days,' Morgan declared. 'Always mouths to feed,' your father said. A depressed market for the coal there was, Master Phillip. Times were hard. Mind, they're even harder now. Too much has been shut down here in this valley. Everyone is edgy these days. Can I smoke a pipe Mr Phillips?'

I nodded my assent.

'The day of the disaster, Thomas Seymour, the new pit manager was more on edge than most.' The old collier shook his head. 'Bit of an outcast in the village, him. Down from the North he was. We didn't take to the man.'

'Managing a pit in troubled times must make for tempers,' I suggested.

'Seymour was known for his,' my story teller laughed wryly. 'Down from County Durham - ay, that's the place. Not long settled in the village then. He was a tartar, though - said if the colliers didn't work without breaks there would be no Christmas for anyone. That didn't go down well. Colliers don't like threats.'

Looking closely into my eyes, the old collier leaned forward to stress his point, saying, 'Our safety depended on your father. Trusted him, we did, he knew that, too. I remember your Dada's voice. Sort of musical it was, but firm. 'Safety?' he said to me. There are cuts and shortcuts everywhere. Men want the drams full, he said, Masters want the drams full. He looked agitated as he spoke. I remember that clearly, for he wasn't often stirred. He soon calmed down again. I must go on in,' he said stamping his feet against the cold. 'Jemima needs this water. Said she'd skin me alive if I didn't have it ready for the day.' The old collier chortled. 'Jemima was the boss at *Ty'n y Coed*! All night she coughed, your Dada said. He didn't want her out there at the pump with all that snow. Your Dada looked at me and grinned. 'And the colliers will be waiting on my arrival soon,' he said. 'Shift starts in less than an hour and I haven't had my food.' Lifting the bucket of water, second pail full to overflowing, he looked up as Morgan Llewellyn touched his cap and moved down the lane, quickening pace as he reached the valley floor. We watched him trek against the noise, the thumping of the Pentyrch works - it dominated everything that morning. I suppose it was the snow that made the sound so different - it altered the look of the valley floor. Black towers stood out bleak against the drifts, smoke curled through the falling snow-haze. 'Strange beauty,' your father said. I always remember his words. 'Black grime of men's labour against the white of drifting snow,' he said, 'and it's calling me to work.' Poetic, your father, Mr Phillips. He said to me that we both sang a song of no escape. Knew what he meant, I did, but a strange way to say it. Looking up at the snow clad Garth, he started talking again about the sheep, white on the mountains above Ystrad Dyfodwg - staring, aimless sheep, he said - bewildered by the take-over of their green by the coal fields. 'It's the same here,' I told him. 'It's the coal. It alters landscapes, alters lives. Sad that it runs in our blood.' Your father nodded in agreement. We laughed.

'Where have the years gone, Jemima?' he called to your step mother as she opened the kitchen door to call to him. 'Lost while you gathered coal and water for me,' I heard his wife answer sharply. Time for work it is and you not eating a thing yet. Come and sit down to your food.' He looked fondly at Jemima, Mr Phillips. You can have a second love when you need a wife to look after the children.' Evans got up, stretched and went to the kitchen to make a drink.

'Three buckets stood waiting to be carried in,' he muttered as he came back with mugs of steaming herbs, 'and then your father was off to the coal shed so that Jemima could warm the house and cook. As your father walked across the front, I saw Jemima, reflected in the window panes and could hear her cough from right across the garden. She was not well at all,' Evans said in confidential tone, 'but as usual, she was busy. A good woman she was, your step mother, taking over the family after Elizabeth.' He swigged back his steaming drink in one long go. 'Poor Elizabeth,' he said as he put down his mug, 'She knew about suffering, your mother.'

As I drank the herb tea, I suppressed a yawn. Still my head ached, still I had no information. Still the burning coal was in my hand. 'And the accident, Mr Evans? I heard you tell the Coroner you were there ......'

'That was a dreadful day, Mr Phillips,' Evans said. 'Your Dada was late - the Overman late? Unheard of at the Lan. Your father was rigid with the rules. We can't get started till the Overman is there,' he added. 'He checks it out first. Goes down alone sometimes to take stock. In spite of biting cold, your Da must have felt a sweat break on his neck as he trekked in after time.' Evans shook his head wryly. 'That English pit manager, Seymour, was there, waiting for him. He called the tune, Phillip Phillips, set man against man. Came in from away for just that purpose. His accent was harsh against the lilt of our Welsh. And he didn't know the first thing of our language - *di Gymraeg!* Disgraceful really. In this Welsh speaking village he tried to govern us without our words. No *shw mae* from his lips. No *croeso* from ours.' Evans grimaced. 'The atmosphere had changed since he took over,' he said, 'men were uneasy. Welsh was our tongue and this pit manager, Seymour, straight from England - thought us *twp*. In fairness to the man, Abraham Phillips always admitted Seymour was sharp. Knew the business by all accounts. There was something else, though, that unsettled us. Being Overman set your father a bit apart from us colliers he grew-up with - and we knew that Booker was a bit friendly to him, gave him privileges. That caused a bit of gossip on the side. We pitied him though - he had to deal with Seymour!'

I looked at my mug of drink, slightly embarrassed by what I heard, then back to Evans hopefully.

'By now,' he said, continuing his story with no more delay, 'the sound of steam and the clanking of the fan was swamping the wind that was blowing snow into drifts. It echoed through the valley with the trudge and hammer blows of working men. Late your Dada was - no one can say different. At the Drift, the babble from the line waiting his order to go down surrounded him. He must have heard us carping.'

'Overman overslept, Thomas Llewellyn joked to his son. 'Married, too. Jemima not doing her job! What's a wife for other than someone to poke you awake in time for the shift'. 'No other reason to marry, is there, Da,' his son Thomas bantered back. 'No chance of sleeping late in our house, eh!' The pair chortled with shared thoughts of Mam Llewellyn, up at dawn, hauling them up and out by five for the trek down from Pentyrch. She was in control in there, Mr Phillips,' he chortled. 'A strong woman, her. Famous for it, she was.' As his laughter faded, he took a deep breath to continue. 'David Reece blew on his fingers,' he went on, 'a mere boy, he was already an old hand - been moved on from the ventilation to proper work. 'Wait till you get married, young David,' William Llewellyn chuckled. The two of them often trekked to work down mountain together. William had watched him since he was a child. 'Anyone got a plug for my pipe while we wait for the Overman to get his brain together?' Henry Sant asked. 'If we stand in this line much longer, we'll bloody freeze.' He moved closer to the steam engine. Old Nelson, as we called it, was chugging away, waiting for ventilation boys. 'Where's young Moses today, then?' someone called. 'We can't go down until he is on the doors.' We were all fond of that young-un, Mr Phillips,' he said.

I smiled at him, leaning to put my mug on the old stone flags that made his floor. An intent look fell over his face. 'The lad was dead scared that morning and we were all having a laugh at his expense,' he said seriously, 'swore he'd seen the *'glow'* - the light miners fear, Mr Phillips. Swore he had seen the *'light'* as he went down.' Looking at me, he explained, 'It's a sign someone will die, Phillip Phillips. Well, the superstitious carry that burden, anyway - probably just a bit of phosphorus on ceiling wood - but it scared young Moses. White he was.' He paused then, staring ahead into nothing.

'William Peters had a wife and two children,' he started again, shaking his head, suddenly impelled to continue. 'He was really angry with your Da. Christmas was close. He wanted to be down and working, not waiting in the row. Probably hoped he could get an extra dram filled that day. I remember how he stamped his feet, shouted across to David Reece some comment about your father late. As David Reece turned his thin, white face towards him, William Peters whispered to John Pritchard, 'That child shouldn't be here. Starved he looks. And listen to that cough'. John Pritchard nodded, but I know him well. He will have been thinking of Chapel rather than the boy. It was always *Capel* that he talked about, obsessed by the Revival, him. *Diolch iddo* - thanks for God's mercy - was on that one's tongue day and night. I never listened to the voice of the Minister,' Evans declared, eyes open wide for emphasis. 'No place for God worship underground.'

He did not need my comment, so I sat silently, watching his face as the flickering fire lit his old coal scars. 'John Pritchard was cutting a spoon for a local girl, his head full of loving,' Evans laughed. 'A few men stamped their feet and chanted *dewch ymlaen, bechgyn, dewch ymlaen* - come on, lads, come on. As it turned to a brash chorus, I glanced up at the desk and saw your father there looking at dram counts. I poked John Pritchard to show him, but he was away in his thoughts, away making plans for married life near the Colliers' Arms. He didn't hear the voices around him, Master Phillip. Love does strange things when you are young.' He laughed loudly.

'Lovely it is when miners sing, 'Mr Phillips,' he said after a while. 'Have you heard us sing? Voices lifting and floating around you when you're down there underground - it's comfortable. You know you're not alone. But back to the Lan,' he said. 'The snow was falling and the men were cursing now. I tell you as it was, master Phillips. Blow by blow, as I remember it. I know you want to hear the detail of that day.'

From then, I decided that I would not intervene. Smoked curled up from his fire and I sank back into the shadows, listening. Evans' voice was animated, fast, dramatic now. A play before my eyes:

'Come on, mun. Come on. Overman must be asleep on the job,' someone said.

'Counting his money, he is,' chortled a voice from the queue.

'Counting our dram loads more like. Bet he undercounts this morning being he overslept.'

'No chance of anyone over-counting,' some collier cut in to loud gaffaws.

'He better watch it. Bringing in English Overmen, they are. It's the fashion now. I hear they rule in many pits.'

'That's all we want,' someone shouted. 'An Overman who can't speak the language! Bad enough having Seymour. He lives up by Salem now. Stranger he is, mun. Bloody hard, too. Look at that face -

those thin lips of his have never smiled. We could do without foreigners. Irish are bad enough, poor buggers, work for nothing they do.'

'Forget the Irish. Christmas's coming. It's up to the bloody Overman to let us down to get working now. I've got a kitchen full of kids to feed. Can't stand here waiting all day. He's a boss man - up there with the books. The way the palling-up is going between Overman and Booker, Overman will be coming in smelling of mothballs weekdays as well as in Chapel on Sundays.' Everyone laughed. 'Some say Booker has had a brew up at *Ty'n y Coed*.' They were angry with your father, Phillip Phillips. It was all just gossip, you know - and most of us liked your Da, anyway. Had known him as he came up the ranks.'

'Cut it, boyos,' declared an old Collier. 'This Overman is alright. I've worked for worse. Fair is Abraham Phillips.'

'Murmurs rose from the ranks of men, buffeting agreement against that swirling snow. Your father knew his job - was well liked. Just that the men were impatient to start. You always get an argument when we are stuck in line - '

'Mr Phillips,' a collier's voice cut through the hum of waiting men, 'Mr Phillips, Mr Booker's agent was here. Seymour is looking for you. Angry he is. Had to go with Booker's man before you got here.'

Abraham Phillips signalled this thanks and headed for the office where Seymour stood, books open before him. 'Mr Seymour,' your father said, touching his cap. Seymour did not look up. 'You called for me, Mr Seymour,' said your Da.

'*Hwyr* - LATE,' the Pit Manager, spelled out as if your Da was stupid - no language to be fluent in that one. He poked his finger into your father's chest spelling out HWYR.'

'Aye. *Mae'n ddrwg.*' Waited then, did your Dada.

'Booker's man was here, Phillips,' Seymour barked at him. 'It all looks bad. Markets for coal are collapsing and we are not getting out the coal quickly enough to fill orders. The iron works we can supply - but nothing left for Cardiff. Do you understand me, Phillips?' He waved his hand over the graphs and columns in the books, which filled the gaps in language. I moved over to listen, Master Phillip. This was worth the hearing, I knew. If the Pit could close, that would be an end to more than Christmas in this village.

Abraham Phillips scanned the columns quickly, his fast eye knowing what was at stake. 'Aye, he answered. '*Y mae hynny'n wael* - It is bad.'

'If we don't do better soon this pit will close, Seymour bellowed at him. 'And you come late to work. Not good enough, you hear? You understand my English?' Your Dada nodded. No language needed to tell him what he knew. 'Get the men underground, Phillips,' Seymour cursed. Get them working hard. NOW. More trams I want today and all filled with good coal. Stand over them, man. The survival of this pit is up to you.' Your father stood before him like a child in school. 'How many men do we employ?' The Manager spat. 'Three hundred, Mr Seymour,' said your father. 'You know that well.' The Pit Manager did not wait for a translation.

'Get them working, Phillips, or you will have the poverty of three hundred families around your neck for Christmas. You dare come late, Overman. The men are waiting. I am waiting. Get them down NOW. Seymour banged the ledgers shut, pages cracking as he shoved the book about. Vicious, he was Phillip Phillips. Your Dada just turned his palms upwards, lifting his shoulders, a look of resignation on his face. Then, touching his cap again, he headed for the Drift entrance.

The line of colliers was rowdy by now, taking risks with their comments. 'Seymour mouth you off for being late, did he?' one man called out. Chuckles spread into guffaws as your Dada ignored his comment and took command.

'Have the firemen been down?' your father asked, ignoring our laughter. If we had guessed what was to happen there would have been no laughter that day.' The old collier's eyes clouded. 'Are the men ready?' your father asked.

'A word with you, Overman,' William John called, his voice lost in the belching of Nelson's steam and the babble of the colliers.

'Fireman wants a word, Mr Phillips.' The words were passed along the waiting men to Abraham Phillips. I hear it still, the repeated words drumming along the line, man to man. It interrupted your father as he stood at the pay office nearby. He looked up for a minute. Colliers were busy in the yard, checking drams, others tallying their dues ready for your father's books. Abraham Phillips scanned the dram numbers, assessed the productivity. Seymour would be on his back if it was down. I bent over to tie my boots again so I looked busy while I stopped to hear.

'The Firemen stood alongside Abraham Phillips. It was William John's shift and he spoke. Worried he looked. 'I've been down to Brass Vein, Mr Phillips,' he said, 'and I recorded gas.'

'Your father paused a moment, then, without a flicker of doubt showing in his face, he gave the order to Will John and his mate: 'Brush it out lads, Brush it out.'

'William John, an experienced fireman, looked at your father long. We all knew he had reported bad air before on several occasions lately. As I listened surreptitiously, I heard him say, 'I spoke to Seymour about it the other day. He said to tell you. Said that you were above him now Booker had made you Under Agent.

'Your father did not rise to his bait. Maybe he felt sore at Seymour, but would not admit it openly. He just stood there, staring into the fireman's eyes. My ears were on the alert, Mr Phillips. Gas at the face is no joke underground, as you well know. We've brushed it out before, but knew the risk.'

'There are problems with the ventilation, Mr Phillips,' I heard the fireman say. His voice trailed to silence as Abraham Phillips replied.

'Remember, William John, I am your master. I tell you to brush it out.'

The men's eyes met. Both knew the danger, both knew the drams had to be filled - non better than the Overman. Both knew productivity was low. We had looked at two exploratory levels some time back, but the quality of coal was poor. Time it had taken, Mr Phillips, time when the drams were not filled - and that means, for working men, no money.

'We are only working out some old pillars,' Abraham Phillips said staring directly into the eyes of William John. 'It's not a long job - we will soon be out of there.' The Fireman had heard it before - we had all heard it before. In truth, air had been bad this many a month, especially near the roof. 'It won't take long,' I heard your father repeat. The airways are not worth repairing now,' he said. 'Brass Vein is spent. We'll get good coal today and that will finish work in the Brass Vein.' Right he was, your father. We all knew there wasn't much coal there. We all knew, too, that since we abandoned the poor work seams there had been roof falls. We knew the air was bad. Your father and the fireman knew as well. I comforted myself that we were only working the last coal pillars between the old working and the cross heading and we would soon be out.

Will John stood waiting there. His mate looked cowed by all the argument. 'Brush it out, boys,' came your Dada's voice again. He was impatient now.

'There was silence, then. A long pause while the fireman and the Overman stared at each other. It was just three days since New Tredegar. Both knew the odds but only one could rule, the other but obey.

'I have put it in the book Mr Phillips,' Will John said hesitantly. 'Records, you know. I always put it there.'

'Then erase it, William John,' your father said.

'That is irregular, Mr Phillips,' Will John protested.

'I am your master,' ordered your father curtly. 'Do as I say.'

The old man shrank back into his recollection, living each moment as he spoke to me. Quiet I was, stunned by this retelling, living each graphic step he took me through. 'You look pale, Mr Phillips. Do you want to stop here? It is not an easy tale to tell.'

'I have heard you thus far, and have to know,' I said quietly, my hand on the knurled and damaged hand of my informer. After a minute, slight moisture clouding his eyes, Collier Evans leaned back and recounted more.

'6.30 in the morning and still dark,' he said looking directly at me. Then, his eyes losing focus, he went on, 'Lamps were checked at the surface. Drams clanked against the wire pulleys. Throats were cleared. Few of us had bothered with God, few knew the Commandments. Most could not spell or write. Few prayed. Hand to mouth we were, us working men. If we had worries, they were put behind us - or drowned up at the Colliers' Arms. We all fell neatly into the pattern of our work. A bit of bantering and then, the occasional name lifting above the melee, and we're in our world together and alone.

'Shadrach Davies,' move will you, came the command.

'Evan Davies, get a move on.'

'Lamps were checked again, gobs of Raleigh discarded, pipes pocketed and the lights of a hundred and fifty men flickered into action as the queue moved methodically down the incline to the drift. Naked lights illuminated faces of men and boys heading for the upper seams, some as young as twelve heading to work the ventilation doors. All men together we are underground. So, man after man, collier, haulier, cutter, filler, we moved down the slant to the seams of the pit, towards the Forked and the Hard Veins. Those moving to the fiery seam should have abandoned naked lamps outside the heading. Regulations. But Regulations are just that. Hats on backwards, peaks down for those with naked head lights and into the Brass Vein. Drams were waiting for the product of our labour, drams that would be hauled up the slope by Nelson, the sturdy engine on the bank, already spewing its steam out into the cold

December air. Left, right to the darkness.' Collier Evans paused to light his pipe. He looked at me. 'The new Lan had not long been opened,' he said, 'You know the Old Lan was worked out. Already the new mine was our world. Both men and boys already knew it inch by inch, danger by danger, damp and flood.

'So, down the incline we went, the occasional crude remark about the old woman from the Level house, who sat at the door basketing. Cruel comments about her body given her face was black from the dust of good coal and slag brought ribald laughter. I felt ashamed, really. Full of rheum were her old eyes, a wetness that furrowed the dust as it ran over her work-worn cheeks. She was hollow with age and sadness, but we laughed at her. Past her sad eyes, shovels, buckets, wheel barrows were trekked down to the dram. Coal levels were sunk for the exploitation of our valley and its proud people, Mr Phillips, but we laughed at that old woman who was proud. You have never been underground - I only have to look at the nails there on your hand - so you will not know how harmless is the careless talk of men.' He stopped again to serve his fire. 'Better work in the coal, we all agreed, than in the iron pit. We didn't have the chance you had in Liverpool. Levels were everywhere - Garth Rhondda, Coed y Bedw, the disused Cribbwr level just below your home – and even that has been reopened by Owen & Watkins for the Brick works. Work underground was all we knew.'

'Tell me about the New Lan, Mr Evans,' I asked, hiding my hands deep in my pockets. 'I never had the interest of our John.'

'Down there, headings have been driven to one side of the incline through several veins. The cross headings branch-off at right angles, running parallel with the incline. Men and boys file to their place of work, mandrels ready. Only the children yawn. No-one asks questions. Second home it is for all of us. Now, when we worked New Lan, the older workings were left with a pillar of coal between them and the cross heading where the men were working. We used to sing, Mr Phillips. All of us. Singing spread, note on note, taken and floated in counterpart. The voice of collier in harmony with collier is deep and mellow, lad. It resounds against the black wall of the coal. Singing was our security, you know, our sense of being together. Everyone would join in. Little gangs of men would cling together, take turns at the face, cutting or working on the pillars, while others packed the roof, or drew the coal aside for the drams.

'Brattices of wood and canvas flapped cool air on our faces as we progressed towards the veins. The children on the ventilation doors froze while we men were sweating cobs. Past struts of oak, of elm, and larch, we colliers tramped through coal dust. No wonder we are ingrained with it,' he muttered looking at his hands. 'It is shelved along the heading, the levels and the trolley ways, clinging on to ledges, sinking into the very substance of the wood. Ingrained with coal it is, long since out of the forest, dead. So, on we trudge, over sleepers or alongside tram roads, pitch pine and oak, flat side to the ground. But we go singing, throat clearing, arguing, through the fir poles in the galleries and drifts. It's another world, I suppose. A world that's underground.' Evans lit his pipe again. Sighed heavily. 'You get the best of worlds and the worst of worlds down there,' he said. 'It's the companionship, you see. We have to trust each other.'

'To get back to that day,' Evans said, perhaps noticing my impatience with his tale. 'To get back to that day - William Llewellyn, who was just twenty-nine and married, led his gang to where coal winning would commence. We gathered around him, each to our own task. Before long, the sounds of our picks, shovels, hammers - our hacks, slotters and mandrels took on a life of their own as we all swung into action. 'Evan,' Will Llewellyn shouted, 'Evan Howell.' Howell grinned at him, busy sticking his candle to the surface with a lump of clay. 'Give us a hand, mun. Bring your wedge over. There's some large mass here that I just can't get.' Will Llewellyn did not respond immediately. He was out and away with his new missus in his head. 'Stop your dreaming, boyo, work to be done,' Llewellyn bellowed. 'Shut it, Llewellyn. If I don't get this candle firm, you won't see beyond this pillar. I like to see the flame long and blue before I get going. Air is not that good at this height,' he added, fixing his candle to a ledge below the ceiling. 'We have to be bloody careful not to hit an old gob. I'm going to go at the cross today,' he declared, 'Feel like a bit of peace from your stupid jokes.' He grinned, indicating a little gang of colliers laughing raucously further down, working the heading which branched-out from the incline. They'd had a good night at the Colliers', I heard, young Mr Phillips,' he said turning to me. The young'un was only just wed - he'd learn, we chuckled together. Then, turning to Evan's candle, I said, 'It's good enough, boyo. Look at that little brown tip to the flame. A little beauty she is! Like his girl's hair when she leans over him in bed,' I shouted to the others. Coarse laughter rang through the gallery, ending in coughing and spluttering as the dust was gulped in. 'Now get over here to shave this lot if you can't wedge it,' someone called. 'Worth its weight in gold, your little tallow stick,' someone commented to unsuppressed sniggers. 'Have to tell myself that when they deduct each payday!' came back from one of the innocent.' A normal day below, Mr Phillips.'

I nodded, shifting in my chair beside his fire. Wind had blown fire-smoke down into the room. Evans paused to throw on another lump of coal, but was still drifting in his story like the smoky air. As a flame burst from the fire, he continued speaking.

'Just another day,' Mr Phillips, he repeated. 'Morgan Morgan, stop chewing those tiger nuts,' I said. 'Makes me on edge to hear you crunching just behind me. Bloody sewer rat you sound like. Get stuck in before the Overman catches you standing there. Christmas soon, mun,' I said to him. 'Don't you want to get the drams full? But don't shave it off the pillars, boyo. Easy pickings, I know, but it'll end in grief.' 'Ay, ay,' Morgan called back to me. 'Didn't come down here today for the first time. Save it for the young. Hey, Moses, did you hear what he said? Don't shave it off the pillars or you'll have him to answer for it.' Morgan whispered to me then. 'Young Moses saw the light as we came down today. Dead scared he is. White with it.'

'The light?,' I questioned.

'Didn't I tell you that before? Some call it the light, others, the glow. Superstition it is,' he said. 'Some think it precedes death.'

I smiled wanly at the man. I was dazed by his command of words and truly tired by now. But I had to hear him out.

'Now, where was I,' the old collier breathed. 'Ah, yes. You know already that the youngsters work the ventilation doors? 'How are you doing,' I asked young Moses as I walked down. He started to tell me he had seen the light but the creaking of the ventilation door drowned any words the child could give. Cool draughts flooded down around him, stirring the dust on ingrained ledges. Daniel Evans was wedging props. His pick haft hit the roof, methodical, and in time with his breathing, the wedge sank and coal trickled down - nice it is to see a working man swing his tools, Mr Phillips. A craft there is to it. Young David Rees, a boy but man already, paused to watch a moment then went on working. 'Good level this is,' he commented, 'it's damp but has no standing water. 'My mam said there was two colliers drowned at Ely colliery in *Penygraig* the day before yesterday. Can't think of it can you? Makes you shiver.' Daniel Evans' pick hovered. 'Riots started there, boyo. Cambrian. Men disputed the price of working the new seam. Locked out, they were.' David Rees stared, his eyes white against his coal blackened face. 'I don't know no history, Dan,' he said, 'I can't read and Mam never said. Anyway, better not tell me now. We'd better get crackin' or the Overman will be on to us.' 'He's alright, is Abraham Phillips,' I butted in. 'Mind, he was late this morning. Seymour weren't pleased by what I heard. Enough to turn any Overman into a slave driver.' Everybody laughed at that.

'Methodically the colliers worked while others hauled. Shovel, bucket, wheel barrow to the dram, the hammer and clink of drills resounding, laughter and effort bouncing round those walls. You have to hear it to know what I mean, Phillip Phillips. Picks, shovels, sledgehammers, spluttering candles - deducted from our wages - they all have sounds we know. Somehow, the noise is comfortable. It helps. Down there we hear the brutal sound of men ripping out the wealth of the earth for Masters that we do not know, mixed with the voices of companionship of men we do. I loved the lilt of singing against the constant rattle of the drams. It's like sharp drum beats, that sound of mandrel and hammer on the coal. It wins you over, calls you to the coal. Those of us who went to school thought lessons were a chore - we spent our childhood wanting to be down.'

At that moment, old Mrs Evans put her head around the kitchen door. We looked at each other, wondering how we could speed up the telling. 'Is he going on again?' she asked apologetically. 'He never stops, that one. Got too many words, he has.'

'Go on woman, back to the kitchen,' Evan laughed. 'I'm telling Mr Phillips what he needs to know.' Mrs Evans sighed, shut the door and left us sitting by the fire together.

'She's always got her eyes on me since the accident, my little woman. Worried about me, she is. Afraid that in the telling I will suffer. But back to the Lan, Mr Phillips. Little gangs of us walked along the pack walls to the drift.' Evans looked at me. 'Men stood aside to let the drams go past. In that place the pillars were ten, twenty, thirty yards apart, standing there - a dark mass of coal against the sweating hulks of us men. Words - our words punctuated our chatter as we walked - you must have heard them from your father, son - some talked of galleries, headings, others of levels spaced alongside the trolley ways. You wouldn't think,' he chuckled, 'that those thick black hands winning the coal with pointed tips of iron, ash handles grasped tight, were the same hands that loved our women, held our children or raised pint glasses while we won halfpennies playing pitch and toss. I suppose we wash-up well.' He chuckled to himself.

'The men worked, watching the flame of their candles silently,' he said, face still again, 'all making fortunes for the Bookers of this world. Men, and boys who are men before their puberty, all of us there in the lamp light, or candle light, using our muscle, metal ringing on the coal. Thomas Llewellyn Senior was explaining a point to his son Thomas. 'We've made two exploratory levels in Brass

Vein, lad,' he said. 'Workings are limited - too many faults, see.' 'Is there gas, Dadda,' his boy asked him, 'that's what I want to know. These naked lamps bother me when there have been roof falls. You told me many times gas rises to the ceiling.' 'Safe it is, here, lad,' his father assured him. 'Ventilated it is.' 'But, Da, I heard the ventilation was poor since the roof fell away,' the boy insisted. 'The airways must be restricted, Da.' 'Your lad giving you lessons is he, Thomas Llewellyn,' I asked. 'What about doing a bit of work then.' I paused, looking at the younger man. Tired I was. I placed my mandrel down beside me, rummaged in my pocket for a pipe. 'Coal here is poor quality,' I murmured, pipe sticking to my lips it was that dry. 'We'll have to work the pillars if we are to fill these bloody drams before it's Christmas.' Evans sucked harder at his pipe, struggling to get it to draw. 'Hot down there, it was,' he started again as his pipe glowed lit. 'Aye,' complained Shadrach Davies, who was sweating cobs. 'What's happened to the bloody ventilation. Boy gone to sleep again, I reckon.' We all laughed wryly. I heard that some of those kids were doing two shifts as Christmas approached, Mr Phillips. 'Saw that poor little blighter from the Level Houses - ravaged he looked,' said Shadrach Davies. 'His Pa is laid up on the straw after being splashed. There's sad it is. A kid taking over and working night and day.' They don't take home much even if they keep awake, Mr Phillips.'

Collier Evans stared at me for some response. I nodded my agreement. 'Shameful,' I said. Time was passing and still he had not told me of the accident. Hannah would be concerned about my whereabouts by now. I knew I should leave his house but could not go.

'Poor little buggers,' Evans went on. 'Morgan Morgan pitched in then. 'All been there of course,' he said. 'Sleep on the job is something youngsters are good at,' he chuckled. 'By now my pipe was drawing well,' he went on, 'We collected around the cross heading, hands on hips, rubbing our bedraggled faces with coal strewn hands, breathing apace. 'Coming up to nine o'clock,' I muttered. 'Been down nearly three hours. I need a break.' Evan

Howell from the Old Level Houses took a hunk out of his door step. 'That kid working two shifts,' he said, 'his Mam is down, too. Ill she is. Saw her this morning. Not long for this world I would think.' No one responded to his words. Words got drowned by our thoughts, Mr Phillips. It was time to have a break. Men leaned against prop hammers, sat on tumps of hewn coal. The strains of *Oh comfort ye my people* drifted up from the silence - Thomas Llewellyn, it was. Chapel man. He knew the tune, anyway.'

'Daniel Evans's voice rose and fell as he told young Reece about the National Unions - fervent, was that lad. All for unions. A lot of us paused, listening to what he had to say. 'Air down here has been bad for months,' he was telling David Reece. 'We all know it. Ventilation's not really working. Too expensive for the Masters to give time for repairs. Profits always come before men's safety.' Men grunted in agreement. But we all knew there was no point asking, Mr Phillips. I give you we could still work but Dan said Unions would demand that repair, not let us Colliers take the risk. You get my point?'

I nodded. The room was colder now the sun had moved round to the back, the fire dying. I pulled my jacket closer round my chest. The old collier packed another pipe as he continued talking, almost to himself by now.

'*Diawl*, mun!' Henry Sant cut in across Dan's words. 'We don't want your politics here. None union men, us. Got to respect the Masters. Where would we be without them? Look at that Guibal fan outside. Fair investment that was.' Men muttered their approval. There was ambivalence - conflicting ideas amongst the men. Masters were hated and feared. Masters were respected. Masters were just that ... Masters. Another breed, Mr Phillips. You know what I say?'

Again I nodded. I had not come for politics nor to hear the life of working men. My interest was in death and if my father carried blame. The man stared into his memory, while I sat quietly and waited.

'Daniel Evans stood up, climbing higher on the coal tump,' Evans pitched into this with vigour. 'It's not exactly asking you to be Scotch Cattle,' Dan said. We didn't want Scotch Cattle on our hill, Mr Phillips. You understand?' I tightened my lips and nodded my agreement.

'We had a right torch-light meeting, anyhow,' he laughed, 'the lot of us together with our lights. Enough to get the troops alerted if we met like that on the Garth hill!' I nodded as he spoke. 'John Flyn from up the Gwaelod started digging. 'If we stand here much longer, Abraham Phillips will be on our backs,' he said. The gang of men agreed and picked up their tools to start again the hacking, wedging and the loading. Daniel Evans ignored their return to labour and raised his voice against their hacking. 'Look yer, you are not *twp*,' he declared. 'Don't you see that we work so that the Masters profit? How many of you have got houses like they have? 'Well, I ain't exactly working for nowt either,' cut in John Thomas. 'I want to get wed next spring - I've already cut my girl the spoon. No money to start us off with if I don't get going. Something is better than nothing.' 'Look at the children, boyo,' Dan shouted at him. 'How many colliers bring theirs down for an extra hand? What point the Mines Act outlawing children underground when a Dada brings his boy down?' 'Or his girl, for that matter,' cut in someone. 'Money it's about,' Dan shouted, 'money and Food.' By now, we men were listening to him.

'Look yer, I am not withholding my labour for your say-so,' chipped in sixteen year old John Pritchard. 'Mam needs me to work underground. Our dada did till he copped it. My turn now. Better keep those thoughts of action hushed, eh? You may get support where you live in Tongwynlais - but not down here or up at the Colliers'. We don't want to go begging to anyone. Gwaelod proud, me.' Daniel Evans was full voice now. 'Begging?' he shouted. 'Who asked you to go begging? Wages haven't gone up for years ... twenty, thirty, maybe. What d'you think John Pritchard?' John Pritchard ignored him, swinging his pick into the Drift wall. Drams rattled on the lines. Men shovelled hard to fill the empty trucks. 'You just wait till you have a girl and little ones,' Daniel muttered at him. 'You'll learn that ever reduced wages and the chance of copping it make life bloody hard. Shouldn't be like it, mun. You know it and I know it. Pulling together is the only way. Just because the Masters have thrown up cottages for you to rent doesn't make them gods. Look you, they have sent us underground to serve their pockets. They breathe fresh air while we crawl about like moles. Not natural. Not for us or those poor ponies, either. Blind they are. Wait till your eyes go like theirs. Wait till the lines in your faces are scarred with the coal dust and your limbs bent from the crawling. It's all there for us ... the union movement. We need to back it, join together. But you lot are blind already. Blind to what is happening to us all. Slaves we are. Frightened slaves to coal.'

'Lines pulled the full drams up the incline. The sound of picks swinging, coal falling, drowned even the pioneering voice of Daniel Evans. Little David Reece stood alongside him. 'Dan, if we withheld our labour, what would happen? Wouldn't the troops come in like you told me? Shoot us down, like you told me?' 'I don't know, lad,' Daniel Evans sighed. 'We are not unionised in this pit and little chance of being. Men won't join and no one of us can do it alone. We'd better get on now. Overman is on his way. Watch me swing this pick, boy, watch me get it out of my system with work.' He laughed loudly as his body force went with his breath deep into the coal face. 'Black mood into black gold,' he laughed. 'Let's serve the bloody Masters who cut wages, cut corners; let's work for tiger nuts till we drop; let's count our wages in death and poverty; let's accept sudden death and disfigurement. And let's drink ourselves to oblivion with the coppers that are left. The whole sodding system insults us colliers and Henry Sant worries about the Masters!' His pick swung violently.

'Abraham Phillips was standing at the fork in the rail watching us men load the trucks. By then we had coal-painted faces, sweat riddling our bodies. Drifts of our conversation must have floated past him. I noticed he was quiet. If he heard our Dan on his soap box shouting about unions, goodness knows what was going on his head. The men often jested about his father and the Ivorites. You know your grandfather's passion, Phillip Phillips.' Laughing, he called out, '*Ifor Hael* - Ivor the Generous!'

He was laughing at me. I felt uncomfortable. My old feelings of paranoia swamped me. More than ever now, I wanted to leave. But I knew that Evans was all I had to find the information that I sought. By now, my head echoed with the rattle of imagined trams. *Cyfeillgarwch, Cariad a Gwirionedd* - friendship, love and truth, Grandfather Shôn's words swamped my mind against the rhythm of imagined picks. My father had not wanted the Lan unionised. If his men had been in unions, I knew they would have been protected from starvation, at least … nine shilling a week and a bit extra for each child. I felt pity for the men, felt pity for myself. Even, I felt pity for my father. Fifty-three and a lifetime underground. I knew men worked underground into their eighties - a cruel price for survival. My father must have felt his years that day.

'The colliers might do better unionised, Mr Phillips,' came Evan's voice across my thoughts.

'Working men helping working men,' I agreed. 'No one can fault those Ivorite rules - you know - man standing for man, high morals and good behaviour, help in sickness and in health …

'I did not mean the Ivorites, son, with all respect to your grandfather. Unions are another matter. More fundamental and more powerful, they say.' Evans went back to his story. 'Drams from the other levels were rattling by,' he continued after a pause. 'Productivity good today,' your father said as the men acknowledged him. 'Christmas and the colliers trying for extra drams,' he joked to me. I nodded. 'Looking good, lads,' your Dada commented as he walked though. 'Drams are going up fast today,' he said. 'Be in the Colliers' later, will you,' he joked to a young collier. 'A quart for the extra, eh!' 'Not me, Mr Phillips. My missus wants to make the best of Christmas before the young uns have to come down here with me.'

Shadrach Davies chuckled. 'I got to poach a chicken for Christmas - unless you have got a spare bit of your pig going without a home.' Cheeky was Shadrach, but your father laughed. He would joke with us, Phillip Phillips. The men liked that.'

I knew that there would have been an agony in my father's laugh, for he knew that many of these men could not adequately provide, that Christmas would be bleak for them and for their children. Candles they would have, paid for from wages earned underground. Coal they would have if they were lucky. But provisions - he would have known how sparse their Christmastide would be.

'We were proud, we were, Phillip Phillips. Welsh proud.' Evans grinned. 'Your father dug Shadrach Davies affectionately in the ribs,' saying, 'Get that bit of slag moved, Davies.' He indicated a waste pile, 'We don't want that noted in your dram at the weighbridge. You know as well as I do, you'll get nothing for your work if it holds slag.' As Shadrach set about his sorting, your father said, 'I'm going further in to see what's going on down there.' Thomas Llewellyn and Evan Davies skulked back a bit, anxious to get in a smoke before they started hacking into the face again. 'Hey, Tommy boy,' I said as I drew deep on my pipe, 'who has stuffed that cavity up with hay?' 'Where now,' questioned Thomas Llewellyn, more interested in getting his smoke. 'Oh, aye.' By the light of my candle clayed to the ridge, the rough repair was obvious. 'Been like that for days,' said Llewellyn. 'Must be straw in that hole to stop the air. Ventilation shaft gets it over-cold some days.'

'I stood up, refreshed and ready to work, my pipe still in my mouth. Comforting it was, lad. Pick in hand alongside the naked flame of the light, I approached the coal pillar. Belting the roof for the bell stone, I breathed, 'Here we go then, boyo. This one is for Christmas!' Weighing my pick with the careful practice of years, I swung hard into the coal face. My mandrel struck, the coal face was riven. 'What the hell was that,' exclaimed Evan Davies. 'I just saw a flash of fire on the roof above our heads.'

'As he spoke, a force rushed out at me. I am an old miner, Phillip Phillips - I know the odds, knew what I had done. My stroke had gone through to an old gob, cut right through the coal face from the relative safety of the new Lan to ultimate hazards of the Lan old workings.

As the gas rushed out with ferocious energy, I took to my heels bellowing.

'Gas boys.

'GAS.

'OUT.

'NOW.

'Breathless with effort, high with the energy of fear, like an animal, I ran, shouting out GAS as I progressed along the corridor, passed cross heading after cross heading. Men heard and followed, rushing for the world outside. Fear ruled. An innate instinct for survival dominated, as man and boy, we found energy we did not have. Half naked and sweating, men and boys ran, yelling, screaming out into the snow. Trembling through air heavy with drifting dust, lamps and candle flames wavering, a shimmering line of light danced everywhere as we ran for our lives, for our children, for our women.

I noticed that as her husband's voice rose, Mrs Evans came from the kitchen, stood there in the doorway, her hands wringing her apron in renewed distress. She looked at her husband, moved forward to his side, but he pushed her away, his face animated with relived fear.

'An almighty explosion rocked us as the gas caught light,' he whispered. 'Its violent, vivid flame ran free along the incline. Abraham Phillips came running towards Brass Vein with two colliers as William Peters rushed towards them, engulfed in fire. Your father gave Will Peters what help he could, shouting, 'God alive man, what has happened?' as he frantically put out the flames. Your father was impressive, man. He saved Will Peter's life. No concern for his hands as he beat out those flames. At that point, a horde of men rushed past intent on getting to the surface. Peters, burned and suffering, joined the two colliers in a rush towards the exit, but your father stayed. 'Keep calm, boys,' he called, *'cymryd pethau'n dawel,* take things quiet.' As he spoke, the force of an explosion hurled a dram from off the tracks and into him. I turned to see your father, Abraham Phillips, hanging there, broken, between the wall and the truck that crushed him. There was nothing I could do. At that moment, simultaneous to the blast, an inferno raged around him.

'In an instant, men were thrown down by the explosion.

'Human flesh was burning to a cinder. The smell of death was everywhere. The noise incredible.

'Then there was silence.

'Endless silence.

'Just a sound of the drip of water from the roof.

'Hollow silence.

'Seconds later, though it seemed like an eternity, I heard the thump of coal falling, rock falling, roof falling, rock hitting rock. Then a thunder, a chaos of blackness. All vestige of light gone, darkness and that ominous drip of water. The gallery where the men had worked in Brass Vein was now still. A huge fissure glared where I had so recently but struck my mandrel.

'Rock fallen on rock.

'Dark.

'Still.

'The silent grave of men killed by firedamp, the dreaded methane.

'Around me, boyos lay in perfection, dead, like bodies that were sleeping. Further in, the order created by man fell around them. Pit props bent and snapped, coal fell about the bodies of collier and haulier trapped at pillars and fire raged, burning full grown men to cinder in a flash. In the tunnels, roofs fell and in the dank air, injured men screamed out and scratched or prayed. Someone called out for his Mam. *'Maddau i mi nawr'*, he screamed, asking that she saved him now - a futile prayer on many a dying breath.

'Coal dust trickled over bodies, into mouths as the whole Vein shuddered. Evan Howell and William Harding lay, seriously injured, man against man, scratching at the coal that now entombed them. Little Moses Llewellyn, but twelve years old, was dead, never again to see to his Mam.

'It was 9.30 in the morning, Phillip Phillips. Above ground, the pit was working as usual, unaware of the catastrophe below. Surface workers were blowing fingers in the cold, some huddling for warmth near the steam boiler to have the comfort of a pipe. Hungry weighbridge workers blew their finger nails, the basketers ever busy, barely spoke, piling slag away from coal. There were all the usual sounds - the fan humming and clanking, the rattle of drams as they were hauled up the incline, and the high pitched voices of the children trying to scratch a copper in the snow.

'At the exit, drams were being accounted, entered in the books as usual. Then, in a frenzy, the first three of us rushed out, screaming breathless the news of the explosion. As the workers gathered, as the news spread, as more men running up the incline burst outside, faces in the yard looked on in disbelief.

'Explosion in Brass Vein,' I shouted breathless, coal dust choking, anguish swamping, guilt at getting out and leaving men down there. 'Gas,' I gasped. 'Gas from the old workings.' My face was badly burned. I was exhausted by the running, by the shouting, exhausted with shock and effort. Diminished, I sank to my knees and sobbed there like a child.'

There was silence in the tiny cottage as collier Evans paused for breath. Sweat hung in beads on his old face, ran down the puckers of his burns, now etched in coal. His wife moved and stood behind him, her hand smoothing the bent shoulders of his grief. How long we sat in silence there, I do not know, but the grandfather clock ticked the minutes unobserved and the light faded on the afternoon.

Slowly, after what seemed like a long sleep, old Evans spoke again. 'Seymour heard the clamour,' he said, 'Came running to the Drift head from the fan house. Horror froze his face. 'Explosion in Brass Vein,' echoed one of the men. 'Serious. The men are still down there.' Seymour saw me on my knees and came to me. 'Are there men and bairns down there,' he asked, hand on my shoulder. I nodded. 'How many went down for this shift,' he asked.

'Door boys, there are - and some cheeky brat ran in some while ago,' said a collier standing at the surface arch. 'I couldn't stop her, Seymour. 'Message for her Da, she had. Child from the Level Houses, I think.' Seymour did not understand or did not hear. 'How many Booker men,' he barked. 'Hundred and fifty, Mr Seymour,' came from the men flooding out. 'It's Brass Vein. We weren't all in there. We're out of Hard Vein - no trouble there - it didn't get to us. Bloody good to be out in the air and safe.' He took one look at Seymour and at me. 'Back down now is it? We've got to find the men.'

'Seymour stood. 'I'm going down the incline now. Who will join me in the rescue party?' He had no Welsh but we understood the sense of what he said. Strange how superfluous language is at times, how without barriers is the vocalisation of distress. *Cymaeg*, English. Manager, collier. The divide was voided as the search party assembled. Seymour was brave, Mr Phillips. We never had time for him, but he was first to head us down. Getting to my feet, I stood to go back in. 'Your face, Evans,' Seymour said. 'It needs treatment. You should not come.' 'I will go down with you' I said.

Evans' wife looked up and spoke. 'Bad news travels fast, Mr Phillips. Murmurs of the accident in the pit, of gas, of explosion, burst into all our cottages. We women shawled-up, ran to the drift. I stood there and saw their hands wringing, babies with them, mindless of the now drifting snow. The relatives of the men gathered quickly. They gathered around the entrance, weeping openly. It was different for me. I knew my man was safe. I did not dare consider that he had again gone down. The haunting sound of Abraham Phillips' daughter, screaming is with me still - your sister Elizabeth I think, but it could have been Susannah. She was uncontrollable - her anguished cries cut through the cold. From Coed y Bedw colliery just yards away in Nant Cwm Llwdrew, colliers came running to the Lan. They always do, Mr Phillips. Colliers watch out for colliers. Firemen assembled, stretcher men, miners. In minutes a search party was entering the drift. I didn't want my man to go back in - '

'What?' her husband cried. 'You would have me stay with you when men were underground? That is not the collier's way.'

Mrs Evans nodded. 'Go on with your story. Mr Phillips must want to go. That young wife of his will wonder where he is. She shrugged her shoulders, went back to the kitchen, shut the door. Evans barely watched her go.

'Instruction passed from men to men,' he said. 'Get to Taffs Well,' he barked to a boy, 'get Dr Edwards here. Fast he will come. Good man for an emergency.' The young boy from the Level Houses ran with the message till his lungs would burst, whistled for the ferry, sobbed to the ferrywoman who took him over the river and waited for Dr Edwards to take them back to the Gwaelod side.

'I gave the directions to the headings in Brass Vein where the explosion had occurred,' Evans said without a movement in his face. 'Seymour was ordering his above-ground work force. 'You, stop staring,' he shouted to a farrier. 'Get on that horse and GO. You,' he called to another lad from the Level Houses who was helping with the basketing, 'you go with the farrier, alert the works surgeon. Get quickly to Dr Franklen Evans of Tynant. Get going now and tell him to come quick.'

'Impressive, he was, Mr Phillips. In spite of the atmosphere towards him, even without our language, he took control and was the first man down. No rescue team came from Booker, lad, no engineers. Instead, the men who had come up unscathed prepared to go back down, led by the outsider. Bravely, he led the party into that inferno, intent on finding my work companions. The fervent noise of men organising themselves, of collier out for collier, buzzed in the falling snow. Miners from nearby collieries, from Coed y Bedw, from Garth Rhondda and Cwm Dews arrived at the scene in no time and went down with the two doctors, who were soon there on the scene and ready to go underground without a thought for their own safety.

'In the yard, men employed for surface work stoked up the steam engine to power the Guibal into overdrive. There, in the swirling snow at the pit head, groups of gaunt faced stokers stood watching hopefully as the fan sucked out the deadly methane - the *chokedamp* - so feared by all us mining men. Few spoke. Men went about their tasks with silent diligence.

'The rescue party literally ran down the incline - I had it from the men. Air fetid, water trickled from above. A ghostly shadow-play moved on the walls, doubling the rescue party in a ghostly, useless dance. Frightening it was. No-one spoke. The dank smell of explosion, of death, of dust, hung in the corridors. Sweat dripped from the faces of the men who had gone back in, exhaustion just a step away. Slow I was, my burned face raw, my burned hand useless, but I followed them.

'Down went the men, through shafted galleries, stepping over abandoned picks and shovels. The cool draught from the ventilation doors belied what we would find. Sweat poured down our faces, black with dust, grim with anticipation. I saw gaunt hollows in my butties' cheeks - they could not raise the energy to lift their mouths to speak. Lit by our lamps, we were a ghoul-like crew, sweating, gasping, some coughing as we approached Brass Vein. The gallery was empty now, final flames had rapidly extinguished. Seymour leaned against the wall, spitting out dust. Boulders of rock were strewn over floors where earlier us men had worked. I watched his eyes, saw him take in the shimmer of the dram rails, saw he wanted to cry out like a child. Saw his pain and shared at last his true humanity. At the seat of the fire, we were. I looked at what I had left. Dead bodies, undamaged, lay as if asleep in cruel replica of life. 'Firedamp death,' I muttered to him. 'Have you not seen all this before?'

'Not this, Evans,' he said to me. 'Not this.' His words were choked, spat out with the dust. 'Come on chaps,' he muttered. 'This is where we start.' I followed his eyes to where, lying unconscious in the arms of Evan Howell, was a child, her father, dead. A sound of sobbing choked throughout the blackness. Men, hard mining men, were crying loud. '*Arglwydd, achub fi nawr,*' I muttered. Lord save me now.' I was unprepared for this. Leaning I touched the little girl. Cold she was. She could not have been more than five years old. Fair curls, she had, curls full of coal. Dust blackened locks fell over her small face. Her father's dead arms around her, she still grasped his finger tight. There was silence in the Vein by now. 'Breathing she is,' I said looking up at Seymour. 'That bairn is one that will not appear on official lists,' he muttered under his breath as he unfolded the arms of the dead miner and picked up the child. Looking up at me, he said, 'Get this child out - and do it quick. We did not see her, Evans. You hear me? Do you understand? That bairn was not down here.' Nodding, I took the child from him, held her in my arms. I rubbed her gently to create some warmth. She whimpered quietly, 'Da, it's dark,' and then she shut her eyes. I cried, Mr Phillips. I had never seen the like and cried. I could not move - I could not take my eyes from her. As the wetness of my tears fell on her face, I stood there, stupefied.

'If you are not going up yet, Evans,' Seymour said urgently, 'pass that wee girl out. Someone - take her to the surface while we work.'

Death was everywhere. Thomas Llewellyn lay there, burnt. 'Poor bugger. A cinder he is,' I gasped. 'I work with him some days.' As I spoke, voices of other rescuers came through the darkness of Lan hell, falling, crossing, one voice over the other:

'*Maddau i mi nawr!* Look here! His boy burnt too. Just had his sixteenth birthday,' someone said.

'I thought he was on the ventilation doors,' said Seymour. 'What is he doing deep in here?'

'Thomas liked to have him by to give him hints,' I said. 'Teaching him, he was. Some homecoming for that poor woman of theirs.'

'Seymour, here quick, mun,' called another, 'Look at Will Llewellyn here ... *diawl!* What injuries. He must have suffered hell.'

'Robert Taylor here, Seymour. Can't bear to look at the poor sod. Look at his head, man, not a chance he stood.

The raw sound of a miner sobbing echoed through the devastating scene. 'What's up, man,' asked Seymour going over to look. 'It's young Dai Reece, mun. Look at him. Head smashed in at the back. A boy he was, just bloody boy. What makes us let children come into this hell.'

'It's all we've got, man. We all have to live,' the voice of an old miner chirped up.

'Live? So that's what that kid died for, eh? He lived for what? To die? Look at him. Scarcely any flesh on his young bones. When did he ever get a chance to live?'

'Over here, doc.' An urgent voice cut in, as through the glare of his lamp Dr Evans shape appeared. 'Behind this fall, doc. There are injured men ... Look here you. Come now. Quick. It's Evan Davies, doc, and he's alive.' As the doctor signed that he would come, the miner leaned low over his mate. 'It's fine, man,' he said softly to the injured man, 'we're getting you out of this and home to Pentyrch pretty damn quick now. The doctors are both here.'

'Tallow lamps vaguely lit the heading. In the moving gloom, Charles Mills and John Flyn were slumped one on the other. A rock fall pinned them down. Rapidly, Franklen Evans, surgeon of the works, moved to them, working where he could to relieve their pain as other men hauled the fallen mass from their crushed frames. 'This chap must have staggered to the entrance,' he said. 'Still breathing but bad injuries to the head.'

'That's Will Harding,' Dr Edwards offered, turning from John Flyn.

Franklen Evans nodded. 'His injured body took him some few steps before he collapsed here. Looks bad, he does, but he is still alive. He is just about breathing. Can you deal with him, Doc Evans. while I move on. All a bit different from your practice in Taff's Well, eh.'

'The injured collier's back arched as doctor Evans tried to tend him. His dull groan resounded through the hell of Brass Vein competing with the voices of other colliers who were yelling out names of the injured from further down the incline. 'Shadrach Davies here and still alive,' called one. 'Unconscious, though,' another called. 'Here's Will Evans,' called another voice. 'Walked in all the way from Radyr to this hell-hole today,' a rescuer muttered. 'I recognise the lad. His missus is going to be lost without him. They were close.'

'Can you come further down the incline, Doctor Franklen,' Seymour called, stripped to his waist now in the heat. 'There are more men here alive but injured. They need the attention now and not the dead.' I ran with the doctor to the place where Seymour stood.

'Abraham Williams from Tongwynlais lay awake. I leaned over him, knelt down by his side. 'No feeling in my legs, mun. Bad, it is, I know.' His voice was weak. His eyes stared at the tallow candle of the doctor kneeling there. 'I've caught it this time, doc,' I heard him say. 'So much for my lucky penny. I don't think your black bag'll sort out this down here.' He shut his eyes in pain. 'Is young Sam Evans alive?' he asked as he opened them again. 'We come in together, see. Can't think of the walk here from the Ton without that boy.' 'Don't use your strength worrying, Abe,' I said. 'There's going be a bit of a trek to get you to the great outside. Snowing it is. You think on that. Forget about those legs of yours. We'll get you out anytime now.'

Doctor Evans put his hand on my shoulder as the man's eyes closed. 'That face of yours needs some attention, too,' he said. Strange that, Mr Phillips. I had forgot my injury.

'Seymour had come upon Sam Evans by now, gravely injured but awake. On his knees was Manager Seymour, on his knees, wiping the coal dust from Sam's mouth. 'Doc Evans is down here, boy,' he was saying, 'we'll get a stretcher to you any minute. Just breathe slow.' 'What the hell are you doing underground,' asked Sam, trying to raise himself. 'What's going on?' Unable to take weight on his arms, groaning, in deep pain, he fought to take another breath, but fell back into semi consciousness. Seymour looked at his eyes, assessed his half naked body, saw his broken youth, his vigour gone. Ashen, torn, he looked at me in grief as Sam opened his eyes. 'Don't tell my Mam, Mr Seymour,' he murmured through his pain. 'Don't tell her, mun. She won't be able to take it.'

'I saw Seymour stand and survey the carnage around him. 'I am all-in,' he said. He looked it, too. Sorry for the man, I felt. Five months in the job and all our hatreds aimed at him. Colliers were still yelling messages one to the other, everyone working to save the injured, count the dead. 'All we need now is fire to spread here,' I said to him. 'Time we were out?' he asked. I nodded to him. He stood up and spoke to the rescuers close to him. 'Get them out as fast as possible,' he said, his voice suddenly tired, lost. 'Stretcher them on what we have. Use the brattice cloth to cover them.' I wished he had the Welsh to give them comfort, even to give them orders in our tongue.

'More help came pouring down the incline; stretcher men with planks, doors, barrows. Their additional lights showed-up the fissures in the heading where I had worked. Bodies were put on the make shift stretchers, recognised, wept over with open tears. Men who fight with fists for Colliers' Law know how to cry, Mr Phillips. Tears of exhaustion, tears of ripe futility fell from men who had worked long shifts before turning round to man this rescue.

'The names of the dead passed along the line of men - Thomas Llewellyn, the father and son who shared a name, now shared their grave, buried deep in coal. John Pritchard, Henry Sant, William Peters, Robert Taylor, Daniel Evans from Tongwynlais, William Llewellyn - and then, the names of the children, David Rees, John Thomas and little Moses Llewellyn. All dead. Just names to pass like tokens along the line of us dejected men. Traumatised by the rescue, stumbling, exhausted by moving roof falls, we men were weary from clearing boulders and rocks thrown by the explosion like dice from a mighty hand. Lost in the hopelessness of exhaustion and dead colleagues, were we.

'A call came from further down the heading: 'Abraham Phillips here,' cried the voice. 'He's dead. The Overman is dead. He's hanging here, crushed against the wall by a dram. It must have pinned him there in the explosion. There's a ghastly sight - Abraham Phillips pinioned against the wall. Poor bugger. A horrible death - and way out of the main gallery, too. Must have caught him a bit later than the other poor sods here.'

Collier Evans paused in his reliving, paused to look at me. Stunned, I sat there silent in my grief. Evans leaned forward plying his dying fire with more lumps of coal. I looked at this old collier who had seen such sights, his scarred face gentle now in his reality. '*Heb iechyd baich yw bywyd*' he said, quoting the old saying. 'Without health, life is a burden. Even if we had been able to get your father out, Phillip Phillips, his life would have been broken, such were his injuries.'

I nodded, unable to find sound let alone make words.

'Back to the telling, then?' Old Evans asked me. 'Are you sure you can take more?' I gestured him to speak. He continued without lead in, deep in the labyrinthine caverns of his mind. 'Let's get them out, boys,' shouted Seymour.' Evans continued recounting his agony, his quiet, measured words falling like gentle rain. 'Like a row of working ants, the exhausted men carried their mates,' he said, 'placed them as best they could into the drams that were still standing. Covered the men in brattice cloth. Then, one after the other, crawling, bending, manoeuvring the roof falls, we escorted out the injured and the dead together. Sweating, defeated, but intent.

'The journey up the incline from the hell of Brass Vein to the surface was an eternity of groans and sweat. Some of the injured had suffered terrible burns; worse - some of the dead had been burned to unrecognisable cinder - spent humanity. Somehow we got there, somehow the endless trek turned into light. Best we could, we lay the living on the straw of the nearby stable. Wives and mothers, sisters, women of the village were there to tend to them. Some had stood in isolated vigil while the snow fell round them, waiting, waiting for their men.'

Leaning over to poke at the spent embers of his fire, Evans kept talking. 'One o'clock,' he said, 'and Seymour noted that the final search was completed by the men. Exhausted colliers all, we had by now combed every vein and every level. 'You are sure no one has been left below,' he asked. All of us in the exploration party replied to him in Welsh, *Nac oes.* 'There is not.' Seymour read the answer in our face.

'As I stood there, I overheard Dr Edwards mutter to the works surgeon, Franklen Evans, 'The pit manager is all in. He didn't expect this five months into the job.' Evans agreed, replying, '*Duwedd!* He is learning the human cost of coal, if he didn't know it already.' Sighing, he turned back to his work, continuing to tend the wounded in the straw. 'Can't say I haven't seen it all before myself,' he added. 'I feel so helpless. I examine them, list their names and direct the rescuers to take them home. Strong women they must have.' 'When they look under the brattice they will need to be,' Dr Evans muttered. 'Some of these men will die on their way home, some will be disabled - what will those strong women do then? Get down there hauling themselves or go to Ponty workhouse? A bad business, Franklen. A bad business.' Dr Evans looked shaken as he packed his bag.

'Gradually, each of the injured was stretchered to his home; crude stretchers made from doors, from planks. We carried them, Mr

Phillips, carried every one covered in brattice cloth, a little group of village people following each cortege. On the longer treks, men from this following changed places with the carriers - sharing the load, you see.' Collier Evans was halting now, his speech slower, more deliberate. I waited, hung to his every word, my heart aching, head swimming with horrific details I could never own.

'Each of the dead was returned to the woman they had loved,' Evans said, adding bitterly, 'and to the children they had left fatherless behind. I walked with some of them in that dreadful cortege, carrying men and boys through villages where earlier they ran. We stopped at the cottages of the dead and injured, greeted and thanked by sobbing relatives. Neighbours, distressed onlookers, eager to do what bit they could, were standing everywhere. We all felt hopeless, lad.'

'You went with the cortege to my father's house,' I asked, no longer silently waiting at his pace. Collier Evans nodded. Taking my hand in his distorted grasp, he said to me directly, 'At *Ty'n y Coed*, Jemima Phillips waited, watched as the stretcher bearers arrived at Abraham Phillips' house. Your sisters Susannah and Elizabeth were following with us. Quietly, Jemima Phillips thanked us as we prepared to lower your father to his ground. 'Are there many injured men?' Jemima asked. 'Aye. It's a bad job,' I said to her. 'Men and boys both. There are few in this village not affected by this at all.' By then, I was too tired, too overwrought, to say more words, my own injuries at last taking their toll. Gently though, we lowered the planks carrying the body of the Overman.

'And my Abraham?' Jemima asked.

'He is here, Mrs Phillips,' I said to her. 'Right peaceful now he is.'

'Dead is he? Jemima asked.

'Will you manage Mrs Phillips,' I asked, head down.

'I have to manage, she said quietly. 'He is my husband.

'I watched in silence as she lifted the brattice cloth and wept.'

1886

The Book says, *And ye shall know the truth, and the truth shall make you free.* I was not set free by the knowledge Collier Evans gave. My nights following our meeting were terrible, my days a passing dream. My father led the men to gas and death. So how could I be free? I travel with my order book. Have not the stamina to speak with John. Grief falls on grief, incongruous as withered leaves in Spring.

I am conscious of my heritage, know that my roots are fixed in coal, yet I am stateless. In the confines of this valley, I am aware of its harsh workings, hear its plaintive song and feel my sadness that it lives engrossed in myth. I see in the construction of my country, its deprivation. I see its people living their short lives in stress. But I find no answers to my lingering grief. In 1885, Susannah, my faultless sister, who cared for everyone, fell ill and died. In *Ty'n y Coed* my fires burn low. For months now, I have been in pain. My face is sallow, my urine turns to black and I fear death. My stomach pains me, my breathing difficult, but I fulfil my order sheet and travel when I can.

In the kitchen, steamy from Hannah's soup making, I over-heard my wife whisper to Elizabeth, 'Phillip is pale today.' As I watched from the void of the hallway, she went over to my sister, who was at her books. 'Lost, your brother is today,' she said, wiping her hands. 'Lost in his thoughts and his anxieties. No chance of getting him out to the pump for water.' I stood watching as she reached for her shawl. 'I worry about him, Elizabeth,' she said. 'He is not himself and has not been for days.'

Indeed, I am not myself. I watched as Elizabeth shut her books and smiled. 'I'll go for the water, Hannah,' she insisted. 'You watch the soup. But do not have concern. Phillip was always one to disappear or dream.' She spoke cheerfully. She does not know. 'Details haunt him,' she added as she put on her shawl. 'He is probably working out accounting for his work.' She was at the door, and turning as she spoke. 'When does he set off again?' she asked. 'A commercial traveller can sink within his orders and his schedule, as you well know. Getting you water will be so far from his mind.' She laughed.

'It is more than that, Elizabeth,' Hannah intervened. 'He is riven with anxiety. I think he suffers from melancholia.'

Elizabeth grabbed her shawl against the wind. Perhaps my wife is right. I moved to the hall window to watch my sister at the pump. Snow propelled itself against her face, cooling the red of her cheeks. The hill was above her, sound muted, sight of it blurred by driving snow. Dragging the water bucket, she made her way up the steps to the top garden, where the spring still forces through. I see my face reflected in the window, see indeed that I am pale. Stopping in her tracks, Elizabeth looked up to Maes Gwyn, the track pure white, no footsteps yet disturbing the new fallen snow.

'If I am ill,' I said to myself, 'she faces soon another death.' I thought of my father standing at that pump, had watched him often filling water jacks. As I stared, a thin wisp of smoke rose, cutting through the mist of falling whiteness. No-one about at all, the world empty, I watched Elizabeth. Saw how she loved the isolation, loved the cottage and was glad that Hannah and I had shared our life with her. Gwaelod y Garth was home. Pace after pace, I watched my sister in the snow. My father's life-time echoed with her steps. Around

Elizabeth I could see the snow piling in little drifts, caught on the frozen blades that edged the track. As the weather worsened, tiny trails of men scurried on the hill, strode or dawdled to their place of winning bread.

Hannah did not turn as I went into the kitchen. I moved to the window, morose with guilt and saw Elizabeth still at the spring, ashamed I had not taken that work from her. I did not speak. I did not raise my eyes or go to Hannah at the sink.

'Why did you bring me here, Phillip,' she said quietly, aware of my deep sadness. 'I know you think still on your father and the accident. But we cannot live always with the dead. This place is full of it, too full of your distress.'

'There are too many dead, Hannah. Would there have been less dead within this village had my father been less dominant?' I said.

'Hist, Phillip. Not that again. *Cariad annwyl.* Let Abraham Phillips rest in peace. The inquest blamed no one.'

'John is destroyed,' I shouted bitterly, 'he thought our father was invincible. Lucky for Evan - he did not live to doubt. That doubt all falls to me.'

'Phillip Phillips, stop shouting. I have had enough,' Hannah expostulated, hands on hips. 'There are men and boys working out there day and half the night if they are lucky in this slump. The entire village has been plunged to poverty now that the Iron Works is closed. The mine has ceased production, so hand to foot they live, their worry to get food for hungry mouths. You are more fortunate. No iron splash, no pit explosions for you, your hands are lily white. Why do you not count your blessings, for you have many, and overcome this blackness which dominates your soul?'

'I will renounce probate on this house, Hannah. I will take you from it,' I sighed. 'Not that anything can change the burden that I bear. But at least we will leave behind my father's house and this god-forsaken village.'

As I spoke, at that very moment, Elizabeth came in. Head up from her task in an instant, she heard my words and cringed. 'Leave this house, Phillip? Has there been foreclosure?' she asked in great concern.

'Nothing like that, Elizabeth. I pay the bills.'

'Then why must we leave?' She stood before me, challenging.

'Because I am unhappy here – ' She did not let me finish.

'Because you are unhappy here?' she shouted, incredulous. 'We leave Dada's house because you are not happy! This is our childhood home, Phillip,' she cried out. 'Leaving here would be too hard. It is convenient for your work, and for me, the school is close. Soon the Board school will be done. I can be a pupil teacher there. The track is easy in good weather. No struggling with the mountain path.'

'I have already renounced our rights, Elizabeth.'

'No, Phillip. Not that. Dada built this place with his own hands. I know every blade of grass. It is wrong you can renounce our rights and leave me nothing.'

'Or so you think, Elizabeth,' I spat. 'You are a woman. You have no rights.' Suddenly, I felt ashamed. 'You do not see the devastation that holds me in its grasp,' I muttered, 'the poverty, the desolation of the valley floor. The black of industry lies all around you. You only have to turn. And you do not carry the anxieties that keep me sleepless.'

'I love the cottage,' Elizabeth cut in. 'I am just starting to live again after Susannah's death. While I was filling the water buckets, alone at the spring, just now, I looked up at the Garth and it was wonderful.' Her big eyes stared, unflinching, into mine.

'Renounced our rights, Phillip?' Hannah declared. 'Then where shall we live now?'

'Father signed that lease with Booker to give us a home for all our history,' Elizabeth shouted, fiercely defiant. 'He told me so himself, said he had made this place so we could be secure. And now you renounce our rights without even asking me.' Gathering her books, Elizabeth left the kitchen, near distraught.

'So, are we homeless now,' Hannah cried. 'What has brought this crisis to our lives?'

'You do not like it here and we shall go. But before I leave this place, I had to know my father's guilt, Hannah,' I said, ignoring Elizabeth's sudden exit. 'I went to see old Collier Evans. What the Inquest heard was true.'

'Why can't you let things lie, Phillip. You will never really know the pressures that your father had.' Hannah looked angry as I knew she would.

'Don't you understand that I have to know? I cannot let my father rest in peace while I have doubt.' Turning to her, I said, 'I should not have left home to travel. I should not have gone to live in Liverpool with Evan. My place was here with them.'

'Torture yourself, will you? There is no answer,' Hannah said coldly. 'A good man was Abraham Phillips - and you lived in Liverpool with me. Does that mean nothing to you now?'

'Hannah, I do love you. I have brought you to my home, but we are not welcome here. Do you not feel it? There is an undercurrent - voices stop as I approach.'

'Dark are your thoughts, Phillip. I have noticed no bad feelings. In this village the Phillips are respected. Old Shôn o'r Lan, your grandfather, Abraham, your father - respect is all I notice here.'

'But those words, Hannah, that order father gave. Brush it out. How could he say that? He knew the danger. How can I rest? He has stained the name of Phillips. I feel the eyes of all the village on me still. How can Elizabeth grow up here free of guilt?'

'As you will, Phillip. But leave Elizabeth out of it. She has her life ahead of her. The children in school love her. Saddle her with your doubt, and you will destroy her, too. She adored her father.'

I walked to the front sitting room, leaving Hannah unanswered. In the gloom of the room, its ornaments, its heavy curtains, my steps were muted. Air was stagnant with its bareness. The old wooden dresser, stripped of Jemima's china, cried to the emptiness I felt. I stared out of the window to the Drift. Hannah followed me, standing in the doorway, silhouetted against the sun streaming over the snow, lighting the empty room. I knew she stood there but did not turn.

'Wordless are you?' she muttered in despair. 'Wordless.' Straightening her apron, she sighed and left me there to my endless questioning. 'Dead men can't talk,' she called, moving quickly to the kitchen. 'You can never know the truth. That has died with your father.' As she kneaded the bread dough, as its soft thump hit the table, I heard her say under her breath, 'Cold it is. This cottage is always cold. The bread will never rise.'

As she worked there, flour on her face where she had brushed back her hair, Elizabeth burst in, happy, through the door, face white, struggling with yet another water jack. 'Hannah, it is magnificent,' she laughed. 'I cannot stay distressed. I had to break the ice out there. Look, I brought you in a bit.' I watched as she thrust the sliver of frozen water into Hannah's mouth. Laughing, they sat down together at the table, their heads deep into books.

Wet drops fell to the cloth from Elizabeth's long hair. 'You are drenched to the bone, Elizabeth,' I said, storming into the kitchen. 'Why do you go in the cold without a wrap?' She did not look up as I came through, did not listen as I spoke to her. Lost she was. Ignoring me or lost in words. And deathly cold. I was angered that she did not answer me. I saw her drenched and shivering form, but had no mercy. 'Books, Elizabeth. They are our downfall. If I had been like John, I would have been here to take some of the strain from father. But books, books, books. Evan's brain took him to Liverpool - books and my anguish to see the world led me to follow. What price books and learning? Knowledge but no wisdom. A clerk to a cotton merchant? Death for Evan. What price clerk to a provisions merchant for me? Eternal guilt. And you, Elizabeth, you with your head full of books, soaked to the skin and shivering. You have no sense so where will it lead for you?'

'Phillip. Quieten. Do not bring your guilt down on us all.' Hannah stood up from the table where she read with Elizabeth. 'Here, eat your food,' she said. 'Angry you are. Musing on the past like this is self indulgent.'

She moved towards me then, gentler, softer, trying to appease. 'When we go from here, the anguish will all cease. It is this place. These cold stone walls devoid of sun. It is not the history of your family that makes it cold. It is what it looks at. What is it, this cottage? Isolated. Stone. On the side of a hill made hostile by what has been taken from it. This is Wales, Phillip - the land which provides rich pickings for the industrialists and scraps for those who serve. What did the Scotch Cattle fight for before you? Ultimately it is about food. That is why our men work for low wages - to keep their children fed. Their hollow eyed women work, large with child year after year, women who themselves have soon enough been underground or in the iron workings. Eat, man. And you, Elizabeth, too. You are too thin. Phillip, your delving will be the death of me, and then, you will have another guilt to worry about. Were we not happy up in Liverpool?' She had said more than she intended, said more than she had ever said before. Wiping her hair from her eyes, she went upstairs to cry.

The next morning, Elizabeth did not come down from bed. Within days, fever had taken her away. In the autumn of the year of 1886, as the leaves turned golden, as they fell from every tree, I had to take my beloved young sister to St Catwg's to lie in peace with her father and her mother, young Deborah and her brother Evan. I am inconsolable, Hannah strong.

We had the coffin made, the eulogy read. Leaves swirled around us as made our way. I can remember nothing more. Head bent, I lay my sister in the earth and went to pay the grave digger his dues.

'We Phillips do not live long,' I said. 'How can I leave her here.'

'No better place to go back to the earth,' the grave digger said. 'Look at that spire - it takes your eyes to heaven. Peaceful it is in the dip of the hill. She will be safe here with her Da.' Leaning back, his spade stuck in the earth, he looked at me with honest eyes and said, 'A good man was her father, Abraham Phillips.'

My head was spinning from his words. I looked at him. 'You knew my father, then?'

'I was a haulier down the Lan with him,' he said, 'and better it is to be digging graves than to lie in one like many of the boyos that I knew! Kept his calm, your father did when fire broke out that day and we were sweating cobs and running riot. 'Calm boys,' he said, in that fine voice of his. 'Keep calm boys - but then he caught it, too.' Cleaning his spade then, the man looked up at the sky.

'Did he ...,' I started but could not find words. Clearing my throat and putting my muffler straight, I thanked the grave digger for his work, gave him the silver coin and left him standing there before Elizabeth's grave.

1887

The wages of sin, the Book taught me at my mother's knee, *is death,* and I have sinned. I walk from the front room to the kitchen wordlessly. I ponder alone the doctor's letter which tells me that my liver is infected, that I soon will die. I dutifully take my medicine three times a day - a tablespoon with one of whisky and more whisky before sleep. I do not talk with Hannah or tell her of my distress. Each step I take is painful, each day too long. And at night, I dream of Collier Evan's tale of hell. The sins of my father haunt my waking and my dreams. I read the Book but find no consolation there, for its God is a jealous God *visiting the iniquity of the fathers upon the children unto the third and fourth generation.* Our family is not destined to find peace.

Another year, and Deborah has been taken. I do not feel distress but punishment. John does not visit me. Anxiety isolates me from my wife. I have a sense of dread. People in the village ignore me as I pass and rumours about me spread. I cannot rest from travel. Railways press forth to ever new horizons. I go to places where there are no orders. My books are empty and I fear I head for destitution soon. I cannot sleep or sit but pace the boards of this ill fated house. I had never faced the subterranean world my father and my brother knew. I know my privilege but find no solace for I, too, am destroyed by coal. I read of accidents. I cannot work or pray. Hollow with living death, I ignore the close-knit family I knew. How do they thrive? Are they immune to death? That I cannot grieve my sister makes my tears more horrible. I know I live yet no one seems to care or know. I have no friends. Hannah forsakes my company and I am tossed from day to day in woe.

I have sent my water to a doctor, have visited the curative waters of the Cheltenham Spa. To fill my time, I write my story in this empty order book. Will Evans brings me papers from his shop. I scan them only for more punishment. I turn the pages of the Western Mail, the London Illustrated Gazette, or anything he brings, and search for articles related just to coal. 'Ynyshir and thirty-nine miners die firing a shot'. I lick my pencil, note it down. I list the deaths from mining, underlining numbers of men killed. Sinking a shaft in Cilfyndd: more lives lost to coal. The year Susannah died, eighty-one dead at Maerdy and on the Christmas Eve. It never stops. I turn to the Rhondda Chronicle and read how '*a loud retort was heard the loudest and most fearful of the kind that they* - the workmen at the surface - *have ever heard*'. I copy it in my hand for future reference. Is there a future for Phillip Phillips, I muse as I write, '*The explosion damaged the pit top and the winding gear delaying rescue efforts so that the first rescuers could not descend for three to four hours.*' I pore over each tragic detail. It all gives a reason for my misery.

I look up as Hannah opens the door, then look down again as if busy with my work.

'You have many orders to collate?' she asks.

I nod my head as I read to her, '*Twenty-nine uninjured and nine injured survivors of the explosion followed by six bodies.*' I hear the gentle rustle of her skirt, assume she has left the room, assume myself alone. *Thirteen horses* I write, saying out loud, 'and three men dead.' My heart beats faster as the newspaper describes the '*most marvellous' escape, that of Samuel Strange employed as an ostler at the mine, who was discovered burnt but alive, while all around him were twenty three horses and three men all dead*'. I follow my finger tip as I scan the columns for more detail, note that a hundred men were underground, while two hundred others waited for instruction to go down. And I ponder greater carnage that did not happen on that day. My hand moves swiftly as I record the verdict: a shattering infringement of the 1872 Coal Mining Regulations Act - proceedings taken out against the Manager. At least no one took proceedings against my father, I think thankfully.

As the day moves slowly on, as the clock ticks mindless minutes, as Hannah brings me food, I carefully cut an item from the Western Mail to mark the opening of another pit. For three years now Albion steel have been sinking shafts at Ynyscaedudwg Farm - another blow against the rural life of Wales, another village sacrificed to coal. 'There will be more deaths,' I say to Hannah as she puts down the tray. 'Another shaft sunk means more men dead. it is inevitable.'

'It's work for people, Phillip,' my wife responds. 'Think of the positive not just on death. Why do you fear death so?'

'Because we live in troubled times where children die - scarlet fever, typhus, visitation by their God. The spectre of death walks everywhere. With workhouses like prisons, the squalor, grief and ever present fear of poverty, death stalks the bare boards of all the cottages. The women must talk of little else but death.'

'If they talk of death it will be talk of Jack the Ripper and Whitechapel,' she laughed, knowingly. 'Not always do they think of mining death.' Leaning over my table she glances at the pages I have read. 'Look, Phillip,' she says, 'a ship from Norway carrying timber is stuck on a sandbank in Rhossilli Bay. They were awaiting a pilot to take them down to Swansea, but the weather changed and now the cargo is all lost.'

'It was Norway spruce for pit props - better lost to the sea,' I mutter. I hear Hannah sigh as she takes the tray and leaves me with my food. I eat abstractedly. My health is now my great concern. I have seen a doctor who has given no good news - another truth that does not set me free, *for everyone that curseth his father shall be surely put to death:* How do I tell my wife there is no work? How do I tell her that

I am ill? How do I tell her that I have brought her to the house of Abraham Phillips and for my sins, I die? How do I tell her that my mind is damaged by Isaiah's burning coal, that I have opened the forbidden door and all the sorrows of the world came in.

Suddenly, I notice that Hannah has not left the room. She stands in the doorway erect and proud. Late sun lights the floating strands of hair around her head. She is watching me, head on one side, much as my mother had once done.

'What do you write, Phillip?' she asks gently.

As she walks towards me, I hear only the gentle swish of her skirt, her footsteps on the bare wood gone. As I look up at her, a shadow moves across her face. 'It is not orders, Phillip, for I know you have no work.' Softly, she moves to where I sit. Putting her hands on my shoulders, she whispers, 'Why do you lie to me? I know you are troubled, know that you are ill.' Her hair is touching mine now, her head resting heavy on my head. As I feel her tears wetting my neck, she whispers, limp like a fading flower, 'I have seen the doctor's letter, Phillip. I have seen your physic in the small backroom. Don't be ashamed of what allowed you to survive. We must love until you die.'

1891

Death stalks the rooms of every house. Here, under the dark eaves of *Ty'n y Coed*, death called to me. Pains in my chest now, a cough I could not quell and fever raging every night, confined to bed and Hannah doing all my work. Dark was my mood, but deep my love for Hannah grew. I could not bear what I was doing to her now. Oftentimes I thought back to the way she crept into my life. It was not love then, but shared experience has made love grow.

'A visitor you have, Phillip.' Hannah's voice drifted through to me. 'Will you see him now.' Before I could say yes or no, she beckoned the caller to my bed. 'The Grave digger from St Catwg's,' she whispered quietly.

'You come for me, already?' I joked to the poor man, who stood there cap in hand before my bed.

'I heard you were ill, Mr Phillips, Sir.' He touched his cap. I signalled him to sit, indicating my cane seated chair. There was no embarrassed silence. 'I'm not one to beat about the bush,' he said. 'You don't do that in my job at my time of life. So I have come to tell you outright.' If I looked bewildered, my visitor did not notice. 'You asked me once, 'did he...' and you couldn't finish, Sir. I know what question you would ask.' Clearing his throat, his voice came slowly. 'The answer, Sir, is yes. Your father sent men down to gas. He took a risk - he had no option for the mine would close. Stark it sounds against the accident.' The grave digger sat upright, formal by my bed. 'We probably had breached a coal barrier with the old workings,' he went on, 'that's where the rush of gas came from that day - then got ignited by Evan's candle burning there. We live with gas below, Mr Phillips. It isn't as unusual as someone who works above the ground may think. Sometimes the firemen ignite it purposely - send all men out, then use the firing line - it makes a hell of an explosion when they do.' He cleared his throat and shuffled in his chair. 'That accident,' he said, 'it's the works themselves to blame. There were roof falls and the ventilation poor. Your Dada took a risk against the odds and lost. Think of it, Mr Phillips. If he didn't get out coal the mine was shut, if he went down - well, we were used to gas. Remember always he was down there with the men. He did not send them into gas alone to die.'

And ye shall know the truth, and the truth shall make you free. The words at last brought meaning, registered somewhere in the depths of my poor soul. I could not speak.

'Are you tired, Phillip?' Hannah asked, concerned. As I became silent, she smoothed the quilt.

I shook my head. 'Will you take food with us?' I asked the man. He nodded his assent and within minutes, Hannah was in the kitchen and minutes more, beside me on the bed. As my visitor pushed down cheese and bread, Hannah beckoned me closer to her, pushed back the hair from her face, tossing her head as she did when we were alone.

'A cold job you have,' she said politely to the man, indicating the falling snow.

'You know what I say, Mrs Phillips. Better to dig the graves than lie in one.' He smiled at her and continued eating, indicating he would tell more when he had fed.

Hannah held my hand while the bread and cheese was swallowed down. Finishing, licking his fingers clean, the grave digger said, 'Your father was late that morning, as I think you know. I saw him, scarf flying, striding fast down the track, heading through the snow to the Lan. He was a fine figure of a man, you know. We all admired him. Well liked was Abraham Phillips. A fine and honourable man.' The grave-digger's words faded into nothing. Uncomfortable he looked now, sitting there incongruous beside the bed of someone still alive. He took his cloth cap in his old bruised hand and handing his plate and cup to Hannah, stood up to go.

'You just remember, lad,' he said, as he moved towards the door, 'your father was down there with the men. If there was a risk, he took it with them.' He scuffled through the door scarcely turning to say goodbye. I thanked him for his words, offered him more tea. But he had said his piece and left.

'This house entombs me, Hannah,' I said quietly when she came back into the room, her hand in mine. 'In the months since Elizabeth's death, I have not got stronger. No longer am I able to mount the stair, my bed here in the room where my dead father lay.' I looked into my wife's eyes, saw sadness there and courage.

She nodded to me and smiled. 'I have watched,' she said.

'Will you live here after me, Hannah?' I asked gently.

'No-one is coming in after us, Phillip,' Hannah murmured this to me as she lay beside me on the bed. 'These old stones, this hearth, will have time to settle now. Ghosts will occupy the rooms, move from hearth to hearth as the wind blows down the chimney ash. There will be nobody here to answer the knocks at the door, no coal to send the trails of habitation to the sky. Leave your memories behind, Phillip. Let them have peace within the cottage walls.'

'Thomas Jones knew what he was doing for mankind with his Ivorite movement,' I whispered, love, friendship and care. I have seen them all in you. My grandfather worked for the language and the Welsh way of life and my father spoke only Welsh, but it is not the language that marks Wales, it is the love you have shown. We are a kind and generous people, Phillip. And most of us know how to love.'

'Abraham Phillips. An honourable man.' I smiled, repeating the gravedigger's words - words I had so much wanted to know. I held them like nectar on my drying lips 'I remember that my father signed Thomas William Booker's lease for *Ty'n y Coed* with a cross,' I said.

'And with a wry smile in his heart,' Hannah laughed. 'Why write his name on an English written document, especially while his father fought for the language. Abraham Phillips made his mark in more ways than one.'

Suddenly, I could laugh again. I took Hannah's hand and rubbed it gently.

'And me, Phillip. What do you recall of me?' she said.

'Oh, Hannah. I still hear your voice behind me on the Garth and I see your golden hair tossed by the wind. You know I love you, though I do not say.'

I could not look at her. 'There is mud there on the floor, Hannah,' I said to her gently. 'The grave digger has left his footprints to the door. We must leave the place clean when we go. Brush it out, will you.'

We looked at each other and smiled. In that instant, years of human love, our love, expanded and encompassed everything.

Hannah started to sing, her face turned to me, my hand held tight, the words of Annie Hawks hymn saying what words could no longer say:

> *I need Thee every hour, most gracious Lord*
> *No tender voice like Thine can peace afford*

Tears in my eyes then. With effort I strove to join her singing, the old words of *Calon Lan* ringing through my soul, resonating from me as never before. I sang out to my beloved wife -

> *Gofyn wyf am galon hapus,*
> *Calon onest, calon lân.*

I ask for a happy heart, an honest heart, a pure heart.

Hannah put her head closer to me, her voice quiet but beautiful. 'A pure heart is full of goodness,' she sang, 'more lovely than the pretty lily. Only a pure heart can sing day and night ...

> *Calon lân yn llawn daioni,*
> *Tecach yw na'r lili dlos:*
> *Dim ond calon lân all ganu-*
> *Canu'r dydd a chanu'r nos '*

She turned to me then, whispering in my ear. I took both her hands in mine as my strength faded. Looking at her dear face, I sang haltingly...

> *I need Thee every hour in joy or pain*
> *Come quickly and abide or life is in vain*
> *I need Thee, oh, I need Thee, every hour I need Thee*
> *I need Thee, I need Thee, I need Thee every hour*
> *I need Thee, I need Thee, I need Thee every hour*

'Will you walk to the Garth for me when I am gone,' I asked her, tired now. 'Will you look up at the sky and call to the echoing air my father's name? Will you sing out to this valley that my father was an honourable man.'

Hannah nodded. She leaned over to be closer, her hair softly on my face.

'Tread carefully when you walk upon the Garth without me,' I said kissing her. 'Tread carefully, Hannah, for you will be treading upon my dreams....

> *Oh, bless me now, my Saviour, I come to Thee*
> *Oh, bless me now, my Saviour, I come to Thee...*

My eyes are shut now. And Hannah singing. As I take my final journey into history, it is all said. I have put down the burning coal I carried and have let myself be carried instead by the Seraphim.

To my love's slow fading words, the house of my father becomes distant as I drift to sleep ...

> *I need Thee, I need Thee, I need Thee every hour*
> *I need Thee, I need Thee, I need Thee every hour*

After words

As this story is based around the actual history of Gwaelod y Garth, it seems important to fix for readers what is fact and what is fiction. The people and main events are created from recorded facts, set in a history that is as accurate as I could make it, but their characters and home life are entirely imagined. For instance, while the details of the accident are taken from contemporary reports, there is nothing to suggest that Phillip Phillips met with either the grave digger or Collier Evans.

What is recorded fact is that **Phillip Phillips** was born in 1854. He was the second son of Abraham Phillips. He married **Hannah Thomas** in the March quarter of 1875. After his death in 1891, **Hannah** went to live with her parents in Gwaelod y Garth. In the September quarter 1894, she remarried. Her second husband is named as John Hicks. It is recorded that in 1901 Hannah and John Hicks are living in Gwaelod y Garth with Mary Thomas, widowed, aged 72. John Hicks, listed as son-in-law, is a platelayer, aged 37. Hannah is 44. A daughter, Mary Hicks, aged 17 and a son, Herbert Hicks, 11, are also listed residents - John had been married before. The death of his first wife, Agnes Ann Hicks, aged 29, is recorded in the June quarter 1892, Pontypridd.

Abraham Phillips was born in 1822, first son in the second marriage of his father, **John Phillips** (Shôn o'r Lan).

Abraham Phillips married **Elizabeth Morgan** in 1847. She was the daughter of Evan Morgan, Pentrych. Her great grandfather, also Evan Morgan, rented Tynycoed Coal, situated between Pentyrch and Creigiau. Elizabeth died in 1866, aged 41.

Abraham Phillips married **Jemima Phillips**, his second wife, in 1870. She came from Bedwas, to where she returned after her husband's death, when she is recorded as working as a charwoman.

Abraham Phillips is recorded in his Will as an Overman and Underground Agent. He left effects to the value of £100. His position of Overman at the Lan means he is highly unlikely to have been unable to read and write as his X on the Deeds to Wood Cottage suggest. He will have had to hire men for Booker, keep daily records and be in charge of transactions at the pit.

Evan Phillips was born in 1848. He died in 1872, aged 24. His death is also recorded in Welsh at St Catwg's Church. He worked as Clerk in Liverpool. No record has been found of a marriage.

Susannah Phillips was born in 1849. She married John Thomas, a coal miner, in 1871. They lived in *Maesarail*, on the Garth, with their daughter, Gwenllian. Susannah died in 1885.

Deborah Phillips was born in 1857 and lived for only five months.

Deborah Phillips (2) was born in 1858. She became a maid after her father's death but subsequently left domestic service to marry Thomas Francis. They had four children: Elizabeth, Gwendoline, Catherine and Thomas. She died in 1887.

Catherine Phillips was born in 1862. After her father's death, she is recorded under the name of **Kate Phillips**, living in *Ystrad Dyfodwg*, Abraham Phillip's birthplace. She is noted as an Assistant, working as a Milliner.

Elizabeth Phillips was born in 1864. She does not marry. Her death in 1886, at the age of 23, is recorded in Welsh at St Catwg's Church, Pentrych, along with that of her baby sister, Deborah.

A Memorial Inscription to members of the Phillips family can be seen at St Catwg's Church, Pentryrch.

Memorial from the Welsh:

In memory of Deborah, daughter of Abraham and Eliza Phillips/ of this Parish who died November 5th. 1857/ aged 5 months/ also the aforesaid Eliza Phillips/ who died August 28th 1866/ aged 41 years/ also Evan their son who died June 27th 1872/ aged 24 years/ also the aforesaid Abraham Phillips/ who died December 6th 1875/ aged 54 years/ also of Eliza their daughter/ died September 13th 1886/ aged 23

John Phillips was born in 1852. He does not appear to marry, but is recorded on a later census as an Overman.

Shôn o'r Lan (John Phillips) (1786 -1871) was Abraham's father. For the purpose of *The House of Abraham Phillips*, I have allowed an anachronism around the date of his death. Shôn's first wife, **Gwenllian Llewellyn**, died in 1820. It was in 1829 that John Phillips left Ystrad Dyfodwg to come to Lan Farm, near Gwaelod y Garth. He moved into the village in the 1840s. Abraham's mother, **Deborah Thomas** (1796-1882), was John Phillips' second wife.

Deborah and John Phillips were baptised in the River Taff, near the weir, on April 17th., 1859. The Reverend John Evans, Minister at the Penuel Baptist Chapel in Pentyrch, officiated.

John Phillips (Shôn o'r Lan) was a known Ivorite leader. He had fourteen children and about fifty four grandchildren. The Phillipiaid, (Y Phillipiaid) a 'history' of the Phillips family, was put together by one of Shôn o'r Lan's grandsons (Evan Phillips) in 1942.

The House of Abraham Phillips, Ty'n y Coed is still extant. It has been known as Wood Cottage for many years. During the time Abraham Phillips lived there, it is recorded that Henry George and his wife Rachel and two children, also lodged in the cottage. Henry George is listed as a quarry man and plays no part in this story. His presence is interesting, however, in the change of name from Ty'n y Coed to Wood Cottage. Henry George is thought to have built the row of houses now known as Georgetown. He appears to have moved into the first of the cottages, of which he was the listed owner, taking the name of Ty'n y Coed with him. This cottage is now the home of Arthur and Irene Welsby. After Phillip Phillip's death, Ty'n y Coed remained empty for many years.

The Lan Disaster:

The New **Lan mine** opened in 1872 as a fuel and ironstone source for TW Booker's iron works. The fatal explosion was on December 6th. 1875.

In 1874, the **Iron Works** and associated mines were owned by T W Booker (Junior). Following the rapid decline of the iron trade in the late 1870s, these works, together with the Melingriffith tin plate works were put in administration following the collapse of the West of England Bank, and ceased trading in December 1879, putting 1,400 people out of work during the period 1878/9. The works re-opened under administration in December 1879, although at a much reduced capacity. Booker's estate included

1000 acres of freehold mineral rights, together with cottages and a farm.

The Lan mine continued to operate intermittently supplying coal to the brick works under several different owners up to just before WW1, but at much lower output. The miners of Booker's mine transferred to the Rhondda and Cynon mines, returning home each Saturday afternoon for a short weekend with family.

During the investigations into working conditions of women and children for the 1842 Royal Commission, it was reported that Pentrych Iron Works, then owned by Richard Blakemore, employed 600 men, women and children of whom 150 children were under the age of 13.

In January 1850, the iron works converted to the Messrs Dickson and Budd process of smelting, which was claimed to save some 100 tons of fuel a week.

(Notes above from Reg Malpass. Mining Historian)

Names of the dead are taken from the Coroner's Report, as are details of causes of death. Contemporary news articles record the accident and report on witness' statements. One paper only carries the story of the young child found in the mine. Other men are liable to have died without name, given the method of hiring workmen for the job - few had continuing employment.

William Galloway, Deputy Inspector of Mines and assistant to the Coroner at the Lan Inquest, was born in Scotland in 1840 to William Galloway, a JP and Paisley shawl maker and coal and iron master. He formed the opinion that it was airborne, dry coal dust, ignited by methane gas, that caused the men to be seriously burned far from the site of the original explosion. After years of his campaigning, watering in dry mines to suppress the airborne dust became law.

This practice was first used in the Lan mine following Galloway's advice after the 1875 disaster. He ultimately became Professor of mining at the University College of Wales. In 1924, he was knighted.

The Lan mine was affected, as noted earlier, by the fluctuating fortunes of the Pentyrch Iron Works. In 1879, after the Franco-Prussian War, the West of England Bank failed, calling in its debts. The Booker company had borrowed heavily and went down with it. The Iron Works closed around 1880 and attempts to create a new company came to nothing. Thus, in 1888 much of Booker's property was sold off. Chancery Records hold the case where Booker took his sister-in-law before the judge as she tried to sell-off her share of assets before the company crash.

The village was plunged into great poverty.

The Lan mine was also providing coal and fireclay for the **Pentrych Brick Works** nearby and after a pause in working, continued on a much reduced scale until around 1898.

William Evans' shop traded from 1860 - 1898 It was in Pen y Garn, (Upper Pentyrch). William Evans is listed as 'Tea Dealer, General Grocer, Linen and Woollen Draper'. In 1974, a cache of his papers were found high in the roof of an old stable adjacent to the shop. William Evans had kept, meticulously, all his paper work for every year going back from 1860 to 1898. This included order books, receipts, and poignant letter from the poor seeking credit.

Thomas William Booker was the second son of Thomas William Booker-Blakemore (1801-58) Industrialist and MP. On his father's death, Thomas William Booker Jnr inherited his father's industrial pursuits and became a prominent Master and major employer at Pentyrch and Melingriffith. He married Caroline Emily Slon, from a County family. They had one child, a daughter. When his business failed, he left Velindre House in Whitchurch and retired to his house in Southerndown, on the Glamorgan coast. Details of his bankruptcy are recorded in Chancery papers He died in Southerndown in 1887, aged 57.

In the 1859 Revival chapter, Elizabeth refers to **Evan Roberts**. I have taken the liberty of using his name anachronistically for his involvement in revivalism fits so neatly into the story of the Lan. Born in 1878, Roberts was a leading name in the 1904 Revival. A coal miner, he was in an explosion that scorched his Bible, which is said to have been open at 2 Chronicles where Solomon is praying for Revival. The picture of his Bible page scorched by fire from the explosion made its way around the world.

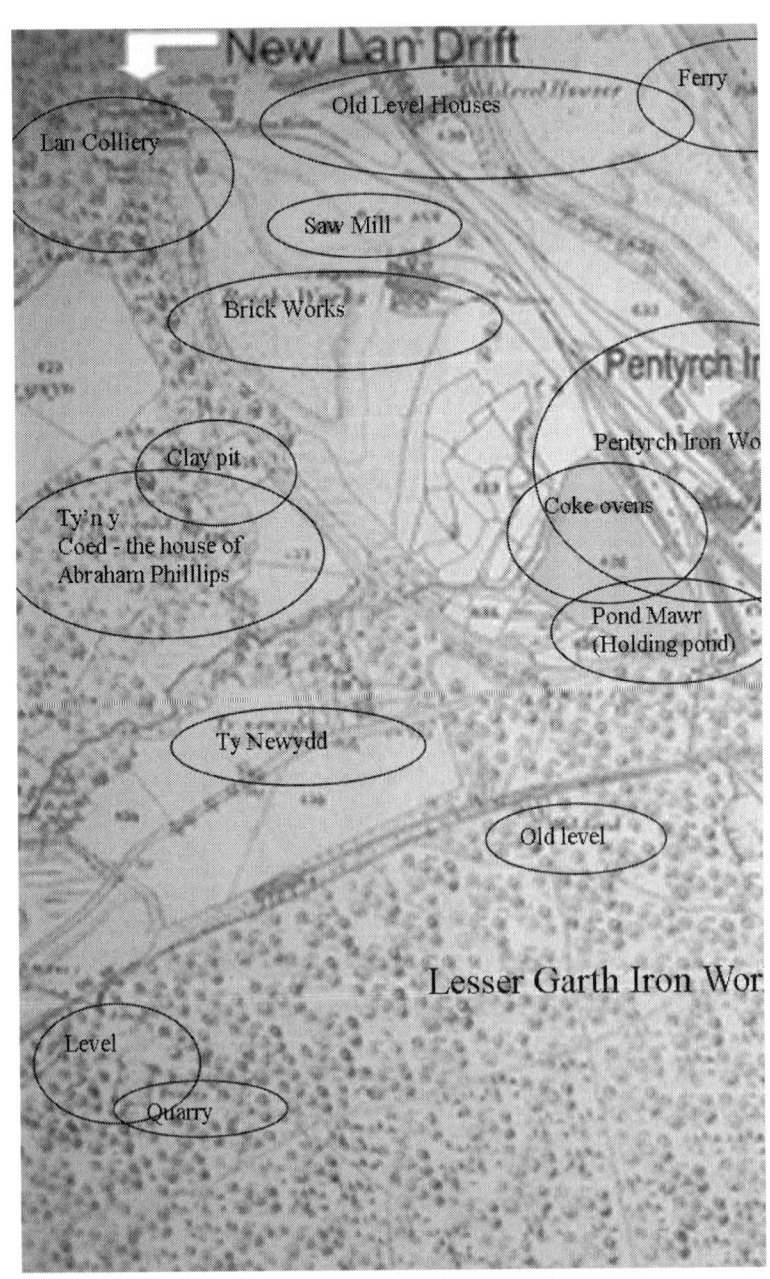

Lower Gwaelod y Garth 1874 - its industrial valley

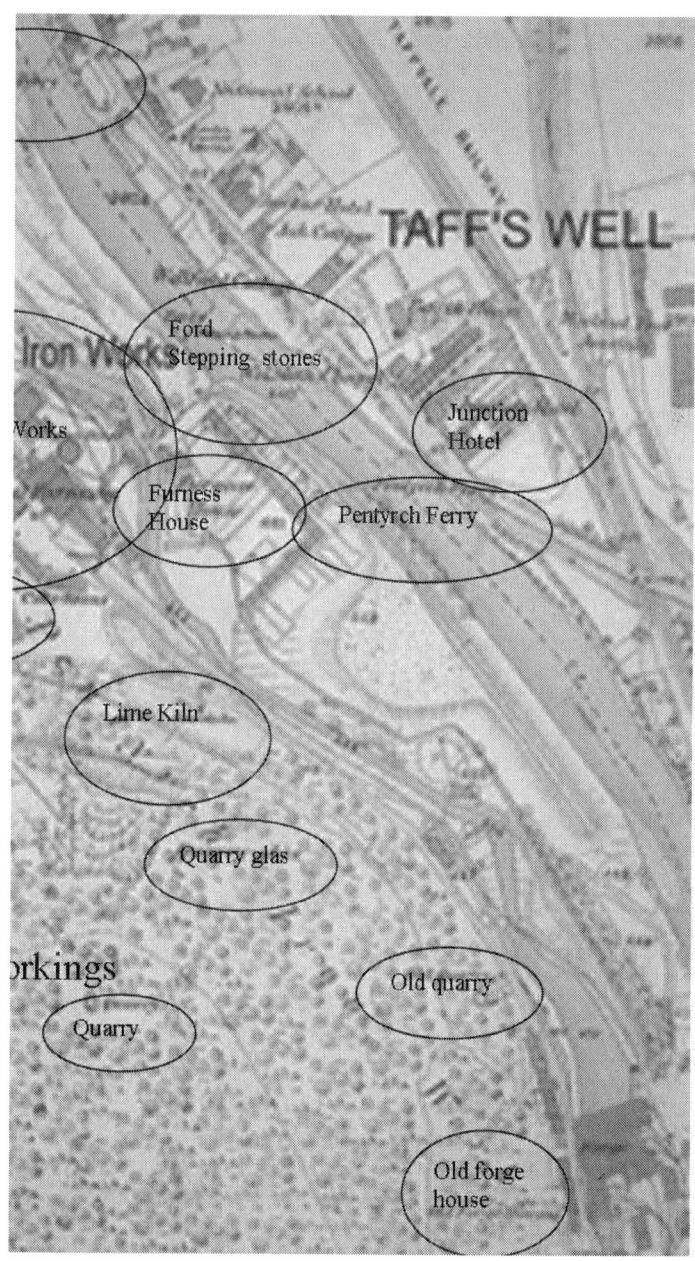

at the time House of Abraham Phillips.

References used

County Families of the UK. (ebook).

History of the Iron, Steel, Tin plate and other trades of Wales by Charles Wilkins

A History of Wales by John Davies

Coal (Garth Domain) by JB Davies and T Ellis Davies

Iron (as above)

Y Philipiaid - The remarkable Phillipses of Gwaelod y Garth. (Garth Domain no 54 Miscellany) Don Llewellyn/ Derek Thomas. Pentyrch and District Local History Society (from *Llyfr Cronicl y Phillip-iaid Gwaelodygarth*).

Archive Photography Series: Pentyrch, Creigiau and Gwaelod y Garth

The Evangelical or Revival Comes to Wales. Eifion Evan - the story of the 1859 Revival.

The Welsh Revival . Thomas Phillips. published 1860.

1876 [C.1499] Mines. Reports of the inspectors of mines, to Her Majesty's Secretary of State, for the year 1875.

1877 [C.1734] Mines. Reports of the Inspectors of Mines, to Her Majesty's Secretary of State, for the year 1876.

1842 Royal Commission Report - Children in Employment in Mines- section re. Lan

Records of proceedings in the South Wales Institute of Engineers Volume XXVIII 1912

Principles of Coal Mining. Joseph Henry Collins. 1875 (g-books).

The William Evans Papers - Garth Domain no.2 1998. Don Llewellyn.

King James Bible

Acknowledgements

My sincere thanks to Derek Thomas for ongoing discussions and detailed local information; to Don Llewellyn for his close reading of the history in my text and for his (and other contributors) work on the Pentrych Historical Society's magazine, *The Garth Domain* and *the Archive Photographs volume*. Both publications have both been a great source of information. Thanks to John Huw Evans for his interpretation of the Freehold Lease of 1861. Thanks, also, to Mel Turner, my brother for his help, and to Osprey and Suz for their notes. Mining Historian Reg Malpass' Flikr site holds photographs and detailed information, which have been invaluable. Dic Mortimer's blog pushed me into an interest in the history of the Lan and the need for a memorial to those who lost their lives. I owe a great debt of gratitude to all who have put on-line extensive records, and to the Cardiff Library Local History Department, that it has recorded contemporary news reports on micro film; to Nicola for reading and emailing them, to Jane who has listened to my musings, and to Tom, who has enthusiastically done the cooking as well as reading the final draft for me.

Norma Procter lives in the house of Abraham Phillips. Born in Norfolk, she came to live in Wales some fifty years ago, when her husband joined the BBC Welsh Symphony Orchestra. Her interest in the story of the Phillips' family arose from conversations with Derek Thomas and research her grandson, Joseph Thorne, did into the history of the cottage for a Young Archaeologists competition. His entry, 'The History of a Welsh Cottage,' is now in book-form and has been a useful resource. During Joseph Thorne's research, the name of Abraham Phillips, the first signatory on the Deeds of Wood Cottage, came to light. His death in the Lan explosion led to a consuming interest that became this story.

In 2011 Norma Procter was awarded the MBE for services to the environment and the village of Gwaelod y Garth.

Printed in Great Britain
by Amazon